Is God Back?

ALSO AVAILABLE FROM BLOOMSBURY

Christianity and the University Experience, Mathew Guest, Kristin Aune,
Sonya Sharma and Rob Warner
Sacred and Secular Musics, Virinder S. Kalra
Capitalizing Religion, Craig Martin
Confronting Secularism in Europe and India, edited by Brian Black, Gavin
Hyman and Graham M. Smith

Is God Back?

Reconsidering the
new visibility of religion

EDITED BY
TITUS HJELM

Bloomsbury Academic
An imprint of Bloomsbury Publishing Plc

B L O O M S B U R Y

LONDON · NEW DELHI · NEW YORK · SYDNEY

Bloomsbury Academic

An imprint of Bloomsbury Publishing Plc

50 Bedford Square	1385 Broadway
London	New York
WC1B 3DP	NY 10018
UK	USA

www.bloomsbury.com

BLOOMSBURY and the Diana logo are trademarks of Bloomsbury Publishing Plc

First published 2015

© Titus Hjelm and Contributors, 2015

Titus Hjelm has asserted his right under the Copyright, Designs
and Patents Act, 1988, to be identified as Editor of this work.

British Library Cataloguing-in-Publication Data

A catalogue record for this book is available from the British Library.

ISBN: HB: 978-1-4725-2903-9
PB: 978-1-4725-2666-3
ePDF: 978-1-4725-2185-9
ePub: 978-1-4725-2840-7

Library of Congress Cataloging-in-Publication Data

A catalog record for this book is available from the Library of Congress.

Typeset by Deanta Global Publishing Services, Chennai, India
Printed and bound in India

Contents

List of contributors

Akile Ahmet is a postdoctoral research fellow in the College of Health and Life Sciences at Brunel University, London, UK. She works alongside Professor Christina Victor on the Leverhulme funded project, 'Care and caring for ethnic minority older people in England and Wales'. A further project exploring poverty and ethnicity has recently been funded by the Joseph Rowntree Foundation. Prior to Brunel she was based at Goldsmiths, University of London, as a research officer investigating progression and diversity of social work students, funded by the Department of Health. Her PhD, awarded from Queen Mary, University of London, explored home and identity for young men of mixed race.

Marta Axner is an affiliate researcher in sociology of religion at the Religion and Society Research Centre, Uppsala University, Sweden. Her doctoral research, which she defended in 2013, was titled *Public Religions in Swedish Media: A Study of Religious Actors on Three Newspaper Debate Pages 2001–2011*. Her research interests concern religion and the public arena in varying ways, such as religion and media/popular culture, mediatization of religion and religion and politics.

Norman Bonney is an emeritus professor at Edinburgh Napier University, UK. His latest publication is *Monarchy, Religion and the State: Civil Religion in Canada, Australia and the Commonwealth* (Manchester University Press, 2013).

Luca Diotallevi is a professor of sociology at Roma Tre University, Rome, Italy. He has been a senior fellow at the Center for the Study of World Religions at Harvard University, US. His recent works include 'Internal Competition in a National Religious Monopoly: The Catholic Effect and the Italian Case', *Sociology of Religion* (2002), the entry 'Church' in the *Blackwell Encyclopaedia of Sociology*, *Una alternativa alla laicità* (Rubbettino, 2011) and 'Catholicisme et modernisation: nouveaux défis historiques. Une analyse du cas italien' in Béraud C. et al. (eds), *Catholicisme en tensions*, vol. 1 (EHESS, 2012).

Paul Gilfillan is a senior lecturer in sociology at Queen Margaret University, Edinburgh, UK, and is the programme leader for the Public Sociology undergraduate programme. His teaching portfolio and research interests include research methodology, nationalism, the sociology of religion, social class and the sociology of contemporary Scotland. His first book, *A Sociological Phenomenology of Christian Redemption*, was published in 2014.

Titus Hjelm is a lecturer in Finnish Society and Culture at University College London, UK. His publications include *Social Constructionisms* (Palgrave, 2014), *Studying Religion and Society: Sociological Self-Portraits* (ed. with Phil Zuckerman, Routledge, 2013) and *Religion and Social Problems* (ed., Routledge, 2011). In addition, he has published several books in Finnish and articles in journals such as *Critical Sociology*, *Acta Sociologica*, *Religion*, *Social Compass* and *Journal of Contemporary Religion*. He is the co-editor of the *Journal of Religion in Europe* (published by Brill) and the founding chair of the American Academy of Religion's Sociology of Religion Group.

Rana Jawad is a lecturer in Social Policy at the University of Bath, UK. She has extensive research experience in the social welfare systems of the region of the Middle East, with particular focus on Islamic welfare institutions. She currently directs an Economic and Social Research Council (ESRC)-funded project on religion and social policy in the Middle East and is convenor of the Middle East Social Policy Network, http://www.bath.ac.uk/ipr/our-networks/middle-east-social-policy/ based at the University of Bath. She is the author of *Social Welfare and Religion in the Middle East: A Lebanese Perspective* (2009) and *Religion and Faith-based Welfare: From Wellbeing to Ways of Being* (2012), both published by the Policy Press.

Steven Kettell is an associate professor in the Department of Politics and International Studies at the University of Warwick, UK. His main research interests are centred on the intersection of politics and religion, as well as the politics of atheism. He is the author of several books, including *New Labour and the New World Order* (Manchester University Press, 2011) and is founder and co-executive editor of *British Politics*.

Alf Linderman is an associate professor in the sociology of religion at Uppsala University, Sweden, and the executive director of the Sigtuna Foundation. Linderman is specialized in research at the nexus of media, religion and culture. He has published work on religious television, media reception, media content analysis, survey research and methodology and has conducted comparative studies of the interplay between media and religion in different geographical regions.

Mia Lövheim is a professor in sociology of religion, Uppsala University, Sweden, and vice-president of the International Society for Media, Religion and Culture (ISMRC). Her current research concerns representations of religion and modernity in Swedish daily press, gender and digital religion, and the interplay between religion and mediatization. Her work has appeared in the journals *Nordicom Review*; *Information, Communication and Society*; *Feminist Media Studies*; *Culture and Religion* and *Nordic Journal of Society and Religion*. She is the editor of *Media, Religion and Gender: Key Issues and New Challenges* (Routledge, 2013) and, with Stig Hjarvard, of *Mediatization and Religion: Nordic Perspectives* (Nordicom, 2012).

Ian Morrison is an assistant professor of Sociology at the American University in Cairo, Egypt. His publications include articles in *Citizenship Studies* and *The Review of European and Russian Affairs*, as well as several chapters in edited volumes. His research interests include continental social and political thought, the sociology of religion and citizenship and nationalism studies.

Raluca Bianca Roman is a PhD candidate in Social Anthropology at the University of St Andrews, UK. Her research interests include visual anthropology, ethnographic filmmaking, phenomenology of religion, studies on personhood, youth and religious socialization. She has published papers on religion, secularization, ethnicity and ethnic identity, including 'The voice of the community? Grassroots interactions between immigrant Roma and social activists in Helsinki, Finland', *Ethnicities* (forthcoming). Her PhD project focuses on the religious conversion and mobilization of Finnish Kaale (Finnish Roma) to Evangelical movements in Finland. She is a member of the European Network for Romani Studies and a policy editor for the University Association for Contemporary European Studies (UACES) Collaborative Research Network, 'Romanis in Europe'.

Kathryn Rountree is a professor of anthropology at Massey University, New Zealand. Her research has dealt with modern Paganism in Malta and New Zealand, feminist spirituality, pilgrimage and embodiment and the contestation of sacred sites. Her books include *Crafting Contemporary Pagan Identities in a Catholic Society* (Ashgate, 2010), *Embracing the Witch and the Goddess: Feminist Ritual-makers in New Zealand* (Routledge, 2004), *Archaeology of Spiritualities* (ed. with Christine Morris and Alan Peatfield, Springer, 2012), and *Modern Pagan and Native Faith Movements in Europe* (ed., Berghahn, forthcoming). Her articles have appeared in a range of journals, including *Journal of the Royal Anthropological Institute*, *Journal of Anthropological Research*, *Journal of Contemporary Religion*, *Journal of Feminist Studies in Religion*, *Body and Society*, *Environmental Ethics*, *Feminist Theology*,

Sociology of Religion, The Pomegranate, Anthropology of Consciousness, History and Anthropology and *Social Anthropology/Anthropologie Sociale.*

Eleanor Ryan-Saha is an ESRC-funded PhD student in the Department of Anthropology, Durham University, UK. Her doctoral fieldwork was concerned with recovery from drug addiction in Sarajevo, Bosnia-Herzegovina. Her current research interests include addiction treatment, future-making practices, welfare provision in transition contexts and religion in south-east Europe. In the past, she has researched the materiality of memory and identity in the Bosnian diaspora and the imaginative nature of tourist and local co-constructions of Mostar, Bosnia-Herzegovina. She is a founding board member of RUN—the Recovered Users Network.

Annette Schnabel is professor of sociology at the University of Wuppertal, Germany. Her research interests cover the questions of why people join social movements, how they form their national, religious and gender identities, and how emotions and rational choices interact. The impact of political and social institutions and their formation form another focal point of interest. The research on these issues encompasses empirical analyses as well as their impact on social theory.

Anna Strhan is a Leverhulme Early Career fellow in the Department of Religious Studies at the University of Kent, UK. She is currently working on a three-year project examining the significance of childhood and parenting in British evangelicalism in contexts ranging from everyday family and church life, to formal and informal educational contexts, to wider public debates about childhood and education concerned with the place of religion and secularity in contemporary society. Her doctoral research was an urban ethnography of the everyday religious lives of conservative evangelical Christians in London, UK, examining their negotiation of different urban moral landscapes. Her publications include 'The Metropolis and Evangelical Life: Coherence and Fragmentation in the "lost city of London"', *Religion* (2013); 'Practising the Space Between: Embodying Belief as an Evangelical Anglican Student', *Journal of Contemporary Religion* (2013); *Levinas, Subjectivity, Education* (Wiley-Blackwell, 2012); and *Aliens and Strangers? The Struggle for Coherence in Everyday Evangelical Life* (Oxford University Press, 2015).

Christina Victor is professor of gerontology and public health and vice-dean (Research) in the College of Health and Life Sciences at Brunel University, London, UK. Her main research interest is social gerontology, with a specific focus on ageing in minority communities, loneliness and isolation in later life, health and health inequalities and the evaluation of services for older people. She is editor-in-chief of *Ageing and Society.*

List of tables and figures

Acknowledgements

Many of the chapters in this book were first presented at the annual conference of the British Sociological Association (BSA) in London, UK, in April 2013. Although the sessions were not limited by topic, I was excited to notice that a common theme around visibility was clearly emerging in the discussions. I would like to thank the BSA for providing a consistently high-quality venue for sociological discussion and debate, which attracts interesting scholars. The Sociology of Religion stream has been my intellectual home at these meetings, and I would like to thank especially Mat Francis and Jo McKenzie for co-organizing the stream sessions with me. Some of the authors joined the project later and brought exciting new perspectives to the collection. A big thank you to the anonymous reviewers who gave their time to make this a better book. Finally, thank you to Lalle Pursglove, Anna MacDiarmid and everyone else at Bloomsbury for enthusiasm, patience and a wicked cover!

1

Is God Back? Reconsidering the new visibility of religion

Titus Hjelm

'God is Back!' screams the title of a recent popular book. In it, John Micklethwait and Adrian Wooldridge ask readers to open their eyes to the continued presence of religion in world affairs (Micklethwait and Wooldridge 2009). Long imagined to be dying, they claim, religion instead is alive, vibrant and stronger than ever. Their book joins a host of others that argue that religion has not vanished from our supposedly secularized world. In fact, a new orthodoxy seems to be emerging: a whole 'religion in public life' industry triumphantly celebrates the death of the secularization thesis. The evacuation of religion from the public sphere – politics, welfare, education, health care, media – has not happened, these scholars claim, the way secularization theories predicted.

Everyday experience seems to confirm the celebrationist view: Even in Europe, long considered the stronghold of secularization, religion has become a topic of discussion in arenas ranging from Parliaments to coffee houses. People who were completely indifferent to religion are now engaging in heated debates about its role in modern society – something unimaginable barely fifteen years ago. Much of this talk is informed by the media, where religion stories are increasingly prominent. Not only has the presence of religion in the media quantitatively increased in the new millennium (Knott et al. 2013; but see Lövheim and Linderman in this volume), but religion also seems to carry more weight as a news item – not least because of its frequent association with social problems (Hjelm 2011; see below). In the post-9/11 world, the most significant reason for religion's 'return' to the public imagination has been the fact that it has been associated with political violence. Whether in political discourse, policing, the media or everyday talk, 'religious extremism' has become a simplistic shorthand for a wide variety of complex structural dynamics.

There is, then, widespread agreement on the increased *visibility* of religion. But what does this 'new visibility of religion' mean? This is different from asking whether 'secularization theory' is right or wrong (cf. Ward and Hoelzl 2008). After all, public presence and visibility is only one aspect of the cluster of dynamics generally subsumed under 'secularization'. Hence, the 'reconsidering' in this book's subtitle refers to the question of whether equating religion's increased visibility with increased vitality or influence on other institutions – as some of the celebrationist accounts seem to do – is justified (cf. Herbert 2011: 632). As Bryan Turner points out, there is a danger of equating social prevalence with cultural dominance, 'confusing frequency with social effects' (Turner 1991: 59). Turner is referring to theoretical accounts of 'civil religion', but his argument is transferable to the question of the public visibility of religion: 'It cannot be assumed that beliefs and practices which are publicly available necessarily have significant effects in the upkeep of crucial social processes and social arrangements' (Turner 1991: 59).

Yet, to separate visibility and social effects completely would also be a mistake. As Nilüfer Göle convincingly argues with reference to the visibility of Islam in Europe, visibility itself can have wide-ranging effects for societies and the faithful alike (Göle 2011: 388):

> Veiling in the public schools and Muslim candidates in the parliament, mosques near the churches and the cathedrals, praying in the streets, all are examples that make 'indifference' impossible for Europeans who find themselves in a passionate debate over the presence of Islamic signs in public life. However, these confrontational controversies around Islam reveal the tumultuous transition and recognition from the status of an invisible migrant to that of a visible Muslim citizenship.

The chapters in this book critically examine what the new visibility of religion means, how religion is contested and renegotiated in the public arena – or rather, in different publics – and what the effects of these struggles are on society, state and religion itself. They do so especially in the framework of Europe, where different historical traditions of church–state relations, varying degrees of significance accorded to religion by citizens and increased immigration all make accommodating public religion a pertinent issue. The two chapters (by Morrison and Jawad) discussing the Middle East are not – despite the obviously different historical, social and cultural contexts – side tracks, but rather examples where fledgling democracies are struggling to create models of governance that stem from the European secular model but that need to accommodate a much more public form of religiosity.

While looking at the connections between visibility and social influence, the chapters converse with a variety of theories and models regarding the public visibility of religion. Most prominent of these is José Casanova's argument about the deprivatization of religion in the modern world, first introduced in his widely quoted *Public Religions in the Modern World* (Casanova 1994). Since many of the authors in this book (especially Axner, Strhan and Diotallevi) examine Casanova's ideas, I will not rehash that discussion here. I will, however, briefly discuss and evaluate some other popular concepts and some less well-known ideas in order to draw together possible theoretical lessons about the new visibility of religion. The list is not exhaustive – mine is not an attempt to summarize the current 'master narratives' about the future of religion (Spickard 2006). Further, my evaluations do not necessarily represent the views of the other authors. Nevertheless, the theoretical discussion helps put the following chapters in context.

Desecularization and post-secularity

Peter L. Berger, the *doyen* of late twentieth-century sociology of religion, has the curious distinction of being probably the singularly most influential proponent of the secularization thesis and, later, a spokesman for *desecularization* and the rebuttal of his own earlier work. In the 1970s, Berger had already started questioning his earlier view on secularization outlined in *The Sacred Canopy* (1967), but the final break came in *The Desecularization of the World* (1999), in which he admitted that he had been wrong and that the world was as 'furiously religious' as ever (Berger 1999: 2). The resilience and resurgence of religion is, so Berger argues, a global phenomenon, and people should look for secularization in the common rooms of elite universities rather than in the world at large.

The problem with 'desecularization' is that it is more a selective description of what the world is like, a 'diagnosis of our times' (Mannheim 1944), than a theory of social and religious change. As Casanova has argued, the permanence or resurgence of religion in public life in different parts of the world does not by itself prove the secularization thesis wrong (Casanova 1994: 212). It does call for the refinement of theory, but without reference to the particular aspects of the thesis they are trying to invalidate, individual case studies can help very little in understanding broader patterns of social change. As Bruce puts it, the religious evolution in Iran does not really refute what has happened in Essex (Bruce 2001: 89).

A problem also arises out of the term itself. The term *desecularization* and references to a 'resurgence' of religion in the modern world imply that secularization *has* in fact happened and what we are witnessing now is a return or a new 'rise of faith'[1] in public life. At the same time, however, many of those arguing for desecularization emphasize the fact that the world (with the possible exception of Western Europe) has *never* been secular. There is an obvious logical discrepancy here. Yet, as I will argue below (see also Hjelm 2014a), desecularization can be a useful term when used with reference to the visibility of religion in particular – certainly more useful than its currently more fashionable cousin, *post-secularity*.

The current faddishness of 'post-secularity' and the 'post-secular' owes much to the weight that the name of Jürgen Habermas has given these notions (e.g. Habermas 2008; cf. Dillon 2010; Bruce 2011: 203). Habermas was not the first to use the term (Beckford 2012), but it was his use of the 'post-secular' that triggered the current flood of discussion. In many cases, however, it seems that there is very little actual discussion but rather an uncritical acceptance of post-secularity as an accurate description of the state of things in the world. There are critical assessments as well (e.g. Calhoun et al. 2011; Gorski et al. 2012; Moberg et al. 2014) but, equally, many studies that treat post-secularity as an empirical premise, no matter how inconclusive the evidence is (see Beckford 2012). In these treatments, Habermas' originally normative use of the concept – that religious arguments have a right to be heard in the public sphere, even if the state should remain secular (Beckford 2012: 10) – is changed into a description of historical change, or rather, historical stability. The 'will to religion' – 'the discursive construction of a normal in which we are all religious', as Lori Beaman beautifully puts it (Beaman 2013: 146) – is, it seems, strong among scholars of religion (cf. McLennan 2007).

The problem of making the conceptual leap from a normative statement to an empirical premise is not the only problem with the uses of 'post-secularity'. A comprehensive review of the uses of the term is offered by Beckford (2012), so I will not go into detailed critique here. Suffice it to say that I have little to add to his evaluation (Beckford 2012: 16):

> The meanings attributed to the 'postsecular' are not only varied and partly incompatible with each other. ... The concept of 'postsecular' trades on simplistic notions of the secular. It has a shortsighted view of history. It refuses to examine the legal and political forces at work in regulating what counts as 'religion' in public life. There is therefore a danger that talking about the postsecular will be like waving a magic wand over all the intricacies, contradictions, and problems of what counts as religion to reduce them to a single, bland category.

What I would like to add, however, is that in light of what is said about the problems of post-secularity and the transition to a 'new era' that it implies, desecularization does not seem such a bad concept after all. As discussed above, it makes little sense to say that the world that was never *actually* secular is now being desecularized. But 'desecularization' can be useful when applied to the public visibility of religion and used in a limited sense. First, desecularization implies a *process* that is dialectical and reversible, not a state of things. In terms of visibility, just think of Beirut and Tehran in the 1970s and then in the 2010s; or think of the role of religion Poland before and after 1989. Certainly, there has been a desecularization – a movement away from the secular – of public space and discourse. Yet, there is nothing inevitable about the current visibility of religion in the mentioned places, or elsewhere. If there is desecularization, there can be *re*secularization as well. Further, 'desecularization' in the sense of visibility does not purport to say anything about beliefs or practices. Finally, the qualitative aspect of visibility needs to be considered: even when religious communities are reasserting themselves as public actors, their discourse can be secular – a point that Bruce makes in reference to the 'culture wars' in the United States (Bruce 2011: 171).

Did 'Welfare Utopianism' kill public religion?

One of the more conspicuous reasons for the new visibility of religion is the increased role that religious groups play in European welfare provision. The usual narrative goes like this: the European welfare states that emerged after Second World War took over most, if not all, of the social and welfare functions that the churches had provided. The nature and extent of the state's encroachment on the welfare field varied according to religious cleavages and class coalitions (Manow and van Kersbergen 2009), but in all countries the churches' role in poor relief and other functions was diminished in an attempt to provide universal healthcare, social services, education and redistribution of wealth, so that poor relief would not be needed in the first place. According to the standard account, this system started to crumble under the neo-liberal drive to privatization that started with the ascent of Britain's Margaret Thatcher in 1979, and was consolidated some thirty years later by the across-the-board acceptance of austerity measures ushered in by global actors such as the US Federal Reserve, the International Monetary Fund and the World Bank.

Adam Dinham (Dinham and Jackson 2012; Dinham 2009) has examined how, in the British case, government policies deliberately marginalized faith-based welfare providers in a push to create an overarching public welfare system. This also had the residual effect, Dinham argues, of decreasing the overall 'religious literacy' of Britons during the 'statist' years, thus decreasing religion's role not only in people's everyday practice but, potentially, in their thought as well (Dinham and Jackson, 2012: 272).

So far, so good. However, where Dinham's account limits itself to the particular fields of welfare and religious literacy, Linda Woodhead's sweeping overview of post-war Britain takes Dinham's idea and makes the welfare state the main factor evacuating religion from public life in Britain. In this account, 'welfare utopianism' – an 'object of faith in its own right' (Woodhead 2012: 1) – was the source of state control, which suppressed religion until 'new opportunities of market and media' freed religion from the chains of the state, despite some backlashes from 're-regulatory' attempts of 'illiberal secularism' (Woodhead 2012: 1, 2013; see Kettell in this volume). Hence, the return of religion is *actually* about the 'crisis of confidence in secularism itself, bound up with challenges to the prestige of science and a loss of faith in utopian post-war secular projects'.[2] The visibility brought about by immigration, religious diversification and the perception of religion as a problem are secularist residues, which have just made it 'easier to focus anxiety and blame on religion, veiled women and Islamic terrorism' (Woodhead 2012: 11). The true source of religion's return, at least in the British context, it seems, is the current unwillingness of the state to regulate religion.

There is more than a little bit of what could be called 'gemeinschaftism' in the 'welfare utopianism killed public religion' account. 'Gemeinschaftism' refers to Ferdinand Tönnies' way of describing the transition from pre-modern communities (*Gemeinschaft*) to modern societies (*Gesellschaft*) as a process of loss (Callinicos 2007: 128). From this point of view, the 'rolling back' of the welfare state and the subsequent new visibility of religion is a return to a natural, normal equilibrium (cf. 'will to religion' above). This rereading of British history is fascinating but problematic. First, despite an explicit aim to consider religion not in isolation but in relation to economics, politics, culture etc., the account mostly ignores the social changes during the period of 'welfare utopianism'. The Britain of the 1950s and the Britain of today are different countries. Immigration, religious diversification and the perception of religion as a problem *have* made religion a different topic from what it used to be before the emergence of European welfare states, as Göle, among others, convincingly argues (Göle 2011). Secondly, the case about the state waging a 'culture war' on religion was much less straightforward than the account suggests. In Britain, as in the Nordic countries, mainstream churches were often supportive of expanding the welfare functions of the state – or, conversely, were against neo-liberal policies that were persecuting the urban working class, as the controversial *Faith in the City* report from 1985 attests (Davie 1994: 151–3; e.g. Anderson 2009). The division of labour in this issue was much more contested in

Catholic majority countries (Manow and van Kersbergen 2009). Finally, the idea that the current re-emergence of religion is somehow a natural – after the abnormality of state-forced absence – or an accidental process, as Woodhead implies (Woodhead 2012) and Dinham and Jackson explicitly claim (Dinham and Jackson 2012: 272), is highly contestable. As Beckford, for example, has shown, governments have very actively solicited 'faiths' to take on welfare functions, especially during the last twenty years (Beckford 2011). In fact, Dinham and Jackson, in the same text where they argue that the welfare period was 'followed by an *accidental* re-emergence of religious social action in welfare' (emphasis in original), also claim that the shift to market-led welfare provision 'marked a *conscious* move towards provision of all sorts of services, not by government, but by voluntary sector agencies' (Dinham and Jackson 2012: 276; my emphasis).

The argument that 'welfare utopianism' killed public religion bestows too much power on the state and sidesteps crucial social changes; it cannot be the full story of the new visibility of religion. Can we really claim that the public attention paid to diversity and the negative aspects of religion are residues of secularist thinking? The war on terror, for example, was not exactly initiated by hard-line secularists. Religious people seem to be as capable of differentiating between 'good' and 'bad' religion as are 'illiberal secularists'. Associating neoliberalism with the new visibility of religion is correct, as I will argue below, but not in the sense of restoring some kind of market equilibrium in religion's public presence after a period of interfering government. The perception of religion as a social problem is as much an outcome of rapid global change as it is of secularist ideology, the neo-liberal appropriation of religion as much an outcome of active policy as 'welfare utopianism' was.[3]

Religion as a social problem

The idea of the welfare state was, in principle, to combat the social problems endemic to rapid industrialization and urbanization, especially during post-war reconstruction. In practice, the motivations for setting up public welfare have been contingent on various political and social factors, but combating social problems has always been the explicit core of welfare provision. In the European context, care of the poor and the sick was, of course, for a long time mainly the function of local parishes and certain religious orders. Later, organizations such as the Salvation Army and the worker priest movement were established on religious principles to combat social problems. It was only in the twentieth century that the state assumed many of the functions that religious communities had traditionally fulfilled. In that sense, the role of religion as a solution to social problems is well established.

During the latter half of the twentieth century – and certainly after 9/11 in the new millennium – religion was, however, increasingly perceived not only as a solution but also as a source of social problems (Beckford 1990; Hjelm 2011). Interreligious strife has, of course, existed as long as there have been competing communities of belief and practice (making *some* religions problematic in particular contexts), and secularist states – revolutionary France, the USSR and China – have at times struck at 'reactionary' religion (making *all* religions problematic in their national contexts). The political attention given to religion has, however, reached new heights in Europe within the last twenty or so years. Fear of 'parallel societies', religiously inspired terrorism, human rights violations and loss of national identity in the face of mass immigration have all contributed to an awareness of religion as a potential source of social problems (e.g. El-Menouari and Becker 2011; Bowen 2007; Cumper and Lewis 2012). When I say 'fear of', I am not implying that the negative aspects of religion are imagined. Bad things that are religiously motivated, or at least religiously legitimated, actually happen. But what comprises 'bad things' is relative, socially constructed (Hjelm 2014b: 37–56). It is easy to agree that bombs or female genital mutilation should be condemned, but what about kosher butchering? Wearing a headscarf? Despite the convergence of governance in Europe, questions regarding religion remain entrenched in national and regional traditions. Indeed, as McCrea argues, the *cuius regio eius religio* theme has been reaffirmed in a modern variation in key EU agreements, such as the Amsterdam Treaty and the Reform (Lisbon) Treaty (McCrea 2010: 114).

The increased visibility of religion as a social problem – whether concerning particular religions and religious practices or the social role of religion in general, as in discussions about French *laïcité* – is important in at least two senses. First, as Steve Bruce puts it, 'Since Jürgen Habermas popularized talk of a "post-secular Europe", there has been much confusion between religion becoming more troublesome and people becoming more religious' (Bruce 2011: 203). On the one hand, the roots of religious violence, for example, are complex and not reducible to this or that religious belief. The more religious are not necessarily the more troublesome, as the case of British 'Islam for Dummies' jihadists demonstrates (Hasan 2014). On the other hand, the fear of radical Islam in Europe is unlikely to trigger a Christian revival, because most of the anti-immigration discourse is secular and because 'most Christians are not xenophobes' (Bruce 2011: 219). Hence, the apparently increased 'troublesomeness' of religion, fuelled by sensationalistic media visibility, is not a measure of increased religiosity.

Second, even if we cannot say much about the return of religion in terms of belief or practice, the construction of religion, particular religions or religious practices as problematic gives us important clues about the struggles to define regional, national, local and individual identity: 'Every version of an "other", wherever found, is also the construction of a "self"' (Clifford 1986: 23). Hence, for example, every European version of Islam, wherever found, is also a construction of Europe (see Hjelm 2012). Defining social problems and their solutions then becomes a question of power: who gets to define 'bad' and 'good' religion? This is an especially pertinent question in a time where religion is increasingly co-opted by governments for welfare and diversity management purposes.

Religion as expedient

One aspect of the new visibility of religion that has mostly escaped the attention of European sociologists of religion is the critical assessment of 'the ways in which governments and other public authorities use religion as a device or resource in the policies for combating social problems' (Beckford 2011: 59). 'Religion as expedient' refers, then, to 'policies and practices that acknowledge the potential of drawing on religious resources to solve problems' (Beckford 2011: 59). In an age of 'big society' and 'rolling back' the state, 'faith' has become a political resource: '"Faith" in policy parlance, becomes something which may (or may not) be useful and, moreover, "usable" by the state and civil society' (Dinham and Jackson 2012: 272). In the United States, the establishment in 2001 of the White House Office of Faith-Based and Community Initiatives (later renamed the White House Office of Faith-Based and Neighborhood Partnerships) sparked a debate about the role of religion in the provision of welfare and the prevention of social problems (Farnsley 2007; Davis 2011). As Europe increasingly embraces austerity and other neo-liberal policies, the role of religious communities in welfare provision and social integration has also become increasingly pertinent. The establishment in 2003 of a Faith Communities Unit in the UK Home Office (later relocated to the Department for Communities and Local Government) is an example of a more formalized cooperation, but there is ample evidence of religious non-governmental organizations (NGOs) playing an increasing role in state or EU-funded welfare provision in Europe (e.g. Lehtinen 2011; Bäckström et al. 2010).

When calling for a *critical* approach to religion as expedient, I am trying to draw attention to the so far, little-examined unexpected consequences of these increased state–religion partnerships (Hjelm 2014c). When politicians and state agencies interpellate or 'hail' (Beckford 2012: 16) religious communities to define themselves as partners in welfare provision and integration, they also – sometimes explicitly, sometimes inadvertently – force these communities to define the limits of legitimate religion and religiosity. The state will obviously only cooperate with communities that do not infringe the rights of other citizens and that support integration into the national community and values – however these might be constructed. Hence, at the more visible end of legitimation demands, we have the case of the 'Muslim vigilantes' in East London. This was a group of young men who posted videos on YouTube showing them driving people who were drinking alcohol or people who they considered 'inappropriately dressed' away from a 'Muslim area'. The response of the East London Mosque – one of the recognized representatives of the British Muslim community – was unequivocal: the patrols were condemned and said to have done 'a huge amount of damage to the Muslim community' (CNN, 1 February 2013). At the less visible end, there have been cases where state demand for gender equality and women's empowerment programmes in development work, for example, have led to tensions within conservative faith-based service providers (Østebø et al. 2013). In both cases, the key issue is that the communities have had to define 'what we are' or 'what we are not' in the face of external interpellation.

So far I have been following in Beckford's footsteps on the issue of religion as expedient (Beckford 2011, 2012). I would like, however, to expand the discussion to the unexpected consequences of the process of interpellation described above. My argument (Hjelm 2014b) is that legitimation is rarely, if ever, a smooth process. Since definitions – in this case, the definition of legitimate religion, religiosity or religious practice – are, by definition, contested, legitimation is always a struggle. In my conceptual scheme, *authenticity* is the flip side of legitimacy, and legitimation always leads to authenticity struggles within the communities. These can range from civilized debate to division. In other words, what I call the 'The Paradoxes of Expediency Thesis' goes like this: *Public authorities' increased tendency to treat religion as expedient interpellates religious communities to formulate legitimation strategies. These lead, by definition, to authenticity struggles which, in turn, can lead to schism, polarization and radicalism.* When politicians and scholars of religion celebrate the new visibility of expedient religion, they would be wise to consider the dynamics of legitimacy and authenticity that may paradoxically encourage the very phenomena that the policies are designed to combat.

Religious 'publicization' and mediatization

No account of the visibility of religion in the modern world can avoid the role of the media, especially the developments in electronic media. Only twenty-five years ago, when selected passages from Salman Rushdie's *The Satanic Verses* were being distributed to offended Muslims, the campaign relied on photocopying and postage. In 2005, the images of the Muhammad cartoons controversy spread like wildfire online (Herbert 2011: 633). On the one hand, the deregulation of media markets has enabled a proliferation of religious symbols and discourse in popular culture, for instance (e.g. Clark 2003). On the other hand, the expansion of media technologies beyond 'mediated quasi-interaction' (e.g. books, newspapers, radio, television; Thompson 1995) has changed the way in which people interact with other people through social media, including religious authorities and resources. This religious 'publicization', as Herbert defines it, refers 'primarily to the public presence of religious symbols and discourses' (Herbert 2011: 627). This, he adds, 'does not necessarily imply that these become more influential, but rather more visible, present and hence available for mobilization, contestation and criticism in the public sphere'. Hence, for example, the proliferation of anti-Islamic online forums is not a sign of the increased vitality of Islam. Nor is it, less obviously, a sign of the increased vitality of Christianity, for that matter.

Another concept that has sought to capture the role of the media in recent religious change is 'mediatization' (e.g. Hjarvard 2012). Since it is discussed by Lövheim and Linderman (Chapter 3) below, suffice it to point out that mediatization conveys the idea that while religion might be more visible through its media presence, it is, in fact, 'tamed' by the media to conform to particular logics of genre and media convention. In early formulations of the concept, Hjarvard emphasized how mediatization creates 'banal' religion, transforming it from a source of identity formation to a source of entertainment. Again, increased visibility does not equal increased vitality or influence.

A brief outline of the book

The chapters below offer case studies of the main problematic in this book: what does the new visibility of religion mean? Are visibility and influence connected? How? Why? Why not? They do so in their own style and from their own premises, yet all highlight the centrality of the questions above in contemporary European societies and, in two cases, in the Middle East. The book is divided into three sections, which reflect the emphases of the articles in each section and highlight the different arenas where the discussion on the new visibility of religion is centred.

The first section, Conceptualizing Public Religion, examines the meanings of 'public religion(s)', a term popularized by José Casanova. In Chapter 2, Marta Axner overviews Casanova's contribution and applies it to a study of religious actors in the Swedish press. Based on this case, she suggests expanding 'public religions' to better cope with the role of the media in modern societies.

Mia Lövheim and Alf Linderman's chapter (Chapter 3) continues on the path set by Axner, this time taking a close look at the prevalence and types of discourses on religion in Swedish editorials over a period of thirty-five years. They argue that 'we cannot assume a direct relation between changes in the visibility of religion in the media and changes in the role of religion in public discourse' (p. 32). They apply the concept of mediatization to the opinion material to assess whether discourse on religion is indeed dependent on the logic of the media and hence limited to particular – often secular – ways of expression. Chapter 4, by Annette Schnabel, changes the focus somewhat. Instead of looking at discourses on religion, she examines the effects of religious belonging and belief on national identity formation. She argues that counter to some theorizations, national identity in Europe does not overwrite religious cleavages but seems to follow them instead. This has far-reaching consequences for the European project, which aims at integrating its peoples – old and new – into a common civil society. Steven Kettell's case (Chapter 5) takes us back to the discursive constructions of the public place of religion. Kettell explores 'pro-faith' discourse in the United Kingdom and the ways in which religion has become a standard reference point for political actors (cf. religion as expedient), particularly in the Conservative Party. As Kettell shows, bemoaning 'illiberal secularism' means different things for religious and political actors and, in the case of the latter, is an ambiguous political choice. Moving from institutionalized politics to 'everyday politics', Anna Strhan (Chapter 6) demonstrates how evangelical Christians negotiate their faith in public arenas that are perceived as secular (especially work). Strhan compares two congregations, examples of what she calls 'conservative' and 'open' evangelicals, and finds that the former, especially, with strict beliefs about gender, sexuality and other religions, experience ambiguities in living their faith beyond the close circle of fellow believers. Long touted as the most visible form of religion in the modern Western world, everyday evangelicalism is a much more complicated story than celebrity preachers tell. Finally, closing the first section is Kathryn Rountree's account (Chapter 7) of Pagan and Native Faith groups in Europe and their connections to ideas of ethnicity and nationhood. Although never numerically large, some of these groups – especially in Eastern Europe – have attracted broad attention because of their openly racist and nationalist views. By looking at different ways of conceptualizing Pagan religions, Rountree argues that contrasting transnational and national Paganisms simplifies the dynamic process of combining traditional beliefs and practices with new organizational forms.

Section two, Rethinking the Religion–State Relationship, examines one of the central arenas where the visibility of religion is contested. Often, in fact, the public visibility of religion is equated with the state treatment of religion. This, as the chapters in this section demonstrate, is a problematic view, as the religion–state relations are discussed, debated, defended and opposed in many other arenas than legislation and the courts. Together, the chapters take a distinctively sociological look at religion–state relations. Luca Diotallevi (Chapter 8) begins with a theoretical overview of two types of religion–state separation, which he calls the (French) *laïcité* model and the (American) religious freedom model. Harnessing the theoretical system of Niklas Luhmann, Diotallevi shows how the two models are – despite both sometimes being lumped under the category of 'moderate separatism' – essentially different. In the *laïcité* model, 'conscience is a space in which the individual can privately maintain his own religious preference, the public expression of which, however, remains strictly regulated by the State', whereas in the religious freedom model 'it is exactly the public practice of religion which guarantees that political power does not occupy the entire public space: it provides for the expression of political, economic, educational, etc. choices and endeavours that are religiously motivated, but not religious in themselves' (p. 110). Chapter 9, by Norman Bonney, analyses the enduring connections between the Church of England and the state in the United Kingdom. Despite perceptions of the state as secular and of secularization on the level of belief and belonging, the Church of England continues to play a pivotal role – despite some concessions to multiculturalism – in popular state rituals, especially those concerning the royalty but also in official forms of state remembrance for the casualties of war, for example. In another case from the United Kingdom – although the independence referendum on 18 September 2014 could have made that political unit very different – Paul Gilfillan (Chapter 10) examines elderly Scots' views on the role of faith in the independence question. Closely examining interview data, Gilfillan argues that his informants' narratives show little or no evidence that the referendum was influenced by their faith or membership in one of the historical Scottish churches. Scottish national identity and nationalism, at least in the narratives of one group of elderly Scots, is class-based rather than religiously operationalized. Religion, in other words, is rarely visible. In Chapter 11, I examine the fate of a Finnish law initiative that proposed to end the privileged position of the Lutheran Church of Finland and thus make it equal with other religious communities in Finland. In analysing three distinct discourses, I argue that the discussion represents a case of 'national piety', a conflation of discourses of religious equality, freedom of religion and national identity that reproduces the status quo. Here, as in many other cases in the book, it is the functions that the 'folk' church provides rather than faith in God that legitimates religion's continuing public presence. Finally, Ian Morrison (Chapter 12) analyses the positions taken by Anglo-American media pundits on post-Arab Spring Egypt. He differentiates between 'optimistic' and 'pessimistic' responses, where the latter, especially, juxtapose the visible rise of Islamic politics and democracy. Using Jacques Rancière's terminology,

Morrison argues that both responses represent a case of 'parapolitics': 'the inclusion or exclusion of Islamists from the post-revolutionary political sphere is determined by a capacity to abide by the rules and embody the values proper to this sphere' (p. 172). Both positions employ 'predetermined notions of democracy as a particular institutional form with a corresponding map of society distinguishing political and non-political subjects (including Islamists) defined by their possession of particular capacities and characteristics' (p. 174). Applying Rancière, Morrison discusses alternative – and more democratic, he argues – views of political participation.

The third section, Religion and Social Action, turns the gaze to the changing field of welfare and the changing role of religion in that field. Staying in the Middle East and North Africa (MENA) region, Rana Jawad's chapter (Chapter 13) explores the different types of Islamic welfare provision. In the MENA region, the role of religion in welfare provision is less contested than in Europe, yet tensions remain in a situation of massive inequality and (external) perceptions of Islamic political groups (e.g. Hamas, Hezbollah) as terrorists. Jawad argues that although religious NGOs have so far had a function as poor-relief providers, rather than agents of social change, any form of welfare provision in the area would do well to understand the role that religion plays in broader visions of a good society. Chapter 14, by Akile Ahmet and Christina Victor, returns to Europe and looks at the role that religion plays in experiences of care and caring among elderly Hindus and Muslims in Britain. Noting the invisibility of religion in previous research on caring, the authors show how ideas about filial duty impact daily practices among their informants. Although working with a limited qualitative sample, Ahmet and Victor's research shows that religion is more visible – at least among ethnic non-Christian informants – than medicalized views of caring may allow. In the next chapter (Chapter 15), Raluca Bianca Roman examines the transnational connections between European Roma communities and the central role that Pentecostalist Christianity, especially, plays in the mobilization of Finnish Roma for international aid and missionary work. She finds that 'religious missionizing among the Kaale appears to be not only individually but also community oriented: it is an individual drive to participate, but the missionary work is almost always conducted in Roma communities abroad, rather than poor communities more broadly' (p. 215). Although grand transnational schemes for a Roma 'nation' – mostly elite projects, as Roman argues – have fallen short of providing grassroots unity, the religious identity works together with ethnic 'togetherness' in mobilizing Roma social activism. In the final chapter of the book (Chapter 16), Eleanor Ryan-Saha looks at the everyday practices of a drug rehabilitation clinic in Sarajevo – the city known as the 'apotheosis of the atheist, socialist dream' in the Yugoslav period and the crux of interreligious strife during the wars of the early 1990s – and reconsiders 'the ways in which public life in Sarajevo is inconsistently and unpredictably constructed as secular and religious' (p. 218). Coining the term 'capricious simultaneity', Ryan-Saha demonstrates how the religious and the secular manage to cohabit everyday practices. Her ethnographic account is a welcome reminder that not every case of the 'new visibility of religion' is a problem.

Valorization of religion, not God

What to make of the above theorizations and the below case studies, then? On the one hand, at the risk of repetition, it is clear that visibility, vitality and social influence are different things. The sometimes barely contained enthusiasm about the new visibility of religion has done a disservice to the analytical study of religion. The celebrationist account seems to be doomed to repeat the sins of the secularization thesis, which was, according to one famous opponent, 'a taken-for-granted *ideology* rather than a systematic set of interrelated propositions' (Hadden 1987: 588; emphasis in the original). Yet, as argued above, visibility can have a potential impact on vitality and social influence, although not necessarily in ways imagined by religious communities themselves. Visibility informs the ways in which we talk about religion – not to mention that, in many cases, it is the reason why religion is back on the everyday political and media agendas in the first place.

On the other hand, judging from some of the theoretical accounts in this chapter and the case studies in this volume, it is apparent that what counts in the public visibility of religion is practice, not belief. Beliefs are not very interesting per se (beyond the occasional tabloid story about the 'weird' beliefs of new religious movements); the practices putatively arising from particular beliefs are. Public controversy about religion tends to be almost exclusively about things such as headscarves, opposition to teaching evolution in schools and the alleged religious motivations of violence. Heresy is not an argument against particular religions in contemporary Europe; immoral – however that is defined – or possibly illegal action by religious individuals or groups is. Similarly, European states are, at least in principle, neutral regarding religious beliefs. Religion becomes interesting when it is seen to contribute positively (as in welfare provision) or negatively (as in 'parallel societies' or violence) to the broader society.

Finally: Is God back? The blunt answer is 'no'. To put it differently: religion, not God, is back. There is an internal secularization of discourse, if you will, at work in the new visibility of religion. Religion, as any cultural phenomenon, is the object of different types of *valorizations* – ascriptions of value – and, despite all the talk about 'faith', it is the social contribution of religions rather than faith that is being valorized (Thompson 1990: 12). In the case of welfare, for example, 'religious groups are recognized for the instrumental role they play in delivery of services and cohesion. It is their public activity which is in focus, not the interior life of faith itself, nor the religious reasons or goals which motivate it' (Dinham and Jackson 2012: 289). Religion is visible because it can be good or bad, but God has little to do with it.

Acknowledgements

An earlier version of this chapter was published in *The Journal of Religion in Europe* 7(3–4), 2014, pp. 203–22. Used with kind permission of Brill. I would like to thank Jim Beckford, Jim Spickard, and Anna Strhan for comments on an early draft. As always, my inability to take good advice is my fault alone.

PART ONE

Conceptualizing public religion

2

Studying public religions: Visibility, authority and the public/private distinction

Marta Axner

Twenty years ago, José Casanova published *Public Religions in the Modern World,* a book which questioned the privatization of religion and changed the debate over secularization in the Western world (Casanova 1994). Since then it has been cited, discussed and used for empirical studies, and Casanova himself has developed some of his points further. At the same time, there has been an increase in the sociological and political debates over the place of religion in modern society. Is there anything new to say about deprivatization and 'public religions'? I believe so, and in this chapter I will go back to Casanova and use a recent study of religious actors on Swedish opinion pages to discuss his concept 'public religion' and how it can be further elaborated and operationalized in empirical studies. I will start by recapping some of Casanova's central arguments and briefly present my study. Then I will discuss four points from my results that are useful for studying public religions. Finally, I will suggest a model or set of questions to use when studying public religions, especially in a mediated setting.

Deprivatization and public religions

For decades, secularization and the privatization of religion had been the focus of most theory and research in the social scientific study of religion (cf. Berger 1967; Luckmann 1967; Martin 1978; Dobbelaere 1981), as well as the paradigmatic political view in most Western countries. In the 1990s, the simple notion that modernity leads to religious decline, or at least the withdrawal of religion from the public sphere, started to be questioned, one of the key works being José Casanova's 1994 book, *Public Religions in the Modern World,* in which he introduced the concept of deprivatization.

Casanova's core idea is that secularization must be understood as three separate processes: (1) as structural differentiation, where every institution in modern society moves towards an increasingly separated and specialized place and refined task. In this process, religious institutions have moved from being general actors in society to having a more specialized religious profile and thereby becoming more marginal in modern society with less influence over other sectors; (2) as declining belief in religious dogmas and declining religious participation on the individual level; and (3) as the privatization of religion in the sense of religion retracting from the public arena, or civil society. Of these three processes, Casanova claims that only the first one has an inherent connection to modernization as such. The other two processes are not necessarily consequences of the first and need to be independently studied empirically in different times and contexts (Casanova 1994: 19–39). The third process is in fact changing, he argues, and participation of religious groups in the public sphere is what he calls public religion. He sets up certain conditions, such as accepting pluralism and participation on the level of civil society, not legislation or state authority, for these public religions to be legitimate in a liberal democracy (Casanova 1994: 50–66). He also sets out at least three instances, or types of issues, where entering the public sphere is legitimate for religious actors (Casanova 1994: 57–8):

1 When religious groups protect not only their own freedom of religion but also other basic freedom and rights, especially against a totalitarian state.
2 To question the ethical or moral basis of political leaders or the consequences of politics or capitalism, such as arms trade or poverty.
3 To protect the traditional life-world from the state – juridical or administrative – and thereby open up a discussion about norms and collective self-reflection.

Casanova discusses the concept of 'public' at length, drawing on Habermas' understanding of the public sphere as the space for open and joint decision-making based on rational arguments (Habermas 1989). Discussing the deprivatization of religion, he is referring primarily to the debates, involvement in collective issues, critique of power and mobilization taking place in the public sphere. As Habermas himself would later argue, religious actors and religious arguments can have a legitimate place in the 'public use of reason', and a pluralist society needs to be able to accommodate also religion and religious arguments (Habermas 2006).

Casanova's (and Habermas') conception of 'the public' is a very particular one, however. Jeff Weintraub has distinguished between two basic but very different understandings of the public and private, which he refers to as the 'visibility' type and the 'collectivity' type. Private and public can hence be understood as (Weintraub 1997: 5):

1 What is hidden or withdrawn versus what is open, revealed or accessible.
2 What is individual, or pertains only to an individual, versus what is collective, or affects the interests of a collectivity of individuals. This individual/collective distinction can, by extension, take the form of a distinction between part and whole (of some social collectivity).

Weintraub further identifies four models of understanding the public sphere that are used in social and political analysis. These are the *liberal-economistic model*, where the state and political decision-making is public and basically everything else (especially the free market) is private; the *republican-virtue approach*, where the public is what is collectively decided upon, and citizenship is key to understanding the public as where individuals come together to take responsibility for the common good; *sociability*, which refers to the public as visibility, or a public space in the physical sense and potentially also the media as public; and, finally, the *feminist approach*, which is mostly a critique of other approaches for not adequately addressing the understanding of the domestic sphere as private and the political consequences of, for example, domestic violence (Weintraub 1997: 7–29).

If the republican-virtue model is a typical 'collectivity'-type model, the sociability model would be the prime example of 'visibility'. If these models are to be compared, it becomes clear that certain phenomena that are considered private in one model can be considered public in another. For example, wearing religious clothing would be a typical example of something private in the republican-virtue model, while it would be public in the sociability model. Placing Casanova in Weintraub's schema, *Public Religions in the Modern World* falls most clearly into the republican-virtue model, with less emphasis on the visibility of religion.

During the twenty years that have passed since the publication of *Public Religions in the Modern World*, the book has been widely cited, and Casanova's theorizations have been further developed and critiqued. Among others, Talal Asad has pointed out the West-centrism but also the Roman-Catholic bias in Casanova's approach, which has coloured his understanding of religious organizations as well as the 'legitimate questions' for a religion to address in a liberal democracy (Asad 2003). Asad also questions the claim that structural differentiation is a defining trait in modernization and the normative stance of Casanova regarding what forms of religion are acceptable in liberal democracies (Asad 2003: 182–4). Casanova has responded to the critique, mainly on the point of West-centrism, and has taken on a more global approach in his later writings. He has softened his view on what spheres are legitimate for religious actors and now finds religious participation acceptable also in the political sphere, not only in civil society. He has also revised his strong view on structural differentiation, in line with the critique from Asad (Casanova 2006a, 2006b, 2008).

Analysing religious actors in Sweden

Starting with Casanova's concept of 'public religions', and with the aim of identifying religious actors in Swedish public debate and examining the way that they participated, I have conducted a study of the opinion pages of three national Swedish newspapers[1] during the years 2001–11 and collected all pieces signed by someone using a religious title or representing a religious organization (Axner 2013). The aim was not primarily to 'test' Casanova's thesis but rather to use it as a starting point. The focus on the participation of religious actors in public debate, as opposed to a study of the contents of the journalistic coverage of religion, was also highly influenced by Casanova's study. The debate column in daily newspapers is a well-established and important genre in the Nordic countries, where people who want to influence public debate can submit pieces. In principle anyone can submit, but the majority of articles are signed by politicians, scholars, journalists, public intellectuals or representatives of organizations. The debate page is mostly an elite arena (Petersson and Carlberg 1990; cf. Wahl-Jorgensen 2004).

A total of 639 articles were collected, and these were coded with attributes of the signatories, such as religion, type of organization, position and gender, but also with codes for the content, such as themes and issues addressed in a more qualitative, exploratory way. The material was analysed first in a quantitative overview to answer questions regarding which religious actors participated in the debate and to what extent; second, in-depth qualitative analyses were conducted, focusing on three topics: the case of same-sex marriage, the position of the majority (former state) church (Church of Sweden), and, finally, the participation of religious minorities. The results showed that Christian organizations – churches as well as non-governmental organizations and other groups – dominated the material, but Jewish and Muslim groups were also present. All actors had to legitimate their participation in the debate but to varying extent: the religious minorities had more limited opportunities to speak out on issues not directly relating to themselves. The most important factor regarding what groups were present in the debate was not size/membership but, rather, history and establishment (not in the legal sense) in Swedish society. This was most striking regarding the Orthodox/Eastern churches that have a high and growing membership due to migration but are almost completely missing in the debate. On the other hand, the Jewish group has a small national membership but a long history in Sweden, and proportionately it is the most published group. The Church of Sweden, the former state church, was the most dominant group on all accounts in the material (Axner 2013: 76–94).

Public religions: Four areas to elaborate

Below, I will discuss four issues that refine and expand Casanova's thesis – at least when applied to a Nordic or northern European setting: the minority/majority dynamics, whether certain issues can be defined as legitimate for public religions, questions of representation and who speaks on behalf of a religion and, finally, how understandings of the public might be informed by a media perspective.

Minority/majority conditions: Who can be a public religion?

One of the main results of the study was the striking difference in conditions and strategies – or at least outcomes – for the different religious groups, depending on their establishment in Swedish society and minority versus majority position. The Church of Sweden, being the former state church with still around 70 per cent of the population as members and having a long history and comparatively good resources in terms of staff, money, national presence and well-known spokespeople, has a very different position compared to the small Jewish and Muslim communities. Church of Sweden actors often write in a 'public religion' way, in the sense that they 'step out' of their own turf and debate common issues defending the common good or criticize power, for example. However, they also debate more or less internal matters, and the issues regarding the Church of Sweden are discussed as a concern for the general public and not only its members. This is in sharp contrast to the religious minorities, who rarely get the opportunity to speak for 'the common good' but instead have to negotiate their own belonging to Swedish society. There are also interesting differences between Christian groups, where mainstream denominations are present in the debate but do not have the same position as the Church of Sweden. The media presence of religious minorities (especially Jews and Muslims) was mostly limited to issues relating directly to themselves (anti-Semitism/Islamophobia, freedom of religion and the conditions of living as a religious minority in Swedish society). Muslims, in particular, often had to defend their faith and pledge allegiance to Swedish society while pointing towards their need for protection as a vulnerable minority.

It seems all religious groups needed to legitimate their public participation, argue why they, as religious actors, had a legitimate reason to participate in a specific debate, or prove their own contribution to the conversation. In this respect all religious actors play an 'away game', not being on their own turf. This did not play out the same way for all religious actors, though: the least established groups seemed to need more legitimizing, and the number of articles and the themes of the articles also point in this direction. The more established a religious group was in Sweden, the more articles were published. This factor was a much stronger indicator of presence than size of membership, for example.

Religious minorities negotiate between being a marginalized group in need of protection and, at the same time, showing support for majority society and the values of pluralism. These strategies are interestingly echoed in another minority/majority negotiation, namely within the Christian groups and in relation to secular majority society, mostly from conservative groups. Actors advocating, for example, a negative view on same-sex marriage or against abortion rarely made universal claims towards all of society; they more commonly argued for their right to a diverging view in a pluralist society and the right to protection as a minority. This argument was also sometimes directed by groups within the Church of Sweden towards their leadership.

The question of minority and majority leads to a more direct question about power. The analysis of the articles by religious minorities led me question whether it is even possible for a religious minority to be a public religion in Casanova's sense. If a group constantly needs to ascertain its own belonging to a society, is it possible to claim to speak out for the 'common good' of that society or criticize power in more general terms?

The tensions or variations between majority and minority positions for religious groups are, I believe, important to keep in mind when studying public religions and are not really addressed by Casanova. The opportunity for a religious actor to act as a public religion depends on its position, in society in general but also within his or her own group. A lot of negotiation and internal debate, partly on specific issues but partly also over who is speaking for a specific group, is at stake. I will return to both these themes later, but I first point to this in relation to Casanova. Though he goes beyond formal leadership and hierarchies, he is still mostly looking at majority or mainstream churches and how they act in relation to a more general public or society. In order to understand the public participation of the religious actors, internal factors and processes need to be taken into account, as well as the very different conditions for marginalized groups to participate compared to the mainstream churches, for example. Questions relating to power and strategies to both legitimate and undermine power structures need to be studied, in relation to a more general societal debate but also within religious organizations and traditions.

Certain issues and arguments – or certain strategies of legitimation?

In his discussion on the legitimacy of religious participation in the public sphere, Casanova (following Habermas) points towards certain issues and arguments that are possible or legitimate for religious actors in the public use of reason in modern, liberal democracies. Without a very precise definition of what these issues are and what constitutes a religious argument, however, they are not very useful, and even with accurate definition they leave questions unanswered. One of the important aspects of participating in public debate is (trying to) frame or formulate the issue at stake, and what the issue 'is' in a certain debate is not neutral or given but, rather, is one of the things up for debate. Whether a question is a concern for the general public, is about democratic principles or about the protection of a marginalized group, is itself one of the important considerations for someone who wants to put an issue on the agenda. For example, should the possibility for a small religious group to practice their faith be seen as a particular interest for that group or as a general issue of freedom of religion concerning the core values of society?

The same problem regarding definitions can be seen when looking at 'religious arguments'. What constitutes a 'religious argument'? In the analysis of the same-sex marriage debate, many potential examples of religious arguments were found, but they were often sweeping, rarely developing theological arguments in detail or giving specific Bible quotes and rarely, if ever, making universal claims. Whether this is due to an expected lack of knowledge about theology or the Bible in the audience (and hence relating to the specific arena of the debate pages in secular media) or something else is hard to tell, but I find it more interesting to look at *how* religious arguments or language are used, rather than *if*.

If it is problematic to define certain issues as legitimate for religious actors and difficult to decide what constitutes religious language, perhaps a different angle is better suited to study these questions. Instead of setting up criteria for legitimate questions, a more fruitful approach could be to study what issues religious actors participate in, how they frame them and how they legitimate their participation in the debate. Further, what strategies are used to argue the issue at hand and how do the actors negotiate their relevance and belonging in that debate or public arena? How does authority – religious or otherwise – come into play, in relation to the other actors involved in the debate at hand but also in relation to other religious actors? This could be especially interesting in debates where religious actors can be found on 'both sides' of an issue.

Representation and the importance of the individual

One of the factors touched upon in the study, but not fully developed, is the importance of the individual writer or actor. A relatively small number, thirty people, signed almost half the articles in the material, and interviews with the newspaper editors confirmed my observation that the writer (together with the news value and the quality of the text) was an important factor when publishing an article. Well-known and respected leaders and intellectuals were published most often. Organizational position is one aspect, but other well-known and established writers without formal positions were also recurrently published. It is difficult to determine whether a writer represents an organization/a religious community or only himself or herself. Sometimes the claim of representation is very clear: when the entire leadership of the Swedish Christian Council sign an article, they are formally representing their churches. In some cases, writers are very clear that they only speak for themselves, relating their own opinions and experiences. Often, however, the lines are blurry, and this raises questions regarding who can speak for a tradition or a creed and whether it is possible for someone with a position of religious authority, such as a bishop or a rabbi, to speak publicly as a private person and not as a representative of her or his faith.

Another interesting phenomenon is when people who have no formal position in their faith community but, by their profession or otherwise, are well-known and respected – sometimes even famous members of society, such as authors, journalists or publicly elected officials – write articles presenting themselves as religious or speaking from a position as a Christian, Jew or Muslim, for example. This was quite common among Jewish writers in the material, but several examples of Christians were also found. This raises questions about authority and legitimacy in another way: in regard to these actors and how they (try to) take on religious authority outside the traditional structures of religious communities, but also in how they might challenge traditional leadership and religious authority. The clearest example was the strong support for Israel among the leadership in the Jewish community, while Jewish peace activists, some of them artists and journalists, questioned both the Israeli position in the conflict with Palestine and the leadership of the Jewish Central Council's right to speak for all Swedish Jews on this issue.

The issue of 'who' the public religion is, that is, who speaks for a group, is not discussed in any length by Casanova, but the religions are mostly seen as the same as their formal leaders. This might be an effect of the aforementioned Catholic bias, where a hierarchical church structure is assumed. This points towards the need both to take in further analytical concepts and to evolve methodology. Questions regarding authority and power need to be taken into account not only in regard to religion versus other actors but also within the different faith communities, organizations and traditions. I also believe text-based studies might need to be complemented with other methods, especially when it comes to negotiations over power and tensions within specific organizational structures. Though some aspects of these negotiations over authority can be studied with discourse analysis, this only reaches the parts taking place in the media or in other public documents. Traditional sociological methods, such as interviews and participatory observations, can give insight into both how these different actors themselves experience participating in the public arena and how these public interactions change or at least affect the non-mediated parts of a religious community and could also provide background to conscious strategies as well as unintended effects of participating in the media or other public forums.

Taking the media perspective seriously: Visibility is not necessarily authority

Though the concept of public religion as coined by Casanova is not equal with 'media religion', it is difficult to imagine a study of public religion without a reference to media. This is perhaps even more so today than when Casanova's book was published twenty years ago. It is important to see that not all attempts to influence public policy or general opinion take place in or through the media, but the specific logic of varying media needs to be taken seriously. The concepts of media logic and mediatization are not unproblematic (cf. Lundby 2009; Hjarvard and Lövheim 2012; Lövheim and Lynch 2011; Couldry 2008), but they can prove useful in helping to qualify the conditions for the public participation studied. At least some sensitivity towards the genres and types of media, as well as knowledge of the infrastructure, economy and technology of the media studied is necessary in order to avoid underestimating or overrating the importance of media logic in a specific context.

This takes us back to where we started: different understandings of the public, or types of public/private distinctions. Some media participation might very well be an example of participating in 'public use of reason' or influencing political agendas in the collectivity sense. But other instances of mediated religion are 'public' solely in the visibility sense. As Göle argues, the physical presence and visibility of Muslims and religious buildings and clothing in European cities is connected to power in the public arena (Göle 2011, 2010). However, instances of visible religion in the media should not be confused with the influence of religion or seen as a sign of desecularization or 'return of religion' without further qualification or detailed analysis.

In the context of mediated religion, I would firmly argue that visibility is not enough. Many media studies approach religion by studying the extent of religious language, or key words, usually using content analysis (Niemelä and Christensen 2013; Knott et al. 2013). Although these are interesting and well-made studies, using that kind of data for making big statements on the return of religion or the end of secularization means using studies of visibility to assume effects on the public without qualifying what is meant by the public, potentially implying impact on the public in a collectivity sense. An increase in visibility of religious actors, themes or content is not necessarily an increased influence for religious authority. On the contrary, the increased visibility could be due to greater scrutiny, negative press or the use of religious symbols in popular culture taken out of context (cf. Hjarvard 2012).

Instead of studying the numerical increase or decrease of religion in the media, or studying whether and to what extent religious groups participate in public arenas, I would suggest moving towards studies of how religion, religious language and authority are being used to create or uphold legitimacy. Legitimacy is a key issue in struggles over representation and authority within certain religious groups and in negotiations over different understandings of the place of religion in the public arena (however defined) in late modern societies (for a more elaborated discussion on this point, see Lövheim and Axner 2014).

Suggested criteria for studying public religions

I would like to end this chapter by sketching a tentative set of analytical questions or themes for studying public religions. These themes are developed for studying religious actors, and while they have grown out of a media study, I believe they are relevant and useful also for other studies of religious actors in the public arena.

Type or definition of 'the public'

The first step, as argued above, is to determine what understandings of 'the public' are present in the case studied. Obviously a careful definition is needed for the study itself, but this is also an interesting theme to analyse in the material itself. If religious actors or others are discussing the place of religion in the public sphere, what are their understandings of the public? In what way are they trying to achieve or restrict public religions?

Claims, authority and legitimation

Who do religious actors claim to represent when they participate in debates, lobby politicians or in other ways move into the public sphere? Do they claim to represent a faith community, or are they speaking out of their individual position? How are they legitimating their participation, and with what authority do they speak, both in relation to their own group and in relation to the wider society?

Intended audience and aim of the participation

This point follows partly from the previous one. In the study of newspaper debates, some articles were clearly directed towards legislators or the general public, while others were directed towards the leadership of the writer's own organization. However, sometimes the intended audience was not completely clear, or there seemed to be an underlying aim for participating in the debate, for example confirming the identity of the group itself while formally addressing the government. Examining the overtly stated as well as potentially underlying aims and intended audience may shed light on further dimensions of legitimacy and authority.

Types of issues, or the framing of these issues

Instead of starting with a set of issues defined as legitimate for religions to address in public, a more useful approach would be to start from a less normative point and map the issues actually addressed. To move beyond just a descriptive study, studies should show how religious actors frame issues to make their own participation relevant or legitimate their point of view by appealing to values or perspectives generally recognized by a wider audience (see Lövheim and Linderman in this volume). Instead of claiming that public religions are legitimate when defending democracy, the focus should be on how religious actors construct democracy and thereby (try to) achieve influence and legitimacy.

Use of religious language or arguments

This point connects to the previous ones in leaving the normative perspective and instead studying the way religious language and arguments, and in that sense religious authority, is used in a specific case by a specific actor. On a more aggregated level, it examines how religious language and symbols are used in a type of medium or time period to achieve influence or to connect religion with negative attributes.

Media logic of the genre used

This is obviously a key aspect in media studies, but I would suggest also paying attention to genre when studying other contexts. Texts are always written in a genre – opinion pieces and news articles as well as reference statements, reports and sermons. Other types of public participation could also be studied with this in mind – a town hall meeting, a Sunday service, a Friday prayer or a political rally all have their 'logics' or patterns of interaction that the researcher needs to be aware of in order to interpret the meaning of textual content in particular contexts.

Final remarks

The idea of 'public religions' has not lost its relevance over the twenty years that have passed since the publication of Casanova's book. Rather, the theme is more relevant than ever and can be used for empirical applications as well as more theoretical analyses. The reflections and suggestions made here are based on experiences using Casanova's concepts and aim to provide perspectives to further nuance and improve the empirical understanding of how religious actors participate in public and how mediated arenas become venues where the place of religion and the nature of a public space are negotiated.

3

Religion, media and modernity: Editorials and religion in Swedish daily press

Mia Lövheim and Alf Linderman

The beginning of the twenty-first century has been marked by the debate about a resurgence of religion in public life. In the Nordic countries, mass media have become the prime sites where people in general encounter religion in daily life (Lövheim 2012; Hjarvard 2011; Lundby 2010). Previous research analysing changes in the visibility of religion in Nordic media over recent decades shows an increased diversity of topics and perspectives. Whether this also means that religion has returned to the political and societal agenda is, however, a question that requires further discussion. This chapter will contribute to the critical assessment of the new visibility of religion through focusing on the use of religion in opinion material, more precisely editorials, in the main Swedish daily newspapers from 1976 to 2010.[1] Our argument is that we cannot assume a direct relation between changes in the visibility of religion in the media and changes in the role of religion in public discourse. The relation between media, religion and the constitution and negotiation of modernity is more complex. In this chapter, therefore, we will present our findings regarding changes in the amount of references to religion in Swedish editorials, but we will also discuss how media representations of religion can be seen as part of the process of constituting and reconstituting core values of modern Swedish identity. Here, we explore how a ritual perspective on media might be used as tool for understanding this role of mediated religion in contemporary society, particularly within editorials as a genre focusing on continuity of political positions and arguments.

Religion, media and modernity in Sweden

The Nordic countries constitute an interesting case for analysing the relation between media and religion in highly modernized societies (Hjarvard 2012). In Sweden, as the first of the Nordic countries, a formal disconnection between the Evangelical Lutheran Church and the state took place in the year 2000. The post-war period saw a large decline in church attendance. In 2012, 67.5 per cent of the population of nine million belonged to the Church of Sweden, but not more than a few per cent attended services on a regular Sunday (Svenskakyrkan.se). Sweden has also, since the late 1980s, experienced an increase in religious and cultural diversity. The largest religious minority group is Muslims: about 450,000 people or 5 per cent of the population have parents who are born in, or are themselves born in, Muslim majority countries. The share of registered members of Muslim congregations amounts to about 110,000 (Nämnden för statligt stöd till trossamfund 2012).

According to the Swedish sociologist of religion Thorleif Pettersson, low levels of church-oriented religious involvement but also high levels of individualism distinguish Swedish culture in an international comparison (Pettersson 2009). Using a definition of religion that focuses on the sacred nature of immanent values (cf. Woodhead and Heelas 2000), he argues that individual freedom, autonomy and human rights hold a sacred status in contemporary Sweden. The tensions between two forms of sacredness, one referring to transcendent, the other to immanent values and symbols, came to the fore, for example, in the crisis around the Danish daily *Jyllands-Posten*'s publication of the Muhammad cartoons in 2005. One further aspect shaping the relation between religion, modernity and the media is that Sweden in international comparison has very high rates of newspaper circulation and trust in the media (Hallin and Mancini 2004: 21–3). Sixty-nine per cent of the population read a newspaper on a daily basis (Nordicom 2012), and an equal amount express trust in public service media (television and radio). More than half of the population trust the largest morning paper, *Dagens Nyheter*, while 13 per cent trust the largest tabloid, *Aftonbladet* (Förtroendebarometern 2014).

A resurgence of religion in the media?

A main strand in the discussion about the return of religion to the public sphere has been the argument that increased religious and cultural diversity, along with a renegotiation of previous boundaries between state, market, civil society and the private sphere, have created a momentum for religious actors and arguments to play a more salient role in the political debate (Casanova 1994: 57–8; Habermas 2006). In recent years, studies have appeared that show a heightened and more diversified interest in religion in modern mass media over the last decades (Knott et al. 2013; PEW 2011). The comparative Nordic study, 'The Role of Religion in the Public Sphere' (NOREL) (Niemelä and Christensen 2013), showed an uneven pattern: an increase in the number of articles on religion in all countries from 1988 to 1998 but a decrease from 1998 to 2008.[2] The most salient finding was the increased *diversity* of coverage; a clear decrease of the share of articles referring to the Lutheran Church combined with a steep increase of articles on Islam (from 2 per cent to 29 per cent). Furthermore, attention during the period shifted from covering religion as news towards debates primarily focusing on the accommodation of an increased religious diversity. Case studies by Marta Axner and Henrik Reintoft Christensen also show that when religious leaders and topics enter a public mediated debate, they tend to adjust their communication to the format and agenda of the media in question (Axner 2013; Christensen 2012). This ambiguous picture has led to a discussion about the risk of conflating the visibility of religious actors in public debate and the impact of religious themes and arguments in society and media discourse (Köhrsen 2012; Beckford 2012; Lövheim and Axner 2014).

These results connect in part to the mediatization of religion theory presented by the Danish media scholar, Stig Hjarvard (2011, 2012). Mediatization describes how the growing importance of technological media during the twentieth century affects other forms of social and cultural life. Hjarvard argues that mediatization may contribute to an increased visibility of religion in society but that this visibility, to a larger extent than before, is constructed in accordance with the institutional, technological and aesthetic preferences of certain media genres. In news media, religion becomes represented according to journalistic criteria of newsworthiness, and in entertainment media, religion becomes represented as *banal religion* – a mix of institutional and popular religious elements mainly used to fulfil purposes of drama and excitement.

The validity of this thesis for analysing the interplay between media, modernity and religion has been debated in Nordic research (Lövheim and Lynch 2011; Hjarvard and Lövheim, 2012). Lövheim and Lundby, in their 2013 study of Norwegian newspapers, argue that changes over time are mediated by the particular religious history of a region and the readership culture guiding editorial decisions (Lövheim and Lundby 2013). It is thus clear from previous research that the presence and role of religion in the media – here, in particular, daily press – is more complex than a linear decrease or increase. In order to assess the impact of increased mediatization on religion, the relation between religion and the modernization of a particular society needs to be taken into consideration.

James Beckford argues that in Britain, the current attention to religion does not signal a new role for religious organizations vis-à-vis the state and polity but rather as part of the neo-liberal government's strategy of managing and controlling religious and ethnic diversity (Beckford 2010: 132). This idea of a continuous but renegotiated contract between the political sector and religious actors in a situation of increasing religious diversity offers an interesting perspective for understanding the use of religion in Swedish media, with clear connections to the role of religion as vehicle of core social and cultural values. The concept of ritual has previously been used within media studies to analyse the role of the media in processes where core values, identities and social relations in society and culture are constituted and reconstituted through, for example, large-scale media events (Dayan and Katz 1992; Curran and Liebes 1998), media coverage of national tragedy (Sumiala 2013) or the production of news (Ettema and Whitney 1987). A ritual perspective starts out from an idea of shared conventions, boundaries and authorities in society that are repeated and supported by the media, but it also makes explicit their performative and constructed nature (Sumiala 2013: 36; Ehrlich 1996: 7; cf. Couldry 2003).

Editorials as case for studying the role of religion in society

Our choice of case for studying the relation between religion and modernity in Sweden is based on the historically important role of editorials in Swedish public debate through their close connection to political parties and debates (Nord 2001). This means that editorials as a genre are formed by ideas about the media as an arena for democratic deliberation and by ideals drawn from a humanistic enlightenment tradition, such as freedom of opinion, rational arguments and a balance between various opinions and special interests (Nord 2001: 74). Furthermore, the editorial can be described as evaluative rather than following news criteria. Thus, editorials can be expected to express continuity in opinions over time to a higher degree than other media genres. This makes editorials an appropriate case for studying the articulation and negotiation of core values in Swedish society and the role of religion in this process.

Method

The material used in our analysis comes from editorials in the eleven largest daily newspapers in Sweden,[3] meaning those that have a circulation of 80,000 or more, between the years 1976 and 2010. From this total material, we selected a sample of 4,865 newspaper editorials from 30 to 32 systematically randomized publishing days per year. The sample includes all editorials (main and smaller) in one of the newspapers for every selected day.

The presence of religion in these texts has been analysed through a quantitative content analysis using a set of search words, grouped into larger categories that represent various indicators of religion (cf. Knott et al. 2013; Niemelä and Christensen 2013). The indicators cover a broad spectrum of religious references, including all the world religions and spirituality.[4] Indicators of modernity in the editorials have been analysed through the use of another set of search words.[5] In total, the number of editorials including any indicator of religion amounts to 481.[6] We also looked for co-occurrences of indicators of religion and indicators of modernity in the texts. Our analysis showed that the most frequent co-occurrence was between indicators of religion and one of the indicators of modernity ('politics'), which is composed of the search words equality, democracy and welfare (Linderman 2013). In total, 119, or 25 per cent, of the editorials containing an indicator of religion did also contain this indicator of modernity. The second phase of the analysis consisted of a qualitative content analysis of the material, focused on how references to religion are used in the editorials, relations between indicators of religion and modernity and patterns of change over the time period.

Religion as description, metaphor and topic for discussion

A first reading of the editorials showed three main ways in which religion was used: as a description of an individual, group or country; as a metaphor; and as the main topic for discussion. The material was coded into these three categories, as well as for the religious tradition referred to and the geographical location of the subject matter (national–international).[7] The largest category, 213 (45 per cent) of all editorials containing any indicator of religion, refers to religion in descriptive way. Seventy-one of these articles include references to Christianity, such as priest, bishop, pope, church, Protestant or Catholic. Sixty-three use words that refer to Islam, such as Muslim groups, Muslim countries, Islamic fundamentalism etc. References to other world religions or alternative spirituality are very few. Furthermore, more than half of the articles in this category, 55 per cent, describe an event or situation in an international context. Many of those are ongoing wars or conflicts between or within nations. This editorial from *Svenska Dagbladet*, 17 September 1993, commenting on the war in Bosnia, is one example[8]:

> The bombings of Serbian positions do not help the Muslims in Mostar contained by Croats. They probably will not prevent new massacres in central Bosnia either where Muslims and Croats compete in cruelty against each other.

The second largest category, 159 editorials (33 per cent), uses religion in a metaphorical way. The majority of the words or expressions used in these texts relate to a Christian, biblical tradition, such as prophecy, preach, doomsday, martyr, sacred, hell, blessing and devil. As shown in this example from *Sydsvenska Dagbladet*, 28 May 1995, the majority of these editorials also comment on national, political events:

> Swedish politics have long been one-dimensional. It has been based on simple, easily distinguishable connections and a number of eternal truths of an almost religious character.

The smallest category, 104 texts (22 per cent), consists of editorials where religion is used as the main topic for discussion. Of these, fifty contain indicators that refer to Christianity, while seventeen refer to a Muslim tradition. Thirty editorials refer to an international context. One of the earliest and most salient examples is an editorial about the 1979 Iranian Revolution in *Dagens Nyheter*, 13 March, with the title 'Can the fanaticism in Iran be stopped?' As this quote shows, the angle of the text is often negative towards religion:

> The women's demonstrations are not the only sign of how the fanaticism and the religiously colored intolerance that Khomeini and the militant clergy expresses frightens many groups in Iran.

Patterns and changes over time

The quantitative analysis of the material showed a slow rise from around 8 per cent of all editorials including indicators of religion in the beginning of the period to more than 11 per cent in 2001–5 and a decrease to 9 per cent in the last five years. If we use the editorial page as a whole as case, we find that 22 per cent of all editorial pages included a reference to religion in at least one of the editorials. For the years between 1996 and 2000, there are references to religion in 45 per cent of all editorial pages. After that, there is a decline. For the last five years, the percentage is just above 30. There is a slight increase in references to Islam in 1991–5 and 2001–5, and there are peaks for Christianity in 1982, 1996 and 2006. The clearest sign of a peak in co-occurrences in editorial texts of indicators of religion and modernity (equality, democracy, welfare) can be found in 1996–2000.

The analysis of the material shows an increase in all of the three categories described above (description, metaphor and main topic), particularly in the period 1996–2005. This tendency is most salient in the category where religion is the main topic of discussion. Here the number of articles increased from eight in 1991–5 to twenty-two in 1996–2000 and to thirty-two in the period 2001–5. The last period, 2005–10, contains twenty-four editorials. In the category of articles using religion as a description the pattern is not so drastic, but an increase is clearly visible from twenty-five articles before 1990 to thirty-one in 1991–2000 and rising above forty in the period 2001–10. The category of religion used as metaphor shows a slight increase in the periods 1996–2000 and 2001–5. The last period, 2006–10, however, shows a decline.

A closer analysis of the issues taken up in the various categories shows that in the category of religion as description, the increase seems to follow the outbreak of international conflicts, with a more distinguishable religious aspect in the years 1991–5, most prominently the civil war in former Yugoslavia. Also, in 1996–2010, the issues discussed involving indicators of religion are connected to international events such as the war in Iraq and terror attacks claimed by groups with a connection to Islam in Afghanistan and Somalia. The conflicts between Protestants and Catholics in Northern Ireland and between Israel and Palestine are recurring topics during the whole period of our study.

In the category of religion as main topic, no particular issue stands out to explain the increase of references. Around 1997, several articles discuss the separation of church and state, and in 2001 there are discussions about religious attitudes towards homosexuality following the debates in the Swedish parliament to allow same-sex unions (decided 2009). However, the main tendency seems to be a growing diversity regarding what issues religion has become associated with. An initial focus on Christianity, where organized religion in the form of the Church of Sweden is a salient theme, becomes over time mixed with editorials commenting on issues where religion is connected to Islam, human rights, religious diversity, equality and freedom of religion. In the year 2001, ten editorials refer to religion, which is the highest frequency for one year during the period. Of these, four comment on the debates within the Church of Sweden on same-sex unions, two comment on attitudes to sexuality within the Catholic Church, three comment on Islamic groups in Afghanistan, and two discuss the role of religion in American political life. In the latest period, 2005–10, issues concerning freedom of speech and freedom of religion are discussed in ten of twenty-four editorials.

Religion and modernity

In the previous section we have seen that the number of editorials that include references to religion seems to increase over the period and also that the texts seem to address a broader range of issues. In order to understand more of what these tendencies mean in terms of the relation between religion and modernity in Swedish society, we turn to the editorials where both indicators of religion and modernity (equality, democracy and welfare) occur. We focus in particular on the period 1996–2000, where such co-occurrences peak.

In the category of religion as metaphor, there are several examples of how key words indicating religion and equality, democracy and welfare occur in separate sections of the article, without being connected. However, some examples show how words with religious connotations are used to emphasize a discussion about, for instance welfare, as in this example from *Sydsvenska Dagbladet*, 25 September 2000:

> The main issue for Social democrats should, Engqvist argues, be every citizen's access to the collective welfare services. He writes about the almost religious fixation to the question about mandatorship for these services.

Also, in the second and largest category of religion as description, indicators of religion and of modernity occur most often in separate sections of the text without being explicitly connected. This can be seen, for example, in an editorial in *Expressen*, 22 May 1991, which discusses the murder of Indian Prime Minister Rajiv Gandhi. Here, India is described as 'the world's largest democracy' and further on as a country divided by 'religious, political and cultural contradictions'.

An example of when indicators of modernity and of religion are connected is from an editorial in *Aftonbladet*, 30 May 1996, about the elections in Israel:

> This fateful election was so focused on security and peace that the growing divisions in society were removed from the debate: divisions between rich and poor, established citizen and fresh immigrant, Orthodox and secular Jew, Jew and Israeli Palestinian. Social, economic and religious conflicts can now rise to the surface. The religious Shas-party did f ex [for example] do well: the party supports a politics for peace, but not without conditions.

The road towards an equal, democratic Israel with equally entitled citizens from all groups in the population is long.

These two examples illustrate the general tendency in this category of texts of representing religion as a factor causing division and conflicts between groups in society and thus as a problem for a modern, democratic society.

It is in the third and smallest category of religion as main topic that we find the clearest examples of the connection between indicators of religion and of modernity. In the period 1991–2001, six of the eight editorials explicitly connect religion to welfare, democracy and equality, and in the later period seven follow this pattern. The main issue in the texts is the complex relation between religion as an individual right and resource for Swedish society and the values and rights necessary for the functioning of a modern democratic society. This theme is salient in the following quote from an editorial in *Expressen*, 1 January 1996, welcoming the public presence of Islam in the form of mosques, free schools etc.:

> For the sake of the old and new Swedes Sweden must leave behind homogeneous standard solutions and become a country where people can develop their specific character. Sweden must in earnest give space to other cultures and ways of thinking – obviously while maintaining a core of democracy, tolerance, judiciary and Swedish curriculum.

In most of the editorials, religious freedom is described as a core democratic value that must be respected. Religious individuals and groups are, furthermore, described as having the potential to respect democratic values and rights, and such a religion is seen as contributing to modern Swedish society. These patterns can be illustrated in an editorial in *Dagens Nyheter*, 2 January 2002, referring to a speech by the foreign minister on events during the past year:

> Religion is slowly separated from the political power and the influences of modernization creates a more open society where religion exists more or less in harmony with general and ongoing processes of social change.

However, as indicated in these quotes, some forms of religion are still seen as problematic. Islamic terrorism, for example, is criticized, but so is Islamophobia and the security policies following the US-initiated war against terror in the later part of our period. One of the core tensions seems to be balancing between freedom of religion and intolerance towards the lifestyles of other groups, such as homosexuals, or disrespect for Swedish laws. These quotes from an editorial in *Dagens Nyheter*, 11 December 2008, express the tension clearly:

Freedom of religion should be respected. But this does not apply to all behaviors where one for more or less good reasons refers to religious scriptures. ... This applies also to the refusal to greet someone by shaking hands. Not a crime and certainly something that can work if you live your whole life in a radicalized Muslim context. But undoubtedly an obstacle, not to say impossibility, if you would like to work as a lawyer, dental nurse, medical doctor or journalist in majority society.

Patterns of change and continuity

The analysis shows an increase in references to religion in the editorials from the mid-1990s to around 2005. In the last five-year period, the pattern is more mixed. However, the qualitative analysis shows that the majority of the editorials do not change their way of referring to religion over the period. In most cases, words with religious connotations serve as a backdrop to international events, often conflicts, or to national debates about political core values. Religion is predominantly described as an obstacle to or problem for establishing democracy, equality and freedom of opinion, or for holding a rational, impartial political discussion. In the category of religion as main topic, we see a tendency towards a more benevolent, albeit ambiguous, approach, where religion might be seen as compatible with and contributing to a modern, democratic society.

In line with the findings reported in a previous NOREL study (Niemelä and Christensen 2013), references to Christianity are predominant over the period in all of the categories, and the Lutheran Church of Sweden is frequently on the agenda in the category where religion is a main topic of discussion. References to other religious traditions, primarily Islam, seem to be increasing over the period, chiefly in the category using religion as description. It is also interesting to compare the findings to a study of references to religion in Nordic parliamentary debates of 1988–2008 (Lindberg, 2014), which shows an increase in references to religion in speeches and debates, although least so in Sweden. References to the Church of Sweden decrease over the period at the same time as religion becomes related to a higher number of issues, which can be interpreted as religion entering new areas of the political discourse. Among the issues that have become more recurrent are human rights, international relations, immigration, religious diversity and the use of religious symbols in public settings and among public officials.

In conclusion, it seems that religion as a topic has a small but continuous presence in public discourse represented by editorials in daily press.

The tendency of a peak in references to religion between 1996 and 2005 indicates that religion became a more discussed topic as its presence and role internationally, as well as in the Swedish society, became more visible and complex. This change is most remarkable in the categories of religion as description and religion as main topic. These tendencies seem to coincide with a heightened and diversified attention to religious aspects of political issues which develops parallel to the changes in the religious landscape over the latest decades in Swedish society.

Ritualization, maintenance and renegotiation of core values

As described above, the idea of a continuous but renegotiated contract between the political sector and religious actors in a social situation of increasing religious diversity (Beckford 2010) offers an interesting perspective for understanding the findings in our study. In this final discussion, we explore the use of theories about the ritual role of the media to understand the use of religion in editorial texts as part of a constitution and reconstitution of social positions and core values in Swedish society. As pointed out by Matthew Ehrlich, the manifold use of ritual within media studies has contributed to a lack of agreement on what the concept actually means (Ehrlich 1996). We will start out from Ehrlich's suggested interpretative framework for studying ritual in journalism, where ritual is used as a heuristic device to locate specific practices which display certain 'family characteristics' of the process of ritualization, such as being performed, formalized, repeated, institutionalized, valued highly etc. (Ehrlich 1996: 7). Focusing on ritualization as a process also allows us to discuss the way these practices fulfil symbolic and referential functions by making use of shared conventions, boundaries and authorities in society as well as reveal their performative and constructed nature.

Ehrlich argues for a study of ritual in journalism across three levels of analysis (Ehrlich 1996: 8–9). Our material does not enable an analysis of the individual and organizational levels. Therefore we will, in the following, discuss our material on an institutional and cultural level, which focuses on the relations between, in this case, the press and other public institutions in society such as the polity, the meanings generated in media texts and the role of the media in the production, maintenance and transformation of social identities and cultural values (cf. Glasser and Ettema 1991). It is, however, important to point out that our material does not allow for an analysis of the readers' opinions or the broader political discourse.

Our analysis has shown three main categories of ways in which religion is used in the editorials – as description, metaphor and main topic. We have also seen that texts within these categories display certain formalized ways of using religion that become repeated over time. These characteristics make it relevant to talk about a degree of ritualization in the use of religion in the editorials, expressed as repetition and institutionalization with the function of upholding certain values and positions regarding the relation between religion, the state and polity in Swedish society. However, there are also signs of how these characteristics have a performative function in both repeating and challenging values and positions, as when religion is used in a metaphorical way to frame a renegotiation of political issues or – not least – when religion is made into a case in point to discuss the relation between individual rights and collective norms and values. We will close by presenting some examples of how these ways of using religion can be interpreted as part of the construction, maintenance and renegotiation of societal positions and cultural values in contemporary Sweden.

In the category of *metaphors*, the dominance of references to a Christian tradition and the repetition of this pattern over time are peculiar, given the decline in church attendance and religious literacy over the period. On the one hand we might, using Hjarvard's definition of 'banal religion', say that these references to religion through mediatization are used in a way where their meaning becomes detached from institutional or dogmatic religious authority. However, using a perspective of ritualization, we can also interpret this finding as an example of how editorials make use of and confirm the paradoxical position of religion in modern Swedish society pointed out by Pettersson (2009). Although Christian beliefs are not actively supported by the majority of presumed readers, references to words such as 'sacred' and 'religious' or figures and practices from the Bible become used to underscore the particular and non-negotiable character of certain political issues, such as welfare or the right to individual choice. This can be seen as an illustration of how immanent, political values are given a particular status and become reinforced as such over time through the editorials' use of transcendent religious references. However, the dominance of references to a Christian tradition over the period shows that even in a situation of growing religious diversity, the historically dominant form of religion maintains a privileged position to fulfil this function (cf. Knott et al. 2013: 68).

The concept of ritual may also help us understand why the category of *description* is the largest one in the material. This category displays examples of ritualization in the formalized ways of using religion that become repeated over time, such as connecting religion to international conflicts and framing it as an obstacle for modernization. These patterns can be seen as examples of institutionalization of religion as something predominantly related to foreign countries and events, and therefore outside of Swedish national identity, and as a threat towards core democratic values, such as sexual freedom and equality. These findings are well in line with previous studies of the representation of Islam in Swedish press (cf. Ghersetti and Levin 2002) as something threatening, foreign and problematic. In our material, the pattern applies to most depictions of Christian religion as well. The amount of references to increased globalization, religious diversity and issues of religion and human rights during the period can signal a possible change of this pattern, but predominantly the purpose of religion in this category seems to be to reconstruct a difference between religion and Sweden as a modern, democratic society.

Finally, a focus on processes of ritualization might help us understand changing patterns in the category of *religion as main topic*. In these texts, we see the most signs of a performative use of religion to articulate a renegotiation of the former positions of the various actors in the political discourse and of the relations between values that are claimed to be central to Swedish modern democratic society. An example of the former are the recurring discussions of the Swedish Church position on same-sex marriages, which can be seen as a renegotiation of the position of the Church in society (cf. Axner 2013). An example of the latter situation is the way editorials depict the tension between, on the one hand, religious freedom and tolerance for various cultural expressions and, on the other, equality and individual freedom as being foundational values of Swedish democratic policies. Both of these examples illustrate how the use of religion in this category can be interpreted as a way of mediating a renegotiation of the contract between religion and the secular state and political power in a more diverse and globalized society but simultaneously controlling the role religion can play in this relation (cf. Lövheim and Axner 2011).

Media, religion and modernity: Conclusion

Our analysis in this chapter points to two important insights for further studies. The first concerns methodology. This study has shown that tendencies towards increases or decreases in references to religion, revealed by a quantitative content analysis based on key words, might indicate changes in the visibility of religion, but it is not sufficient to draw conclusions regarding changes in the significance of religion in the public sphere. The combination of a quantitative and a qualitative content analysis in our study shows that indicators of religion encompass very different uses of religious words and symbols. The categories of metaphor, description and main topic have made possible the uncovering and differentiation of various meanings of references to religion in media texts. Furthermore, our analysis has shown that co-occurrences of religion and indicators of modernity such as democracy or equality in a text do not necessarily mean that they are connected in a discussion about the role of religion in democratic society. These insights call for a more careful analysis and critical discussions about the empirical bases for claims about changes in the significance of religion in public discourse.

The second insight concerns how to make sense of the patterns of continuity and change regarding how religion is handled in Swedish editorials. Inspite of the tendencies of increased attention to religion over certain periods in our study, the findings do not easily support theories about the return of religion as an independent political voice in society. As we have seen, the increased attention to religion in the texts instead follows the format and purpose of the editorial as a media genre – to express continuity and change of political opinions in a particular society over time. This might be seen as a sign of mediatization, meaning that religion is moulded according to the preferences of a particular media genre. That this process would weaken the role that religion plays in society, however, is not as obvious. The findings instead point to how religion continuously plays a role in this mediatized political debate even if the issues and the forms of religion addressed are changing. Drawing on a ritual perspective, we have illustrated how patterns of using religion as metaphor, description and main topic in editorials in Swedish press can be interpreted as fulfilling a function of maintaining and reinterpreting the balance between two forms of sacredness – the immanent values and symbols of modernity and the religious heritage of contemporary Sweden.

4

Religious cleavages and national identity in European civil societies

Annette Schnabel

The aim of this paper is to examine the relationship between religion and national identity in Europe. As it is one of the more important policy aims of the European Commission to strengthen and to support civil societies in Europe in order to increase Europeanness and European integration,[1] it is important to know more about the factors that structure such civil societies. As many of the chapters in this volume and elsewhere agree, religion is perhaps more visible than it used to be. However, as many also agree, visibility is not the same as significance or authority. My aim is to examine the role religion plays in the formation of national identity. The results indicate that religion remains important on the individual and societal levels.

Religion as a way of understanding civil society

Sociology of religion suggests that religion on the one hand increases social integration through shared symbols, rituals, norms and networks (Durkheim 2010[1912]; Fukuyama 2001; Putnam 1993, 2000) and has the power to transcend boundaries constituted by factors such as ethnic origin, gender or age (Beck 2008: 75), while on the other hand it tends to exclude those who are not part of the dominant congregation(s) (Bohn and Hahn 2002; Yuval-Davis 2010; Gross and Ziebertz 2010). Religion establishes one of the major societal 'cleavages' as Lipset and Rokkan (1967) convincingly argued.[2] In the light of an overarching secularization trend in Europe, one might raise the question of whether and to what extent religion (still) has the power to integrate and to divide European (civil) societies.

In the context of this question, national identity serves as an indicator for a particular aspect of social inclusion. Historians and political scientists argue that national identities emerged in the wake of the structural crisis of early modern European societies. They helped to overcome religious and class-related heterogeneities at that time (e.g. Hobsbawm 1990: 31; Wehler 2004: 25). Within the borders of the newly emerged nation states, the 'standardized citizen' (Robertson 1990: 49) was established, who received similar rights and duties independently of other, mostly ascribed, characteristics. Sociologically, national identity is a modern form of 'exclusive inclusion', marking boundaries between 'us' and 'them' and enabling imagined communities between people beyond families, clans, religious communities or other ascribed and inherited affiliations (Anderson 1983; Triandafyllidou 1998).

In order to analyse the role of religion in modern societies and the 'exclusive inclusion' through national identity, I want to analyse whether – despite a long-standing discussion on the ongoing secularization of European societies – religion is still a constituent factor shaping affiliations as well as social (national) cleavages through sustaining national identity. I examine religion as a multilevel phenomenon that comprises of individual religiousness but also is embedded in the institutional and cultural settings of countries. Religion consists of long-standing belief systems that are inscribed into political institutions, cultural frameworks and social inequalities (e.g. Lipset and Rokkan 1967; Spohn 2009; Mau 2006). As a structural factor, religion influences individual perceptions, attitudes and actions. The article thereby shows that 'religion' triggers different mechanisms according to the societal level on which it is observed and that individual feelings of affiliations towards the imagined community of the nation are influenced differently by individual religiousness, the religious homogeneity of a society and the state–religion relationship.[3]

Social inclusion, religion and national identity: A close but not too close relationship

European societies are often descried as secular: 'The United States is a religious society, Europe a secular one' (Berger et al. 2008: 8; Davie 2006: 247).

Europe, so it seems, has lost its God; but is that, in fact, the case? And what are the consequences for European civil societies?

Civil societies are the space where collective interests are formed, negotiated and organized. There are as many concepts of 'civil society' as there are authors writing about them. Prominent definitions are provided by Gramsci (1999), Habermas (1992) and Alexander (2006). For this chapter, I follow Putnam, for whom civil societies constitute a level between the governmental and the private, in which private interests are transformed into collective interests and in which participation in voluntary organizations generates trust, commitment and solidarity (Putnam 1993, 1995, 2000). This theory of civil society draws attention to two main aspects of social inclusion. First, civil societies are often seen as providers of important conditions for civic engagement and the social space to articulate, negotiate and organize the interests of citizens. In so doing, they help to maintain and legitimate democracy and redistributive governmental policies (e.g. Putnam 1995: 66). Second, civil societies are still shaped by cleavages, political inequalities and differences in access to resources and social positions. Fukuyama suggests approaching those through the concept of the 'radius of trust': 'All groups embodying social capital have a certain radius of trust, that is, the circle of people among whom co-operative norms are operative' (Fukuyama 2001: 8). It is influenced by group memberships and varies between different social communities (such as religious communities and family- or politics-related communities). The radius of trust has the power to mark the boundary between 'us' and 'them'; it facilitates economic and social inclusion and exclusion and, thereby, political participation and the possibility to be an active community member. If we want to learn how civil societies in Europe are shaped and structured through societal cleavages, we have to understand the factors that shape the radius of trust.

National identities in civil societies

National identity provides one possible way to conceptualize 'inclusion' in civil societies outside governmental institutions.[4] Historians and political scientists argue that national identities emerged in the wake of the structural crisis of the early modern European societies during the phase of nation-state formation in Europe in the nineteenth century. Nationalism must be understood as an 'alternative loyalty commitment' (Wehler 2004: 17) that helped to overcome religious and class-related heterogeneities at that time and, by serving this role, paved the way for the development of modern nation states as a legitimized form of political order (e.g. Hobsbawm 1990: 31; Wehler 2004: 25). Through social policies, education, centralization of administration, increased bureaucracy and compulsory military service, modern nation states generated 'standardized citizens' (Robertson 1990: 49) with similar rights and duties. Citizens became members independently of their ascribed characteristics like gender, clans, family affiliation, religion or work status. Thus, one may even say that national identity provided a particular means for integrating civil societies beyond former social cleavages.

To Calhoun, national identity in modern nation states still is 'one genre of answers to the question of what constitutes an autonomous political community capable of self-determination' (Calhoun 1993: 387). National identity constitutes a basis for the radius of trust among those who are considered 'similar'.[5] Although the imagined community of the nation most often unites around underspecified ideas of similarity that may also change over time, the nation constitutes an intentional object towards which people orient their imaginations, understandings and actions. Nations form a 'community, because, regardless of the actual inequality and exploitation that may prevail in each, the nation is always conceived as a deep horizontal comradeship' (Anderson 1983: 7). This comradeship constitutes a social fact, in the Durkheimian sense, that has the power to rebuke people to overcome their egoistic individual interests. National identity has an emotional dimension of loyalty, affiliation and commitment that is far more specific than general trust because it is rooted in assumptions of similarities (whatever these assumptions are based upon). With these central characteristics of shared identity and belonging, continuity and stability, national identity can serve as a proxy for a special aspect of social cohesion (e.g. Easterly et al. 2006).

National identity is a part of individual identity formation (e.g. Jenkins 1996; Cohen 1996) that provides a means for individuals to understand who they are in relation to others. National identity gains power, however, by providing a clear distinction between 'us' and 'them' or, as Triandafyllidou states: 'The nation thus has to be understood as a part of a dual relationship rather than as an autonomous, self-contained unit' (Triandafyllidou 1998: 594). This relationship exists irrespective of whether those 'others' are situated within or outside the state borders.[6] National identity thus forms a group identity that is related to a particular territory with clear-cut yet negotiable borders. The imagined community of the nation concurs with the citizens of the state (only) when nation and state coincide (Barrington 1997). Often, however, nation and state are not identical, as in Belgium, the United Kingdom or Spain.

National identity gives one possible and quite exclusive answer to the question of 'who are the people?' that differs from the answer of governmental citizenship rules. It establishes an inclusive yet exclusive aspect of civil societies. Some even argue that this aspect, especially, is a necessary precondition for the legitimacy and acceptance of governments (e.g. Calhoun 1993b; Miller 1993; Weiner 1997; Conversi 2007). As such, the concept of national identity refers to (a now-substantiated) aspect of the radius of trust that relates to a territory and comprises the interest of political self-determination.

Religion and civil society: Cohesion or repulsion?

The question of whether national identity as a rather 'exclusive form of social inclusion' is influenced and moderated by religion draws its relevance from sociology of religion. It has been successfully and repeatedly shown that religion has the potential to generate a radius of trust itself that contributes to inclusion of society. The integrative impact of religion has been continuously analysed since Durkheim stated that religion provides the necessary norms, meanings, rites and symbols and the opportunity structure that facilitate interpersonal attachment and, thereby, solidarity and social cohesion (Durkheim 2010[1912]). More recent research argues that there remains a positive correlation between religious membership, beliefs and practices, on the one hand, and social capital and integration, on the other. Religiousness seems to lead to a decline in crime and delinquency (e.g. Hirschi and Stark 1969; Stark 1996; or Stark and Bainbridge 1987) and anomic behaviour (e.g. Bjarnason 1998), and it increases trust, cooperation and the morale of reciprocity (e.g. Smidt 2003; Putnam 2000), which are closely related to social capital. Fukuyama explicitly links religion to the integration of civil society (Fukuyama 2001: 19).

Religion, however, has also been proven to have exclusive powers against those who are not part of the congregations, churches or communities in power, that is, the religious radius of trust does not necessarily comprise all citizens. Some forms of social capital can become exclusive and religion may add to 'bonding' within groups instead of 'bridging' members of different societal groups (Welch et al. 2004). At the same time as it integrates, religion is able to operate as a marker of group boundaries between 'us' and 'them' and thereby facilitates cohesion within the religious group but at the expense of the exclusion of non-believers or people of other denominations (e.g. Yuval-Davis 2010; Gross and Ziebertz 2010). The inclusive influence of religion in those cases is limited to parts of society and constitutes cleavages within the civil society. For Europe, it has been argued that Islam became the most prominent religious 'other' during the turn of the century – most visible in the debates about Turkey's EU membership: As Casanova stated in 2004, 'The first open, if not yet formal discussions of Turkey's candidacy during the 2002 Copenhagen summit touches a raw nerve among all kinds of European "publics". The widespread debate revealed how much "Islam", with all its distorted representations as "the other" of Western civilization, was a real issue rather than the extent to which Turkey was ready to meet the same stringent economic and political conditions as all other new members' (Casanova 2004: 5 and similar e.g. Gerhards 2004; Spohn 2009).

Even if religion plays an integrative role, does this still matter in the light of its decreasing salience? Without intending to go too deep into the heated debate on Europe's secularization, three different dynamics can be distinguished (Pollock 2008): First, drawing from Weber's thesis of the 'disenchantment of the world', secularization refers to the replacement of religious explanations by scientific ones in modern societies (Weber 2006[1922]). Religious interpretations become less salient in modern societies, and religious organizations lose their monopoly of power. An alternative but highly related argument is that secularization refers to the progressive functional differentiation reducing religion to one among other functional spheres in society (Luhmann 1977). Secularization, secondly, is understood as individualization of religion stating that people decide what they want to believe in, independently of the churches' dogma, including changes to esoteric beliefs and alternative religions (Luckmann 1967; Davie 1990, 2001). Thirdly, according to the economic market model, secularization is the lack of sufficient religious answers to a stable and constant demand for transcendence because of a lack of competition between religious organizations (suppliers of religion) due to state control (Stark and Bainbridge 1987).

This gives rise to the question of whether religion still is important for societal cleavages and, if so, on what level and in which way?

Religion as a multilevel phenomenon

Taking the debate about secularization and its different levels seriously, we have to understand religion as a multilevel phenomenon that comprises of more than just individual religiosity. On the different societal levels, religion can be expected to develop three different kinds of influences:

1 Theories of civil society and social capital call our attention to religious organizations, community work and religious groups (e.g. Coleman 1988: 99). Religious structures have the power to create general social capital: 'The social capital generated by religious structures supports not only formal religious volunteering but "secular" volunteering as well' (Greeley 1997: 592). Religious organizations provide a particular norm system and opportunity structure, but also membership and belonging. Believing and belonging, however, can diverge in modern societies (Davie 1990).

2 Religion also develops its influence through communal beliefs and shared systems of meanings, morals and values that have the power

to engage members' allegiance through shared interpretations, norms and sanctions. In this way, religion shapes the understanding of civicness within a society and what constitutes acceptable social behaviour.

3   Religion manifests itself as well within governmental structures as constitutions and welfare policies (e.g. Welsh et al. 1991; Stark 1996; Manow 2005). These shared systems of understandings, customs, regulations and laws manifest themselves potentially on the level of smaller regional communities, nation states or larger cross-border collectives, such as the European Union.

Religion, as a contextual phenomenon, has the potential to influence people's attitudes and behaviour. Religion has the power to alter social capital and thereby the individual radius of trust and the average level of inclusion of civil societies. However, we can expect the influence of religion as a contextual phenomenon to vary according to the type of religious context. Both the way and the degree to which religion is intertwined in civic societies vary across European societies. The argumentation focuses on the effects of three different aspects of religion as a contextual phenomenon, namely the institutional interplay between the state and religion and the organizational degree and the actual degree of religious heterogeneity on the contextual level.

In general, we expect religion to play an important role in creating and sustaining national identity. According to Durkheim and the thesis of the integrative effect of religion, we expect that individual religiosity supports national identity, while, according to social capital theories, we expect a positive influence of active membership and of a higher organizational degree of religious organizations on the country level. The expected effects of religion as a societal phenomenon are unclear. Case study evidence suggests that a strong state–religion relationship may support individual national identity, as in Greece or Ireland (e.g. Halikiopoulou 2008), and from normative political theory we may gain the insight that (religious) heterogeneity might be perceived as threatening the community (e.g. Wolfe and Klausen 1997). However, systematic evidence is missing, and therefore we treat the analysis of the contextual aspects of religion as explorative.

The model

In order to answer to the research question as to whether religion influences national identities in Europe, comparative data on both religious affiliation and individual national identity are needed. The European Values Study (EVS) is a large-scale, cross-national survey research programme that provides insights into the beliefs, preferences, attitudes and values of citizens in Europe. It is the only comparative European data set including both questions concerning people's religious beliefs, practices and memberships and questions on national identity. For the following analysis, we employ the fourth wave of 2008, which covers the total of the twenty-seven European member states (Integrated Data Set ZA4800). Although it means excluding such interesting cases as Norway and Switzerland, we restrict the analysis to the member states of the European Union. The analysis thereby refers to a territory that is politically harmonized in aspects significant for our analysis: the European Union imposes standardized integration and harmonization policies through anti-discrimination regulation and the legal inclusion of churches and religious organizations on all member-states, which influences the national state–religion relationships (Grötsch 2009; Grötsch and Schnabel 2012). In addition, this country selection corresponds with the EU notion of 'Europe'.[7]

In order to measure the 'exclusive integration' of civil societies, we want to refer to national identity. A suitable operationalization of 'national identity' is offered by the questions Q80a–Q80e of the EVS:

Some people say the following things are important for being truly [NATIONALITY]. Others say they are not important. How important do you think each of the following is?

Q80.A To have been born in [COUNTRY]

Q80.B To respect [COUNTRY]'s political institutions and laws

Q80.C To have [COUNTRY]'s ancestry

Q80.D To be able to speak [THE NATIONAL LANGUAGE]

Q80.E To have lived for a long time in [COUNTRY]

The answers are coded between '1' and '4', where '1' indicates 'not important at all' and '4' represents 'very important'. According to literature on national identity, we would expect to find two distinct dimensions of national identity – an ethnic dimension and a civic dimension (e.g. Smith 1991; Hjerm 1998; Jones and Smith 2001). The list of questions of the EVS, however, comprises only five of the original eight items previously used in analysis of ethnic and civic national identity (Jones and Smith 2001). Despite that, an explorative factor analysis indicates that these five items gather into two factors.[8] The first factor comprises of Q80.A, Q80.C, and Q80.E, the second of Q80.B and Q80.D. These factors replicate previous findings (e.g. Smith 1991; Hjerm 1998; Jones and Smith 2001) and correspond to both expected dimensions. The first factor accounts for 47 per cent of the total variance, the second for 22 per cent.

This factor structure of two factors could be reproduced, however, only for eleven of the twenty-seven countries. Although comprising of the same manifest variables, the Eigenvalue of the second factor is smaller than one for the remaining sixteen countries. We may assume that this is due to the shorter list of questions. This, however, indicates that the measurement of civic national identity is not reliable in the same way for all of the European countries. Therefore, we restrict our analysis only to the ethnic dimension of national identity.[9]

The ethnic dimension of national identity mirrored in these questions emphasizes the two aspects of time and space and refers to the individual being part of the *imagined community* of those for whom being born in the country, having ancestors there and having lived there for a long time are important. In this interpretation, the 'nation' refers to an imagined community that is restricted through geographic borders and to those common grounds that constitute a common history.[10]

Contextual level variables

For the following analysis, we want to focus on societal aspects of religion on the country level, since evidence on this level is mainly qualitative. The theoretical reason lies in the close relationship between the nation state and religion in Europe. On the one hand, national constitutions and policy systems mirror Christian social teaching and can be understood as the manifest result of conflicts between different religious and political groups throughout history (e.g. Lipset and Rokkan 1967; Manow 2005; Kippenberg 2006). On the other hand, the national educational systems are major transmitters (and homogenizers) of ideological and cultural perspectives and understandings (e.g. Gellner 1983), and the state–religion relationship is highly significant for religious practices (Fox and Flores 2009). Distinguishing between such country-specific characteristics allows taking diverse governmental settings into account.

In order to tap into religion at the country level, we use two different measures. First, we include the institutional cooperation between the state and religion. We use the state–religion relationship variable from Fox's State-and-Religion data set (Fox 2004). These data describe the intersection between state and religion monitoring governmental policies in favour of or against churches, religious groups and congregations worldwide. We include a measurement of the official state–religion relationship indicating whether a government has hostile (0), inadvertent intense (1), separatist (2), accommodative (3), supportive (4) or cooperative (5) relationships or a civil religion (6) or a state religion (7). This variable refers to the degree of governmental secularization – the closer the relationship, the lesser the degree of secularization. Secondly, we measure the countries' religious homogeneity in order to capture the societal religious context (the Herfindahl-Index for religious heterogeneity is calculated from aggregated EVS data).[11]

In order to consider country-specific conditions that might influence religiously motivated cleavages, we control for the national economic situation operationalized by the gross domestic product (GDP) and social spending as percentage of the GDP (indicating that in wealthier countries and in countries with high redistribution, class-related cleavages are less prominent [e.g. Kumlin and Svallfors 2007]) and immigration rate (data are EUROSTAT-Data from 2007). These data refer to the distributive and thereby more secular aspects of societal integration.

Individual level variables

Individual religiousness is differentiated into belonging to a denomination (Roman Catholic, Protestant, Orthodox, other, and none, coded as dummy variables). To analyse whether the intensity of individual religiousness plays a role in forming national identities, we created a multiplied indicator, 'intensity', from the frequency of church attendance (Q26) and the importance of God in everyday life (Q36).[12] The indicator is standardized between '0' and '1' and captures individual religious behaviour as well as the intensity of the belief.[13]

For sociodemographic control variables, we included the respondents' sex, age, year of completed education, annual household income and general trust in others. Although I am not particularly interested in the effects of these variables, we control for them in order to ensure that variances in the dependent variables are not due to their influence and that the country-specific differences in national identity do not depend on their country-specific distributions.

Although this chapter is about the social cohesion of civil societies, I am, strictly speaking, interested in whether (religious) institutions matter for individual attitudes and affiliations. This is because we consider the degree of social cohesion of a civil society as aggregated from individual affiliations and attitudes (in accordance with Coleman's research programme (Coleman 1994: 2ff.). In our interest in the feedback effects of institutions,[14] we consider individuals as nested within larger institutional contexts – in this case, within countries. As Hox and Kreft stated, 'It is important to note that individuals and the social contexts in which they live can be viewed as a hierarchical system of individuals and groups, with individuals and groups defined at separate levels of this hierarchical system' (Hox and Kreft 1994: 284).

Statistically, such multilevel problems cannot be solved simply by generalizing results from one level to another (Robertson 1950). While wrong translations from a higher (macro) level to a lower (micro) level bear the risk of ecological fallacy because unobserved, intervening influences of higher-level properties can interrupt the relationship found on the individual micro-level, atomistic fallacies are committed when correlations on the individual (average) level are wrongly generalized to the higher (country-)level.[15] Besides the theoretical focus on the feedback effects of institutions on individual-level national feelings and affiliations, statistically, the analysis of aggregated country averages of national identity runs the risk of disregarding the individual-level covariances and may lead to wrong conclusions about the underlying mechanisms.

Because we take country-level properties into consideration, and because we assume that individual attitudes vary according to these properties, a multilevel analysis (MLA) is performed. Even if country characteristics are not explicitly tested, an MLA provides the means to control for differences in country-specific distributions of individual characteristics (Steenbergen and Jones 2002). We use multilevel regression, that is, effectively, an ordinary least squares (OLS) regression, which can handle nested sources of variability such as individuals in nation states. Multilevel regression performs better than OLS regression if macro variables are included. This is because the variation within the dependent variable is due to two sources of variation: variation within groups and between groups. If a single-level model is performed, the assumption of independency of the error terms is violated because observations within a group can be expected to be more similar than between groups, and standard errors are underestimated (Snijders and Bosker 1999; Hox 2002). A minor problem is that the number (N) of included countries is only twenty-seven. The article follows Snijders and Bosker (1999) arguing that if N is equal to or greater than ten, a random intercept model is preferable to a fixed model of regression analysis.

The religious and national landscape of Europe

First, descriptive analyses of the EVS data indicate that the religious landscapes of Europe look quite diverse. It seems to be impossible to geographically localize religiously homogeneous regions within Europe (see Figure 4.1).

There are very few countries with a single clearly dominant majority denomination: Only Denmark has a Protestant majority larger than 75 per cent. The Catholic mono-confessional bloc, with more than 75 per cent Catholics, consists of Ireland, Italy, Portugal, Malta, Lithuania, Poland and the Slovak Republic. Classic representatives like Spain are not in this group. Greece, Cyprus and Romania are countries dominated by an Orthodox majority.

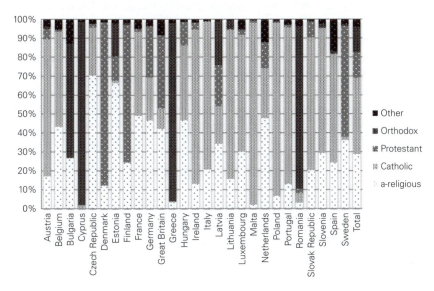

FIGURE 4.1 *Religious landscape of Europe (Denominational distribution per EU member-state in 2008).*

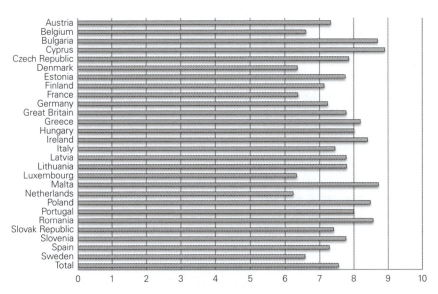

FIGURE 4.2 *Intensity of ethnic national identity.*[16]

Estonia and the Czech Republic have a-religious majorities that are close to 70 per cent.

It is important to note that the European member states are characterized quite differently by the average values of ethnic national identity (see Figure 4.2). On average, ethnic national identity shows a higher intensity in Cyprus, Malta, Bulgaria, Romania and Poland, while the Netherlands, Luxembourg, Denmark, France and Sweden have quite low average scores. These country averages, however, disguise differences and variances on the individual level.

The multilevel analysis

The MLA shows that country-level properties matter for variances in national identities: the empty model (Model 0 in Table 4.1) shows that 17 per cent of the total variance in ethnic national identity is attributed to differences on the country level. An MLA is therefore not only theoretically but also statistically justified.

Because we are not interested in general individual influences on national identity, we are not commentating extensively on the individual control variables. They do not show any irregularities and are in line with former research on national identity (e.g. Jones and Smith 2001: 111): after controlling for country differences, women do not differ significantly from men regarding ethnic and civic national identity, while age, education and a higher general trust increase national identity.

Concerning individual religiosity, the models show that, compared to non-religious persons, Catholics and Protestants show a higher degree of ethnic national identity, while membership of the Orthodox Church is strongly negatively associated with ethnic national identity. The group of 'other religious memberships' is too heterogeneous and too small to be meaningfully interpreted. However, we can assume that being member of a religious minority makes it harder to feel attached particularly to the ethnic dimension of national identity. Although the influence of religious denomination is straightforward in principle, there are some interesting details: Counter to what we might have expected, Protestants have lesser affiliations to ethnic national identity than Catholics. The negative association of Orthodoxy with ethnic national identity can be explained by the Russian minorities in the Baltic states (Estonia, Latvia and Lithuania), who do not develop a national identity in their host countries (c.f. Meur 1999).[17] They constitute a large enough minority in the sample of the EVS that is statistically responsible for a strong negative effect. This effect is not compensated by a weak positive impact of the Orthodox people living in countries with an Orthodox majority.[18] All in all, the results on the individual level indicate that denomination

Table 4.1 Multilevel models for ethnic national identity

	Model 0	Model 1	Model 2	Model 3	Model 4	Model 5	Model 6
Constant		7.336**	7.914**	6.555**	5.917**	9.036**	6.325**
Sex (0 = women)		0.003	0.003	0.003	0.003	0.003	0.007
Age		0.001*	0.001*	0.001*	0.001*	0.001*	0.001*
Education		0.011*	0.011*	0.011*	0.011*	0.011*	0.012*
Income		0.012*	0.012*	0.012*	0.012*	0.012*	0.011*
General trust		0.325**	0.325**	0.326**	0.325**	0.324**	0.319**
Individual religiosity (ref: No religion)							
Catholic		0.214**	0.214**	0.212**	0.212**	0.213**	0.143*
Protestant		0.210**	0.210**	0.208**	0.209**	0.211**	0.121
Orthodox		−0.380**	−0.383**	−0.383**	−0.384**	−0.385**	−0.596**
Other		−0.549**	−0.549**	−0.549**	−0.550**	−0.549**	−0.468**
Intensity		0.067	0.067	0.065	0.066	0.068	0.040
Interaction effects Herfindahl...							
...Catholic							0.124*
...Protestant							0.211
...Orthodox							0.644*
...Other							0.298
National context							
GDP			0.003*		0.003*	0.003*	0.002*
Social spending				−0.082*			
State–religion relationship					0.343*		
Homogeneity (Herfindahl)						1.836*	2.377*
Model statistics							
Residual	3.037	2.794	2.795	2.794	2.795	2.795	2.769
Variance	0.630	0.876	0.755	0.710	0.667	0.651	0.524
% Variance country level	17.172	23.858	21.264	20.268	19.261	18.895	15.914
n		22.208	22.208	22.208	22.208	22.208	22.208

*p < 0.05; **p < 0.001.

still is important for group affiliations and identity formation in Europe but that the religious beliefs themselves are less important.

Models 2 to 6 in Table 4.1 test for country specifics. Although the analysis shows that individual religiousness is effective all over Europe, the increased percentage of the total variance due to the country differences in Models 2 to 5 indicates that there are country-level differences among the member states that are not explained by the variables we tested.

Concerning the social policy-related control variables on this level, the country's GDP and the government's social spending show a significant relationship to ethnic national identity; the share of immigrants had no significant effect.[19] This, in fact, supports arguments stating that the nation's wealth and its distribution bring people effectively together, while the actual share of foreigners per se does not pose threats to solidarity.[20]

The country-specific religious contexts have interesting consequences for ethnic national identity. Looking firstly at the state–religion relationship, we find that the stronger the relationship is, the stronger ethnic national identity is (if the tie between state and religion improves by one unit, ethnic national identity increases by more than 0.3 factor scores). If we understand the state–religion relationship as an indicator for secularization, we may assume that a higher degree of secularization is accompanied by lower ethnic national identity.

Religious homogeneity results in stronger ethnic national identity (see Figure 4.3): if the Herfindahl-Index increases by one unit, ethnic national identity increases almost by two factor scores. The religious homogeneity can be related to societally shared systems of meanings, beliefs, morals and values. This might result in increased feelings of community, sameness and shared origins. The data at hand, however, implicate just one way of a plausible chain of causation; they do not show whether a salient national identity may lead to an increase in religious homogeneity through national naturalization laws or social exclusion, religiously justified violence and displacement.[21]

If people are members of a particular denomination, and if they live in a religiously homogeneous environment, their national affiliation increases: the increase is highest for Catholics and Orthodox, but the increasing rate is highest for Protestants, while people of other religions are always in a minority position that prevents them from becoming part of the ethnic national group. The interaction effects that were tested in Model 6 thereby support our earlier findings: denomination matters and religious minority positions lead always to lower affiliation with the ethnic national group. If Europeans are part of the religious majority they experience being born in the country, having ancestors there and having lived there for a long time as important as well.

The results of the MLA provided a systematic analysis of religion as a context for national identity. Not only individual religiosity but also religion

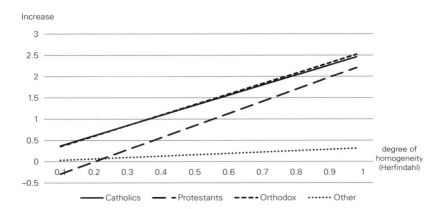

FIGURE 4.3 *Increase in ethnic national identity in religiously homogeneous countries.*

on the country level continue to play a significant role in creating, sustaining and shaping such identity. All over Europe, the state–religion relationship and religious homogeneity are still important for feelings of national affiliation. Further, although the secularization thesis on the micro-level of individual beliefs seem to be the right description of current social developments, national identity in Europe is still strongly connected to denomination and the religious context of the country.

How religion and national identity are enmeshed – discussion of the results

This paper asks how religion is related to feelings of national identity for the average European citizen. It thereby does not so much contribute to minority studies on religious minorities, religious discrimination and exclusion. It instead contributes to our understanding of how different dimensions of religion influence individual affiliations towards the nation. Although there are several case studies on the relationship between religion and national identity indicating that despite all trends of secularization, religion still plays an important role for national identities, there is a lack of quantitative analyses supporting this claim. The study at hand contributes to closing this gap.

The results presented here show that religion and national identities in Europe are in fact still interlinked but that this link is moderated by contextual factors. The analysis indicates that it is important to treat religion as a multilevel phenomenon, the influence of which reaches beyond the level of individual religiosity. In particular, when the civil societies and their inclusion are in focus, it is important to take into account individual beliefs and practices but also the societal contexts in which they flourish. A comparative perspective makes it possible to consider these factors; in this case, it revealed the particular dynamics between religion and national identification in Europe. The MLA helps to understand that it is not the nation state as a geographic entity, but particular – in this case, religion-related – contextual factors connected to the nation state that shape individual national identities.[22] Analysing how such contextual factors influence national identity deepens our insight in how civil societies in Europe are structured and influenced.

Independent of country-specific differences, individual beliefs and actions are important in the way that denomination influences national identity. Catholics and Protestants have stronger feelings of national identity, while Orthodox believers and people of other denominations have weaker national feelings. People in religiously homogeneous environments feel stronger about being part of the *imagined community* of those born in the country, who have ancestors there and have lived there for a long time. In opposition to this denomination effect, the intensity of religious beliefs does not play any significant role. It seems that religious memberships still matter but that the religious content becomes more and more irrelevant. Such secularization on the individual level weakens national identity and thereby the 'exclusive inclusion' through ethnic national identity.

Counter to literature on the development of European nations (e.g. Anderson 1983; Wehler 2004), the analysis at hand suggests that national identity in Europe does not overwrite religious cleavages but seems to follow them instead. For the debates on civil society, this means that religion is still an important marker of such cleavages. But it seems that this marker is more about mere memberships than about shared rites, symbols or beliefs. The denominational cleavages, however, are less noteworthy between Protestantism and Catholicism than between Protestantism/Catholicism, on the one hand, and non-religiousness and Orthodoxy, on the other. With regard to the discussions that took place in Europe concerning the formation of European identity, one might add that there is an additional cleavage forming between Christianity and Islam. Unfortunately, my data do not allow for testing this, and further research is needed.

The analysis supported the claim that the influence of individual denomination is still effective all over Europe: statistically, the associations between denominations and ethnic national identity did not change when controlling for other context variables. Theoretically, such a linkage between denominational membership and national identity might be explained through shared traditions and a collective memory that is associated with ethnic national identity. All in all, civil society cleavages still are structured by denominational memberships rather than differences in beliefs.

While on the micro-level there are some observations that can be witnessed all over Europe, the high percentage of the total variance due to the country differences indicates that there are country-level differences among the member states despite the European Commission's tendencies to homogenize the legal conditions of religion among the member states.[23] One factor that is responsible for these country differences is the state–religion relationship. Although it does not change the individual-level results, it is partly responsible for the country differences. Here religion and national identity overlap as well; a close relationship between state and religion constitutes more intense feelings of ethnic national identity. This can be seen as an indicator for the built-in character of religion; that is, religion in countries with a supportive relationship between state and religion may serve as an integral component of the self-understanding of the ethnic nation. This result supports case studies about the sometimes close relationship between nation and religion, indicating that this relationship is mediated by governmental alignments (e.g. Halikiopoulou 2008).

Civil societies in Europe are neither homogeneous nor necessarily inclusive. Most importantly, the governmental sphere provides the institutional framework for them: when the government has a close relationship to religion and religious organizations, national identity is strengthened. One explanation might be that such cooperative state–religion relationships lessen religious cleavages, which, in turn, tie in with feelings of affiliation to national identity.

Civil societies are shaped by the history and by the design of the governmental context. Our data suggest that it matters for national identity how the organizational specification of religion is interlinked with the state. Civil societies might legitimize or control governments; their cleavages, however, are influenced by the governmental institutions. In this regard, institutions matter not only for individual attitudes but also for the way in which civil societies are structured and how their radiuses of trust are arranged. One might even say that the governmental settings facilitate exclusive and inclusive tendencies of religion in civil society and thereby the possibilities of civic participation.

It is, however, not only the institutional framework that works as a country-level context for the unfolding of civil society's cleavages. Religious homogeneity indicating socially shared values, beliefs and, perhaps, even lifestyle systems is strongly tied to ethnic national identity. This suggests that when religious cleavages are not salient in civil societies because of their religious homogeneity, religion seems to be a *silent* (in the sense of a 'quasi-self-evident') component of the ethnic nation. While some researchers argue that religion and nation coincide mainly in the Protestant North (e.g. Lipset and Rokkan 1967; Riis 1989), our results suggest that this is the case independently of the denomination, including Catholic countries such as Ireland as well as Orthodox countries such as Greece or Bulgaria, where religion is an integral part of what is considered as 'the nation'. When, however, religious cleavages become salient through heterogeneity, religion as part of the nation becomes subject to societal negotiation and the relationship is no longer clear-cut. Such religious differences and distortions then become a characteristic of civil societies, and we may expect the exclusive powers of religion to become more effective. The mechanism here is through religious denominational traditions and their governmental support rather than through beliefs, convictions and shared rites and collective faith in God. This means as well that religious heterogeneity and a secular state–religion relationship makes the exclusive inclusion through ethnic national identity less probable, which may give other more comprehensive forms of inclusion an opportunity to flourish. Civic national identities, solidarity by universal rules and regulations or stronger degrees of functional differentiation may provide such alternatives.

Acknowledgements

I would like to thank Florian Grötsch for most helpful discussions and arguments. His input contributed tremendously to the chapter.

5

Illiberal secularism?
Pro-faith discourse in the
United Kingdom

Steven Kettell

The boundary between the 'religious' and the 'secular' is intrinsically political. Its parameters define the terms of engagement between the two spheres on a variety of political and social issues, and the precise point of demarcation remains a site of ongoing contestation. In Britain, a central feature of these disputes in recent years has been the emergence of a strident 'pro-faith' discourse. Promoted by a variety of leading religious and political figures, this asserts that a militant, aggressive, intolerant and distinctly illiberal form of secularism is seeking to drive religion (and Christianity, in particular) out of public life.

This chapter examines the conditions underpinning the development of this pro-faith discourse and centres on two overlapping, but nevertheless divergent, sets of explanatory factors: 'religious' and 'party political' interests. The former of these have been predominantly driven by concerns around secularization, the latter by the changing nature of governance and the electoral fortunes of the Conservative Party. Both cases highlight the extent to which claims that 'God is Back' are as much about political strategy as they are an attempt to reflect a shift in social conditions. They also highlight the problematic character of pro-faith discourse and the reasons why it is unlikely to be effective.

The growth of pro-faith discourse

The claim that religion is being forced out of public life by a militant, aggressive and illiberal form of secularism has become an increasingly prominent feature of debates around the relationship between the religious and the secular in Britain. This assertion is supported by a wide range of leading religious and political figures. Notable advocates from the former include members of the Church of England, such as the ex-Archbishop of Canterbury, Rowan Williams, who has criticized 'programmatic secularism' for treating religion as a private lifestyle choice (Williams 2012), and his predecessor, George Carey, who has warned that secularist forces are 'hollowing out the values of Christianity and driving them to the margins' (Moreton 2012). Senior figures from the Catholic Church have been critical too. The former Archbishop of Westminster, Cardinal Cormac Murphy-O'Connor, has persistently attacked a 'new secular aggressiveness' marked by a desire 'to close off every voice and contribution other than their own' (Murphy-O'Connor 2006), while his successor, Vincent Nichols, has rounded on secularists for their 'dogmatism' in wanting 'to isolate faith and privatise it' (Teahan 2012).

Similar assertions are also made by a variety of religious groups beyond the main national churches. Prominent examples here include the Christian Institute, which warns that 'the marginalisation faced by Christians is increasing at an alarming rate' (Christian Institute 2009); Christian Concern, which has claimed that Christians are being 'penalised for their faith in the public sphere, often due to equalities legislation and the promotion of homosexual rights' (Christian Concern 2011); and the Evangelical Alliance, which insists that 'secularist policies, far from being "neutral" ... merely replicate discriminatory attitudes towards religion' (Evangelical Alliance 2006: 91).

Leading figures from the political world have also warned of the dangers of illiberal secularism. The former Prime Minister, Tony Blair (now heading his own Faith Foundation), has warned that religion is 'under attack' from an 'aggressive secularism' (Blair 2008), and like-minded sentiments have been expressed by Members of Parliament (MPs) from across the political spectrum. Among these, Conservative MP Peter Bone has warned of a 'creeping secularism in society' (*Hansard*, 19 December 2012, Col. 894), Labour MP David Lammy has protested that 'aggressive secularism' is 'drowning out the ability of people of faith to live with that faith' (Walters and Carlin 2012) and Conservative MP Mark Pritchard has persistently warned against the growing threat of 'Christianophobia' and 'the increasing marginalisation of Britain's Christian history, heritage and traditions' (*Hansard*, 2 December 2007, Col. 255). The cross-party group, Christians in Parliament, has complained of 'a frequently default position of suspicion towards Christianity', driven by 'increasingly secularist conceptions of human rights' (Christians in Parliament 2012).

The most notable attacks on secularism from political figures, however, have come from members of the current Conservative–Liberal Democrat coalition government. Indeed, while the Conservative and Liberal Democrat manifestos made scarcely any mention of religious issues ahead of the 2010 general election, the coalition government has avowedly sought to promote a greater role for faith in the public sphere. One of the staunchest critics of secularism in this regard has been the former co-chair of the Conservative Party and the-then Minister for Faith and Communities, Baroness Warsi. Claiming that an 'aggressive secularism is being imposed by stealth' and that faith in Britain is being 'sidelined, marginalised and downgraded', Warsi warns of a 'deeply intolerant' process of 'militant secularisation' and maintains that secularists are 'attempting to remove all trace of religion from culture, history and public discourse' (Warsi 2012). Making the same point is the Communities and Local Government Secretary, Eric Pickles. Accusing the previous New Labour governments of having allowed 'so-called equality laws to undermine the fundamental right of freedom of religion', Pickles rails against an 'illiberal', 'intolerant' and 'aggressive school of secularism', that, he claims, 'has marginalised faith groups in this country' (Pickles 2010). Such views can be found at the apex of government itself. Professing to have 'never really understood the argument some people make about the church not getting involved in politics' (Wright 2011), Prime Minister David Cameron has hailed the renewed emphasis on faith as 'a Christian fight-back' against secular currents (Sanderson 2012), and insists that Britain remains 'a Christian country'. 'The Bible', he claims, 'runs through our political history in a way that is often not properly recognised' (Cameron 2011).

The emergence of this pro-faith discourse has been driven by a number of interconnected dynamics, processes and themes. These factors overlap on various points, but the core interests and motivations at stake in its promotion by religious and political actors differ significantly. For religious actors, the key motivating issues centre on the ongoing challenges posed by secularization. For political actors, the key issues centre on the changing capacities of the British state and the electoral considerations of the Conservative Party. These points are explored in more detail below.

Religious interests

The use of pro-faith discourse by religious actors (including both groups and prominent individuals) aims to promote and legitimize a greater role for faith in the public sphere. Principally, this has been underpinned by a perception that faith itself (and especially Christianity) is under threat. This perception has been fuelled by a combination of international as well as domestic developments.

High-profile campaigns and statements from the Vatican, such as Pope Benedict's warning (made during a visit to Britain in 2010) that 'aggressive forms of secularisation' were eroding respect for 'traditional values and cultural expressions' (Jones et al. 2010), have nurtured the view that religion is under siege. So too has the emergence of a more overtly visible and politically activist form of atheism (known as 'New Atheism') from the middle of the previous decade. Primarily an Anglo-American phenomenon, and itself largely a response to the growing influence of religion in public life, this denotes a more direct and assertive form of atheism that avowedly aims to undermine religious beliefs in the private as well as the public sphere (McAnulla 2012; Kettell 2013).

Alongside this, pro-faith assertions from many religious organizations in Britain have been influenced by the political strategies of the Christian Right in the United States (Jelen 2005). This has sought to mix claims about the threat faced by religion with a rhetoric of rights, equalities and freedoms, central to which is the notion that there now exists a competing hierarchy of rights and that those of Christians have become subordinate to the rights of other social groups, primarily ethnic minorities and homosexuals. Legal provisions on human rights (such as the European Convention on Human Rights and the 1998 Human Rights Act) as well as legislative measures designed to promote greater equality and fairness – such as the 2003 Employment Equality Regulations, the 2004 Civil Partnership Act, the 2007 Equality Act (Sexual Orientation Regulations) and the 2010 Equality Act – have been instrumental in the adoption of this approach as well (see Stychin 2004; Hunt 2007). Claims that legislative measures such as these pose a direct threat to religious freedom have been accompanied by a series of high-profile legal challenges, most of which have centred on issues of alleged employment discrimination on religious grounds (four of these cases have recently been heard, and three of them rejected, by the European Court of Human Rights).

These issues reflect another notable feature of pro-faith discourse in Britain; namely, its utilization as a form of identity politics (see e.g. Stone and Muir 2007; Muir and Wetherell 2010). In this, claims of marginalization, discrimination and a loss of religious freedoms are framed as part of a defence of minority group rights along with related demands for equal recognition and tolerance. Framing the challenge facing religion in terms of themes of discrimination and the defence of minority rights is strategically useful for a number of reasons. Establishing a sense of injustice can help to foster group cohesion and solidarity, as well as promote activism, while appeals based around the values of group rights, liberties and perceptions of fairness are more likely to connect with the concerns and language of the wider public given the salience of human rights norms and issues of identity politics generally (Knutson 2011; von Stuckrad 2013).

Underpinning these various developments are the challenges posed by ongoing processes of secularization in terms of the declining social and cultural influence of religion in Britain. The Church of England, for whom the decline of religion represents something approaching an existential crisis, admits that the 'exceptional challenge' posed by secularization has made it all the more important 'to counter attempts to marginalise Christianity' and has highlighted the need to devise more effective 'strategies and innovations for growth' (Church of England 2011). A desire to push back against the pressures of secularization was also evident in the response of many religious organizations to the coalition government's 'Big Society' agenda, which was widely hailed as a means of promoting a greater public role for religion. The Church of England's Mission and Public Affairs Council (2010: 14) claimed that the Big Society offered 'a chance to "shift the dominant narrative" about the role of religion in public life' (Mission and Public Affairs Council 2010: 14); the Evangelical Alliance called it 'an immense opportunity' to enhance Christian involvement in social affairs (Evangelical Alliance 2010); and Christian Concern praised the policy for its 'exciting opportunities for churches and other Christian groups' (Christian Concern 2010).

The scale of the problem facing religious organizations is well demonstrated by official census statistics. These show that the proportion of the adult population in England and Wales describing themselves as Christian fell from 71.7 per cent in 2001 to 59.3 per cent in 2011, while the proportion describing themselves as having no religion increased from 14.8 per cent to 25.1 per cent over the same period (Office for National Statistics 2011). Similar findings have been produced by other surveys. Figures from British Social Attitudes show that the proportion of British adults describing themselves as belonging to no religion grew from 31 per cent in 1983 to 50 per cent in 2010, while the proportion describing themselves as Christian fell from 66 per cent to 44 per cent (British Social Attitudes 2012). Attendances at a place of worship also declined. Just 14 per cent of the adult population said they now attended at least once a week, just 9 per cent attended at least once a month and 56 per cent said that they never attended at all.

At the same time, negative public views about religion in public life, driven by factors such as controversies around faith schools, the scandal of child abuse in the Catholic Church, and problems of religiously influenced violence (seen most dramatically in the attacks of 9/11 and in episodic outbreaks of community conflict in places such as Northern Ireland), are also common. Research carried out by YouGov–Cambridge found that 71 per cent of people felt that religious leaders should not be able to influence government decisions (with just 8 per cent opposed), while 81 per cent thought that religious beliefs should remain a private affair (with just 6 per cent against) (YouGov–Cambridge 2012).

Party political motives

While the deployment of pro-faith discourse by religious actors has been driven by the pressures of secularization, the principal motives underpinning its use by senior political figures are rooted in concerns around governing and electoral strategy. The main challenges here are set against a backdrop of transformative social, political and economic developments that have together been associated with a loss of governing capacities, raised questions about the nature of democratic accountability and contributed to a growing sense of public disenchantment with the political process. The economic pressures of globalization, the transference of decision-making responsibilities to non- and quasi-governmental agencies and the development of multilayered governing structures have all been instrumental in this, helping to produce an increasingly pluralized and variegated policy-making environment (Richards and Smith 2002). Socio-economic developments around increased levels of inequality and heightened social fragmentation, as well as tensions around issues of social and cultural pluralism, have been influential too, adding to the strains on Britain's social fabric and creating problems for the legitimacy of state authority by fostering concerns around social cohesion and eroding a sense of overarching national identity (Stone and Muir 2007, Hickman et al. 2008).

One way in which recent governments have sought to address these problems (and one that echoes the theme taken up by many religious groups) has been to promote the politics of identity. A central feature of this has involved efforts to foster the idea of 'Britishness' as a means of inculcating a sense of shared national solidarity and a common set of values (Muir 2007). The idea of Britishness has been typically based on the invocation of ambiguous qualities such as 'tolerance', 'justice' and 'fairness' (Grube 2011), but the notion presented by the coalition government (particularly its Conservative elements) has been readily infused with the ostensible values and benefits of religious beliefs, institutions and practices as well.

Emphasizing a link between Britishness and Christianity provides particular benefits for the Conservative Party, forming an anchor for its ideological position of supporting traditional values and promoting small state politics. Emphasizing conventional bases of social order and connecting the Conservatives to symbolic notions of national identity plays directly to heartland constituencies as well as to assertions about the failings of New Labour, exemplified in the use of party slogans around the notion of 'Broken Britain'. In so doing, this helps to create the impression of a coherent governing narrative imbued with a wider sense of moral purpose. Promoting the idea of national solidarity also helps to divert attention away from divisive economic issues around the imposition of austerity, as does the commitment to enable religious groups to become more active in the supply of public services under the aegis of the Big Society project – a provision that facilitates swingeing cuts in public expenditure while leaving faith-based organizations free to ameliorate the worst excesses of state retrenchment (Kettell 2012).

Attacking 'illiberal secularism' and promoting a greater role for faith in the public realm provides other benefits as well. Significant here is the potential for strengthening the appeal of the Conservative Party among religious and sympathetic sections of the electorate. Although the nature of electoral competition across Western Europe has been significantly affected by processes of partisan dealignment and by the rise of value-based, issue voting, and while the influence of religion has been undermined by secularization, the salience of religious cleavages remains considerable. Religious affiliation continues to be a key factor underpinning patterns of voting behaviour, and the general trend – that members or affiliates of a religious group are more likely to vote for parties of the centre-right – remains a consistent one across the continent (e.g. Knutsen 2004; Van der Brug et al. 2009; Minkenberg 2010; Van der Brug 2010; Raymond 2011).

The influence of religion on party choice in Britain has been less pronounced than in most other European countries, but as Tilly notes, the religious cleavage remains 'an exceptionally good predictor of party choice' (Tilly 2014: 12), even accounting for factors such as class and other social characteristics. Affiliates of the Church of England, for instance, are typically more likely to vote Conservative than Labour, while the reverse remains typically true for Roman Catholics, other Christian denominations (especially from black and ethnic minority groups) and members of non-Christian faiths (Kotler-Berkowitz 2001; Heath et al. 2011; also see Sobolewska 2005).

Figures from the 2010 general election illustrate these trends. These show that 45.5 per cent of Church of England members voted for the Conservative Party, compared to 25.5 per cent for the Labour Party and 20.5 per cent for the Liberal Democrats. In contrast, 39.9 per cent of Roman Catholics voted Labour, compared to 29.3 per cent for the Conservatives and 23.2 per cent for the Liberal Democrats (figures for Christians from other denominations are more evenly split, albeit with a slight leaning overall towards the Conservatives) (see Clements and Spencer 2014; Tilly 2014). These broader links between religion and voting are further illustrated by opinion poll results. According to research conducted by YouGov, 56 per cent of Conservative voters at the 2010 general election considered themselves to be religious, compared to 43 per cent of those who voted Labour and 35 per cent of those who voted for the Liberal Democrats (YouGov 2012).

In this context, attacks on 'illiberal secularism', in conjunction with calls for a greater public role for religion and an emphasis on the Christian basis of British national identity, have the potential to produce direct political benefits. Along with enthusing traditional Conservative supporters, such a combination is likely to appeal to voters who believe religion (and particularly Christianity) to be under threat, and may also attract floating or undecided voters with a sense of (even nominal) Christian identity. Importantly, too, the particular framing of pro-faith discourse also enables these objectives to be pursued without threatening the Conservative Party's claims to have dispelt its old 'nasty party' image. By framing illiberal secularism (somewhat ironically) as being driven by an oversensitivity to the concerns of minority groups, pro-faith discourse provides a coded 'dog whistle' for right-wing antipathy towards issues such as multiculturalism and political correctness, enabling it to play to such concerns without endangering efforts to increase the party's appeal among ethnic minority voters.

The limits of pro-faith discourse

These attempts to promote a greater role for religion in the public sphere through the propagation of pro-faith discourse are problematic in a number of ways. One immediate problem is that there exists no consensus on the meaning of the term 'secularism' itself. Typically, this is taken to indicate a normative commitment to neutrality on the part of the state towards religious affairs; a position that neither favours nor promotes any particular religious viewpoint over any other. However, the idea of 'neutrality', by itself, prescribes no particular set of institutional relations and can be interpreted in different ways (Taylor 2007; Kosmin 2009). In conceptual terms, for example, this ranges from the insistence on 'public reason' promoted by John Rawls and Jurgen Habermas, to more flexible and inclusive forms such as that advocated by Charles Taylor, which call for all worldviews to be authentically expressed and represented (Rawls 1997; Habermas 2011; Taylor 2011). Indeed, commentators such as Tariq Modood and Elizabeth Shackman Hurd maintain that the very idea of 'secular neutrality' is a myth that invariably privileges certain ideas and interests (Modood 2010; Shackman Hurd 2008). Practical variations are evident too. Secular political arrangements can be said to vary here between 'exclusivist' and 'inclusivist' forms according to the extent to which they declaim a need for the state to maintain a distance *from* religion (a public sphere shorn of religious influence and a separation of church and state) or support a position of equity *towards* religion (providing equal recognition for all religions in the public sphere) (see Taylor 2007; Kosmin 2009; Modood 2010; Bhargava 2011).

These variations highlight one of the most important features of pro-faith discourse; namely, that its objections have less to do with the pursuit of 'secularism' per se than the pursuit of an avowedly *exclusivist* variety. Implicit here is the notion that exclusivist secularism is a position at the extremes, a substantial variance from traditional or commonly agreed norms. However, while this presupposes a default position of inclusivist (usually described as 'moderate') secularism against which the designs of illiberal militants can be counter-posed, no such position, given the diversity of secular formations, can actually be said to exist.

A further issue for pro-faith discourse is that its central notion – that Christians in Britain face rising levels of marginalization and discrimination – is difficult to square with the actual reality on the ground, where Christianity, despite its waning sociocultural influence continues to enjoy extensive privileges in key areas of politics and law. The formally established Churches of England and Scotland are obvious examples of this, as is the position of the reigning monarch as head of the former and the fact that Church of England bishops continue to hold reserved seats in the House of Lords (a situation that is unique among advanced liberal democracies). Indeed, the constitutional grounding of the entire parliamentary system, based on the authority of the 'Crown-in-Parliament', is itself said to derive from divine warrant as expressed in the coronation oath (see Bonney 2012). Religious privileges are also evident in a wide range of other areas. These include the extensive involvement of religious authorities in the education system and a variety of exemptions around issues relating to tax and legal regulations, most notably in the case of employment law (e.g. see Sandberg and Doe 2007).

Assertions of illiberal secularism are also at odds with the reality of secularist advocacy in Britain. Alongside a commitment to an exclusivist form of secularism (including the disestablishment of the Church of England), the main campaigning bodies involved in promoting secularism – the National Secular Society and the British Humanist Association – have traditionally supported a range of progressive political objectives. Among these include the promotion of science and reason, abolition of the blasphemy laws (finally achieved in 2008), the eradication of poverty, electoral reform, equality before the law and freedom of expression (see McGee 1948; Taylor 1957). Moreover, such aims are underpinned by a distinctly moral social vision based on the promotion of democracy and the fulfilment of human potential. Indeed, the term 'secularism' itself, coined by George Holyoake in 1851, was formulated, in part, to assert moral capacities independent from religious belief (see Holyoake 1871).

This is not to deny that illiberal secular practices exist (restrictions on religious behaviours, such as moves to ban religious symbols and clothing from the public square in parts of Europe, may be seen as examples of this), or that many religious people may feel genuinely threatened by the declining sociocultural influence of religion combined with expressions of secular assertiveness (the emergence of New Atheism being illustrative here). The key point, rather, is that in using the notion of 'illiberal secularism' as a central part of an overt political strategy, proponents of pro-faith discourse are guilty of either misunderstanding or of wilfully misrepresenting the case that most advocates of secularism – and certainly its principal campaign groups – actually make. Far from being motivated by an illiberal desire to drive religion into the abyss, the real call is an avowedly liberal one: for a free and open public sphere in which all citizens can participate equally, as citizens, without the encumbrances of special religious rights and privileges.

The use of pro-faith discourse by religious organizations attempting to combat the pressures of secularization is problematic for a number of other reasons as well. In a general sense, framing a defence of religious interests around assertions of illiberal secularism entails the subsuming of possible tensions between differing groups and denominations within a broad-based 'Christian' (or, even more vaguely, 'faith') identity. While this may be effective in establishing perceptions of a common threat and in providing a possible unifying spur to action, it remains to be seen whether this can provide a sufficiently strong and practical basis for sustaining cohesion between a diverse range of groups with an equally diverse (and not always complementary) range of interests and beliefs.

The advantages of playing to the theme of identity politics are also less than clear-cut. In contrast to the originating impulse for such an approach, which was based on the desire of genuinely marginalized and under-represented groups to secure greater social acceptance and empowerment, the use of identity politics by leading religious figures represents an attempt to defend established interests and privileges. As such, the extent to which such claims will resonate positively with the wider public also remains an open question, not least given the fact that religious claims of discrimination often rest on top of potentially toxic fault lines involving the ostensible rights of religious groups to opt out of progressive measures on issues such as gender equality, sexuality and reproductive rights.

But perhaps the greatest problem for religious advocates of pro-faith discourse concerns the very nature of this discourse itself. Promoting religion with a language of civic and human rights effectively denotes the use and acceptance of norms and patterns for public discourse that are (or at least have become) intrinsically secularized (for this point in the US context, see Jelen 2005). Putting the case for religion in such a way effectively concedes the point that public discourse in Britain needs to be framed around avowedly liberal secular values in order to have any public influence or legitimacy; a tacit acknowledgement of the weakening sociocultural position in which religious groups find themselves. At the same time, the claim that religious organizations need to be accorded the same formal rights and equalities as other social interests itself only serves to highlight the sectional nature of a religiously based appeal, and, as such, provides no obvious reason why religious groups should continue to be treated differently to other social interests in the enjoyment of special political and legal advantages.

The issue of secularization also raises problems for party political actors. Appealing to religious voters in a context of sustained decline in religious beliefs and practices, and hence one in which religious adherents represent a progressively declining share of the electorate, offers little obvious long-term advantage. Indeed, Rowan Williams has himself recently maintained that Britain has now become a 'post-Christian' country (Ross et al. 2014). By the same token, attempts to link Christianity to conceptions of British national identity are unlikely to provide substantial benefits when large sections of the population hold a rather different and altogether more secular view of what 'Britishness' actually is. The extent to which the promotion of faith issues might be able to improve the standing of the Conservative Party among ethnic minority voters, the large majority of which continue to support Labour and do not consider the Conservative Party to be representative of their interests, also remains an open question (Heath et al. 2011; Sanders et al. 2013).

A political strategy based on appeals to religious groups also poses problems for the supposed modernization of the Conservative Party. More traditionalist elements within the party (including many religious groups) have viewed attempts to move in a more socially liberal direction with open hostility (e.g. Furness 2013), a point that has clearly been seen in the issue of same-sex marriage, a policy designed to showcase the government's modern and progressive credentials but one that strongly antagonized large swathes of religious opinion and alienated many potential supporters on the right.

Conclusion

The propagation of pro-faith discourse has been one of the defining features of recent debates around the relationship between the religious and the secular in Britain. Based on the claim that religion is under threat from an illiberal form of secularism, this seeks to promote a greater role for faith in the public square and to delegitimize secular advocacy by presenting this as militant, aggressive, intolerant and at odds with the British character. The emergence of pro-faith discourse has been shaped by a number of domestic and transnational factors, but the principal religious and political interests involved differ significantly. While the former centre on the challenges posed by secularization, the latter have been principally driven by the changing nature of governance and the electoral concerns of the Conservative Party. At the same time, assertions of illiberal secularism are problematic in a number of ways. Not only do the key features of pro-faith discourse run contrary to the realities of secular advocacy, but the increasingly secular nature of British society also provides a formidably high barrier to overcome for those seeking to legitimize a greater public role for faith. Given these problems, it is unlikely that the continued use of pro-faith discourse will produce the kind of results that its proponents wish to see.

6

Negotiating the public and private in everyday evangelicalism

Anna Strhan

What does it mean to 'do God' publicly as an evangelical Christian in Britain today? In recent years, different evangelical groups have generated very diverse forms of publicity. The positions taken by some British conservative evangelicals on a number of moral, political and ecclesiastical issues – from opposition to women bishops to arguments that religious freedoms are increasingly under threat – have stimulated increasingly polarized media narratives of either a rising 'religious right' or an increasingly marginalized minority. At the same time, some other evangelical groups have generated publicity through their forms of social action in response to conditions of economic scarcity following the financial crisis of 2008, for example, in running food banks. The Archbishop of Canterbury, Justin Welby, from a charismatic evangelical background, has also commanded media attention through a number of media statements, for example, his calls for banking reforms and his desire to compete the payday loans company Wonga out of business.[1]

While these different public engagements by evangelicals might be taken to suggest that God *is* back, how do these forms of media visibility relate to the lives of members of evangelical churches? In this chapter, I seek both to open up diverse ways in which evangelical leaders seek to make faith public in a largely secular British culture and to consider how this desire for 'religious publicity' (Engelke 2013) relates to the everyday lives of members of these churches.[2] Contemporary popular perceptions of evangelical Christianity in Britain tend to emerge both from the dominance of media representations of American evangelicals and from the prominence of a small number of media-savvy leaders in Britain, which feed into overly simplistic portraits of evangelicals as either increasingly persecuted or as right-wing culture warriors. In this broader cultural landscape, my research explores the mundane hopes and habits of members of different evangelical churches in London, exploring individuals' experiences in relation to their urban locations and their processes of subject formation. I draw here on ethnographic fieldwork[3] conducted with two London churches, one conservative evangelical and Anglican, 'St John's', the other open evangelical and Baptist, 'Riverside Church'.

The term 'evangelical' is broad, and scholars – as well as evangelicals themselves – disagree about the question of definition.[4] I use the term here, following David Bebbington, to refer to the tradition existing in Britain since the 1730s, marked by the characteristics of conversionism, Biblicism, activism and crucicentrism (Bebbington 1989: 3). I use the term 'conservative evangelical' to refer to the tradition that emerged following a rift with liberal evangelicals in the 1920s, with differing estimates of the Bible a central point of tension (Bebbington 1989: 181–228).[5] I use 'open evangelical' to characterize a culture united in a dissatisfaction with dominant evangelical 'labelings of faith and belief, and the ways these labels have frustrated what they see as an authentic ecclesiology. In their view evangelicalism has suffocated itself through a tight hold on propositional belief, personal salvation, and overheated conviction' (Engelke 2013: 20). In the congregations I am studying, some members of these churches – their leaders perhaps in particular – would self-identify using these terms. However, not all members of either church would be familiar with, let alone describe themselves, as either conservative or open evangelical. My aim in using these terms is not to reify a particular portrait of 'conservative' or 'open' evangelicals, but rather to open up the diversity of British evangelical cultures and of the complexities and heterogeneities that exist even within the setting of individual churches.

In examining how evangelicals negotiate what it means to go 'public' with their faith in these two churches, I show that members of St John's experience more constraints in this than members of Riverside. I argue that this is related to tensions between universalizing modern norms and conservative evangelicals' beliefs about gender, sexuality and other religions. I demonstrate that while the leaders of St John's encourage church members to speak publicly about their faith in the workplace and other urban settings, individuals struggle to put this into practice, coming to experience themselves as emotionally constrained by their own secular sensibilities in a way that is not mirrored in the lives of the open evangelicals at Riverside. This enables us to see how processes of the privatization and deprivatization of religion can take place in uneven ways within individuals' subjectivities, as their actions are shaped through participation in both church and secular spaces outside of this.

Doing God in public? Conservative evangelicals and the times of secularism

In *Public Religions in the Modern World*, José Casanova argues that religious groups, when disrupted by processes of modernization, can be mobilized to enter the public sphere in response; for example, the religious Right in the United States. Religions today, he argues, are entering the public sphere both to 'defend their traditional turf' and to participate 'in the very struggles to define and set the modern boundaries between the private and the public spheres, between system and life-world, between legality and morality, between individual and society' (Casanova 1994: 6). We might expect conservative evangelicals in a de-Christianizing cultural landscape to be entering the public sphere in the way Casanova describes, and it is possible to understand responses by some socially conservative British Christian groups to universalizing processes extending equal rights in relation to sexuality[6] in these terms.

The Christian Institute is one such group, as I have discussed elsewhere (Strhan 2012, 2014). Among other issues, their campaigns have focused on marriage, the family and sexuality, for example, defending Section 28 of the Local Government Act 1988 when it was on the statute books, and their involvement in the 'Coalition for Marriage', launched in 2012 in opposition to the coalition government's proposed legislation for gay marriage. The Christian Institute has also focused on defending freedom of religion, which they describe as increasingly under threat for Christians. Their 2009 'Marginalising Christians' booklet positioned tensions over 'equality' as central in this narrative, for example: 'This growing sense of intolerance felt by Christians is made all the worse when they face hostility in the name of "equality and diversity" … Christians … feel that a hierarchy of rights has sprung up which leaves them bottom of the pile' (Christian Institute 2009: 5).[7]

The Christian Institute reports a rise in cases of religious discrimination related to clashes over 'equality', and several of these have received media coverage. One highly publicized case was that of Peter and Hazelmary Bull, guesthouse owners who were (unsuccessfully) defended by the Christian Institute against the claim that they had breached equality legislation in refusing a double room to civil partners Steven Preddy and Martyn Hall in 2008.

Another high-profile case was that of Lillian Ladele, a registrar who refused to carry out civil partnership ceremonies, and claimed she was discriminated against by Islington Council.

Christian Concern, together with the Christian Legal Centre, has also generated publicity in relation to cases of Christians who claim to have been victims of religious discrimination, for example, Owen and Eunice Johns, who were involved in a dispute over an application to be foster carers, after a social worker questioned their views on homosexuality. Stories about these cases, originating from press releases from the Christian Legal Centre, have attracted column inches in national newspapers such as *The Daily Mail*, *The Mail on Sunday* and *The Daily Telegraph* (Walton et al. 2013: 54), and through this, a narrative of Christians being discriminated against in the name of 'equality' and 'diversity' has been increasingly disseminated.

Christian Concern has also been involved in campaigning for the public visibility of faith (Strhan 2012, 2014). This can be seen, for example, in their 'Not Ashamed' campaign, the website of which states (Christian Concern, not dated)

> More than any other person, Jesus Christ has shaped our society, for the good of all. The values and freedoms that flow from Him have been embedded in our culture and laws, bringing great benefit to our nation. ... Yet the truths, values and behaviour consistent with that foundation are under attack. ... There is mounting pressure to exclude Jesus Christ from public life, consigning Him instead to the realm of the 'private and personal'. Increasingly, Christians are encountering attempts to restrict their freedom to speak and live in accordance with biblical teaching in the workplace and in public life. ... In these challenging times Christians need to stand together and speak clearly of Jesus Christ as 'good news' not only for individuals but for society as a whole.

Seeking to promote this 'public' articulation of Christian values as 'good news ... for society as a whole', Christian Concern runs a training course, the Wilberforce Academy, which aims, its website states, to train young people for 'Christ-centred leadership in public life, having been equipped with a robust biblical framework that guides their thinking, prayers and activity in addressing the issues facing our society,' in a variety of professions, including law, politics, education and media.[8]

The successful commanding of media attention and (less successful) attempts to influence policy by such groups have contributed to portraits of conservative evangelicals as either a newly mobilizing religious right in liberal sections of the media, or as increasingly marginalized in more conservative sections, with stances on sexuality and equality often defining points of tension. Both narratives are too simplistic, and, as Walton et al. note, evangelicals are far more spread across the political spectrum in Britain than the United States (Walton et al. 2013). Yet there *is*, as Walton and colleagues also point out, a growing prominence to these groups' concerns, which they mostly articulate – and self-consciously so – in the secular language of individuals' human rights being threatened. How do these examples of publicity emerging from organizations linked with conservative evangelical networks then practically relate to and affect the everyday lives of members of St John's?

Both ministers and members of St John's saw their differentiated understanding of gender roles[9] and teachings on sexual relationships[10] as increasingly countercultural and as potentially generating hostility from others if they sought to share their views. Ministers occasionally referred in sermons to publications such as 'Marginalising Christians' to support this. They also often expressed, as I have commented on elsewhere (Strhan 2013a, 2014), a desire for the 'public' expression of Christianity in a context perceived as increasingly hostile to their faith, for example, when David, the rector of St John's, preached that Christianity should be 'energetic and corporate, public and unpopular, and selfless and sacrificial'. He stated

> Christian partnership is ... public and unpopular, contending for the truth, which is objective. ... We contend publicly for the objective truth of the gospel that God has done in and through Jesus Christ, hence the unpopularity of this. ... Wherever the gospel is proclaimed publicly by gospel partners, we find them engaged in conflict, as in Acts. ... As this country careers away from its Christian heritage, we will increasingly be considered immoral, bigoted, out-of-date.

This desire to express faith publicly was not, however, about influencing policy but rather a more traditional apologetics aimed primarily at converting non-Christians. In this theology, there is a sharp sense of a divide between the Kingdom of God and the world, with the world felt to be in need of a salvation that comes through belief in Jesus and an understanding of his death as an atoning sacrifice. The proclamation of this message is then understood here as a central aspect of what it means to be follower of Christ. Yet, David's words suggest that this task of proclamation is felt to be increasingly difficult: this sense that conservative evangelicals are increasingly perceived as 'out-of-date' suggests a temporal orientation that locates conservative evangelical teachings on gender, sexuality and other religions as in tension with a hegemonic narrative of modernity conceived in terms of a progressive account of increasing freedoms, and particularly sexual freedoms (Butler 2009: 109; also discussed in Strhan 2014: 243).

Describing the contemporary moment as 'totalitarian', David said that what today in Britain masquerades under the title 'multicultural liberal diversity' is, in fact, 'illiberal, intolerant, secularist fundamentalism. This is not multiculturalism or liberal diversity. It is totalitarian.' In another sermon, one of the curates described Jesus' disciples as having been 'hated' for 'speaking Jesus' words', and said that if Christians today 'stick with the words of the Bible', they will also be 'hated'. He gave examples of how he had personally experienced such hostility, all indexing a tension with ideas of 'equality', for example, describing how there had been a dispute at their local diocesan meeting about a nearby church performing a blessing on a civil partnership ceremony, and he had taken a stand against that and said 'you could feel the hatred in the room from many of those there'. He stated that the apostles 'stuck with the words of Jesus' and were hated as a result, and said, 'the only kind of Christian that is authentic' is one who is hated for speaking the words of Jesus (also discussed in Strhan 2014: 244).

This, then, is the context in which the leaders of St John's encourage individuals to go public with their faith. David said, in a question-and-answer session following a sermon, that the 'social and political tectonic plates of Britain are shifting radically, as we move from once-Christian – at least nominally – through to post-Christian Britain'. He then asked the congregation, 'Given that the tectonic plates are beginning to shift, well, are you not finding that to speak openly of your faith, to make mention publicly of your views of sexuality, or gender, or other faiths, the absolute supremacy of Christ and the impossibility of salvation through any other religion…, are you not finding that as you say these kind of things, you're facing increasing hostility?' His question implied that individuals were speaking publicly about these issues, and he mentioned individuals in the church who had been challenged by their human resources departments as paradigmatic exemplars of this public speaking. He then encouraged members of the church to speak about their faith in their workplaces and universities, saying: 'if they sack you, the law is on your side, because they are threatening your human rights'.

The church leaders frequently outlined tactics to encourage members to feel more confident in speaking publicly about their faith. When Pope Benedict XVI visited the United Kingdom in September 2010, for example, one of the ministers said to the congregation that the visit was a great thing 'because of the publicity it brings to Christianity'. He said, 'as a Christian, I'm very pleased he has come, as it's a great opportunity to talk about our faith'. He then outlined how they could use this as an opportunity to talk about faith with others, suggesting that most people (implicitly non-Christian) would take two approaches to the Pope: 'you will either find yourself talking to secular people who are very angry with the Pope … or to multicultural people who are very happy with the Pope.' In a conversation with someone who is anti-Pope, he said, 'the temptation would be to say that you are against the

Pope too. ... But that would be wrong. Although the Pope is wrong about some things, like contraception, the issues that the secularist is angry with the Pope about, in relation to sexuality for example, the secularist would probably be angry with us about too. ... Now that may be an explosive conversation for you, but it is worth having'. Other people, he said, are 'very happy with the Pope: ... in some media representations, there is the impression that only a fundamentalist nutter who is intent on dividing Christianity would be negative about the Pope. ... Our response to someone like this should emphasize that we like the Pope, but we have serious disagreements with him about what religion is for.' As well as priming church members for discussions arising from news events in this way, the church also offers a weekly evening course to help individuals feel more confident in speaking about their faith through training in particular techniques of speaking.[11]

Such strategies might appear to fit with Casanova's thesis of the deprivatization of religion. Yet the practical effect of the leadership of St John's saying that Christians will be hated for speaking about issues where their faith is in tension with universalizing modern norms, combined with the media prominence of cases like the Bulls, seemed the opposite of what these leaders and organizations intended. Many church members felt increasingly anxious in speaking about such issues; many felt awkward talking about their faith at all. In the sessions aimed at training church members to feel more confident in talking about their faith, members of the group I observed talked about how they often felt embarrassed in talking about their faith with non-Christians, and they prayed for forgiveness for times when they had felt ashamed. The fact that the church leaders designed this course can be seen as, in itself, an acknowledgement of the difficulty experienced by members of the church in speaking publicly about faith. The training format of the course – with small group discussions and role plays – might be seen as evidence of how it is, today, religious 'professionals' such as church leaders who are able to 'do faith' publicly, while ordinary church members feel that talking publicly about their faith breaches the implicit norms of interaction in secular spaces. A graduate in his late twenties I interviewed said he found it difficult in his open-plan office 'to talk about Christian things, because people can just come in halfway through a conversation, and then it would probably sound quite strange what we were talking about ... It's hard to have a chat about personal, spiritual things. ... I find it quite difficult, but I love it whenever I get the chance to'. This indicates his internalization of a secular cultural norm that faith is somehow 'personal' and 'private' that rubs up against aspirations for public speaking encouraged in evangelical discourse.

A sense of feeling awkward about speaking about faith in public contexts was reiterated by many of those I spoke with. This was frequently narrativized in terms of guilt and shame. David said in one sermon on the book of Hebrews that he had been talking 'to a group of Christian business people, and said ... "what is this costly aspect of being an out-and-out Christian to you at the moment in the office?" And they said, "oh the ridicule, my reputation is at stake, I might be known as a Bible basher"'. David stated that the author of Hebrews 'lines up shame and the social distance that might be placed between an individual and the people of God with sin and the moral battle that's going on in the individual's life. ... And it's my experience that that battle goes on right in the heart of every Christian believer, as the battle is raging morally, simultaneously as the battle is raging socially'. Church members learnt to use this language to describe some of the tensions and internal conflicts they experienced in speaking about their faith. Jane, a teacher, for example, said 'I wonder if it's hard [to speak about faith] not because of the society we live in, it's just that ... we make it hard for ourselves, 'cos we're rubbish, and lack the confidence.' Another speech therapist said, 'Jesus talks about, "whoever will be ashamed of me and my words, I will be ashamed of him"', and stated that this showed that feeling ashamed is the inevitable experience of all Christians (Strhan 2013a, 2014).

Shame can be seen as an emotion arising 'when the dominated come to perceive themselves through the eyes of the dominant, that is, are made to experience their own ways of thinking, feeling, and behaving as degrading' (Wacquant 2004: 393). Shame therefore implies a fracture of subjectivity that is simultaneously determined by and expresses wider diminishing social cohesion (Wacquant 2004: 393). In this context, and as I have discussed elsewhere (Strhan 2013a, 2014), experiences of shame suggest that conservative evangelicals experience their identities with ambivalence in settings where they sense tension between their faith and broader cultural logics of equality. Contrary, then, to linear narratives of the deprivatization of conservative religion in secular modernity, conservative evangelicals' subjectivities are formed through *both* a desire to speak about faith publicly *and* by secular norms locating religion as a private personal matter. As they are formed as 'modern' subjects who value the freedom that the liberal separation of private and public domains allows, they feel uncomfortable expressing moral viewpoints that appear to transgress 'public' impersonal norms by expressing moral convictions that would imply that others' 'private' moral behaviour is wrong. This is most intensely felt in relation to issues such as gender and sexuality where the teachings of the church rub up against broader norms of equality. How does this compare with open evangelicals' experiences?

Open evangelicals and logics of publicity

The *New Statesman*'s New Year 2014 leader article, 'The moral challenges of our times,' argued that the financial crisis and subsequent years of economic scarcity have returned questions of morality to the forefront of public interest: 'How should limited resources be allocated? What constitutes the good society? What are the values that should underpin our economy? Can individualism and the common good be reconciled?' (*New Statesman* 2013). The article noted that 2013 saw the emergence of 'moral leaders outside of politics [who] have shown considerable moral guidance'. It described Pope Francis as articulating a 'vision of a church "of the poor, for the poor"' and a 'moral denunciation of "unbridled capitalism"', and it highlighted some of the stances that the Archbishop of Canterbury took in 2013:

> Justin Welby ... has reaffirmed the Church of England's status as a defender of the most vulnerable. He has condemned the coalition government's cap on benefit increases for making children and families 'pay the price for high inflation, rather than the government', denounced the 'usurious lending' of payday loan companies and criticised the banks for asking what is 'legal' and never what is right'. ... He has demonstrated his Church's values through deeds as well as words. ... One need not share their faith – and the *New Statesman* is a resolutely secular magazine – to respect the moral clarity that both Pope Francis and Archbishop Welby have brought to issues of economic justice.

Justin Welby's background is charismatic rather than open evangelical.[12] However, the political climate that led to his media engagements since taking office are the conditions that also underpin open evangelicals' modes of publicity.

During my fieldwork at Riverside, the church's leader has featured in local and national media, often discussing the church's work in providing services responding to local needs, such as a food bank and debt advice centre. The church has also been involved in creating and entering into other kinds of public space. Riverside regularly organizes a public assembly, in which a variety of political issues are discussed. Riverside's aim in providing this space is to 'encourage debate, inspire innovation and enable social change', and to enfranchise 'those who until now have felt they have been disqualified from taking part and having a voice'. The assemblies I observed have allowed people from the church and the local area around the church, and others interested in the topic under discussion, to debate with and articulate their views to politicians and other public leaders.

The assembly can be seen as a space of both the 'secular' and a space where open evangelicals are able to express their faith commitments: to be open evangelical here is *also* to be secular. Charles Taylor argues for an understanding of secularism as 'an attempt to find fair and harmonious modes of coexistence among religious communities,' and describes this as 'an essential feature of religiously diverse societies, aiming to secure freedom of belief and unbelief as well as equality between citizens' (Taylor 2009: xxi–xxii). In the history of non-conformist Christianity, when marginalized by the established churches, evangelicals often desired and worked towards creating secular public spaces. This understanding of 'the secular' in terms of a liberal space that allows freedom of belief and non-belief can be seen as underlying the norms of interaction in Riverside's People's Assembly. Here, members of the church articulate their views usually without explicitly referencing their faith, and when faith positions are referred to, this tends to be expressed with the pluralist consciousness that their Christian conviction is one possible stance among others, rather than 'the' truth.

Riverside members also make their faith public in other ways, for example when the church was involved in organizing a flash mob at London Waterloo station on the morning of Good Friday in March 2013 (also discussed in Strhan 2013b). At 11.00 a.m. that day, a procession of around 200 people from different churches in the North Lambeth area who had been on a Good Friday 'walk of witness' arrived at the station. A priest carrying a large wooden cross stood this in the centre of the concourse, while volunteers from Riverside wheeled empty shopping trolleys that had been waiting outside the station to stand beside the cross. This was the cue for the other members of these churches who were flash mobbing the station, who were standing by, unobtrusively blending in with the other travellers there. A young man from Riverside started playing a steady drum rhythm, and the woman next to him began singing 'Amazing Grace.' The members of the flash mob joined in with pre-rehearsed harmonies, swelling the volume for each of the hymn's verses, and other drummers joined in verse-by-verse, amplifying the rhythm. As they sang, the flash mob processed towards the cross, carrying tins and packets of food to put in the trolleys to contribute to the local food bank run by Riverside.

As a public event, this captured the attention to those in the station that morning: most passing through stopped to watch and listen, and a large crowd gathered on the balcony above the concourse, filming the event on their phones. Many smilingly joined in the singing, and some donated money for the food bank or bought food from shops at the station to put in the trolleys. The flash mob organizers had been anxious about how the station staff would respond, yet, on the day, many joined in with the song and gave out mini Easter eggs to distribute to passers-by. After the final verse, the singers and drummers dispersed, leaving the trolleys overflowing with food and the wooden cross in the centre of the concourse, so that these remained as public visual markers of the event. In a video that Riverside Church posted online afterwards, Riverside's minister described the event as a way of 'serving the local community.' He said 'the story of Jesus happens on the street, it doesn't happen in the church building, and what we wanted to do on Good Friday is take the story of Jesus, the story of Jesus giving Himself for the world to this, well, it's the biggest station concourse in London, to make this story of Jesus public.' He went on, 'just as people joined in with the singing this morning, people join in with the song of Jesus as they're caught up in the excitement of building His kingdom.'

While St John's teaches its members that Christianity should be 'public and unpopular', so that they feel often divided about the prospect of practically expressing their faith publicly, the focus of Riverside of seeking to 'serve the local community', through church volunteers providing services such as food banks, groups for toddlers, youth groups and mentoring schemes, or English language lessons. These relationships enable them to create 'public' spaces of civic sociality, for example, in hosting 'community fairs' or 'Messy Church', which are attended by local inhabitants of diverse religious and non-religious backgrounds. Although a few members of Riverside expressed to me their sense that the social activism at Riverside appeared in many ways little different from that provided by secular services, they did not feel emotionally constrained or divided about being 'public' with their faith in the same way as members of St John's. Their particular engagement with food banks and highlighting of food poverty has generated publicity for the church across different sections of the national media, following a similar logic to the visibility of Justin Welby.[13]

The *New Statesman* article welcoming the public interventions of Pope Francis and the Archbishop of Canterbury suggested that they provided a moral vision that was lacking in contemporary political life (*New Statesman* 2013):

> The public's disillusionment with politicians can partly be explained by their failure to address these issues convincingly. When politics is reduced to a game in which the parties continually seek to outmanoeuvre each other for tactical, short-term advantage, it is unsurprising that the public turns away. The frequent lament that they are 'all the same' is an attack not, as is often thought, on a perceived lack of policy divergence but on the managerial, technocratic culture that they embody.

Perhaps one of the salient features of open evangelical culture that enables aspects of their work to gain public visibility is an evangelical preference for a mode of 'plainness' or 'simplicity' in style, which shapes their ways of speaking and allows some of their statements on issues such as poverty to capture public attention. An advertising slogan for the work of the food banks with the clear and hard-hitting slogan 'Britain isn't eating',[14] for example, generated significant media and political debate. This is not to say that evangelicals' engagements with these issues are unaffected by cultures of publicity and public relations advisers. However, in the contemporary moment, one of the reasons why open evangelical churches and evangelical leaders such as Justin Welby are able to successfully capture public attention on these issues is bound up with the simplicity with which they articulate a particular moral vision for society that is often otherwise missing in political debate.

Discussion

Steve Bruce argues that the compartmentalization of religion that occurs with structural differentiation – in which religion is at least partly separated out in liberal public spheres into the realm of the private and personal – is a holding process en route to secularization (Bruce 2002: 29). However, examining how members of St John's and Riverside negotiate what it means to be public with their faith complicates this narrative, as well as Casanova's thesis of the deprivatization of religion (Strhan 2014: 253). The tensions that members of St John's experience do seem to imply a secularization of public space, in which speaking of faith is felt as a taboo. Yet members of the church are also conscious of this, and they narrate this tension in their desires in the language of 'shame' and 'guilt', demonstrating their sense that they ought to speak of their faith in these spaces.

As some sections of the media often posit the rise of a new Christian Right in Britain, it is easy to interpret the statements of conservative evangelical leaders and groups such as the Christian Institute and Christian Concern along these lines. But these individuals and are religious 'specialists', whose everyday lives, working professionally within explicitly Christian cultures, are not shot through with the logics of 'secular' workplace interactions in which faith is seen as a personal and private area. In this context, ethnographic focus on the practices of the ordinary members of St John's complicates straightforward narratives of conservative evangelical mobilization. Their subjectivities are formed through both their acceptance of traditionalist teachings on gender and sexuality in tension with universalizing norms of equality, and their simultaneous inhabiting of liberal, pluralist secular spaces that lead them to experience those teachings as a cultural taboo, which they are, in most everyday spaces they inhabit, reluctant to transgress.

Comparing the experiences of members of St John's and Riverside in relation to religious publicity both opens up the heterogeneity of evangelical cultures in modern Britain, helping us move beyond simplistic stereotypes of evangelicalism as a coherent subculture, while also demonstrating a shared concern for faith to be part of the public sphere. The desire to do faith publicly can be seen as part of a broader evangelical theological logic of engagement with the world, where the world is understood as in need of salvation – understood in very different senses across conservative and open evangelical traditions – and it is the church's responsibility to work towards that salvation. At the same time, the desire for religious publicity can be seen as part of a broader structural logic of institutions in a media age. Thus the flash mob's mode of performance draws on secular modes of spectacular public performance to generate interest in the work of Riverside and to demonstrate that 'the story of Jesus' is still relevant. As a Riverside newsletter encouraging members to get involved in a second pop-up church in 2014 expressed this: this event 'gives us the opportunity to publicly witness to the life-changing story of Jesus' death and resurrection and, at the same time, send the public message that we, as the Church, are as committed to following Christ and working together to serve the poor as we have been through the centuries.'

Further ethnographic study of the mundane materialities of attempts at publicity within different evangelical cultures has the potential to deepen analysis of the extent to which God *is* brought back and rendered visible in individuals' everyday lives, as well as opening up the effects of media portrayals on their social interactions. Both conservative and open evangelicals' different modes of and desires for publicity can be seen as shaped by a secularization of public space in the specific sense that it is a 'differentiated and fragmented space marked by specific limitations and affordances for religious activity' (Wilford 2010: 329; Andersson et al. 2011: 629). Further study of the everyday practices of religious publicity has the potential to open up deeper understanding of the complex moral landscapes shaping the co-constitution and performances of religion, the secular, and non-religion and the ontologies of particular kinds of public that enable and constrain these.

Acknowledgements

I am grateful to all members of 'St John's' and 'Riverside' who participated in my study. This research was made possible through funding from a University of Kent doctoral studentship and a Leverhulme Trust Early Career Fellowship.

7

The Gods are back: Nationalism and transnationalism in contemporary Pagan and Native Faith groups in Europe

Kathryn Rountree

I would like to begin by suggesting that any new visibility, resurgence or re-emergence of religion we might currently detect in Europe (or elsewhere) does not necessarily mean that 'God is Back', if 'God' is taken to mean He of the world's well-known monotheistic religions. For modern Pagans – participants in the global new religious movement which emerged in the middle of the twentieth century and grew rapidly from the late 1980s – the God of the Abrahamic faiths is not back and is, at best, receding further into irrelevance. Numerous gods and goddesses from diverse older religions are, however, back with fresh relevance and communities of followers (Harvey 2011; Davy 2009; Pizza and Lewis 2009). Indeed, Europe currently seems to be teeming with deities in all its quarters, although the communities that revere them are highly diverse, usually very small, constantly morphing and often barely visible to the larger societies in which they are embedded.[1]

All modern Pagans share some key characteristics: a focus on attunement with nature (Harvey 1997; Rountree 2012), the valorization of ancient religions and polytheistic cosmologies. However, groups are diverse in their specific beliefs, practices, values and sociopolitical agendas. Some Pagans take up British- and American-derived transnationalist traditions such as Wicca, Druidry, Goddess Spirituality and Core Shamanism, drawing on diverse and eclectic sources from the past and present for their religious ideas, beliefs and practices. Many in these traditions who seek to forge a personal spiritual connection with a particular sacred landscape – or, more frequently, with 'nature' in general – are enamoured with the mythologies of ancient worlds and those of contemporary indigenous peoples (especially those with an animist worldview), shun excesses of consumerism and materialism and may be motivated by an environmental ethics and politics (Harvey 2011; Davy 2009, vol. 2). In addition, those in Goddess Spirituality are likely to espouse a feminist sociopolitical agenda; indeed, they may be feminists first (Christ 1997; Rountree 2004; Eller 1993; Griffin 2000). Some, especially those belonging to Wicca's initiatory traditions,[2] are primarily attracted by the idea of magic, esoteric knowledge, arcane ritual and a gender balanced religious path expressed in the worship of both goddess and god (Luhrmann 1989; Greenwood 2000; Pearson 2009).

Other modern Pagans, despite being influenced to some degree by these transnational varieties of Paganism, are preoccupied with the cultural and religious traditions of a particular people and place and may be driven by ethnic nationalism (Strmiska 2005; Shnirelman 2002). Such groups aim to reconstruct the ancient religion of a specific ethnic group or geographic area and have been interpreted as responses to concerns about foreign colonizing ideologies, internationalization, globalization, cosmopolitanism, crises in ethnic identity and anxieties about cultural erosion (Lindquist 2011; Ivakhiv 2005, 2009; Shnirelman 2002). For some of these groups, or individuals within them, the term 'Pagan' is problematic because it is seen as Christian-derived, and Christianity is perceived as the religion of the foreigner, colonizer or invader. Their preferred alternative terms are 'Native Faith', 'traditional religion', 'indigenous faith', 'nativist', 'reconstructionist' or the specific name of a local group or tradition such as *Rodnoverie* (Russia), *Forn Siðr* (Denmark), *Maausk* (Estonia), *Dievturi* (Latvia), *Hellenismos* (Greece) or *Romuva* (Lithuania).

Among some individuals and groups, ethnic nationalism is explicitly coupled with racism. The politics of White Power, White Separatism or tracing one's ancestry to an 'Aryan' civilization are not uncommon among East European nationalist groups and seem to gather force through the new rise of xenophobic far-right movements. Although the notion of an 'Aryan people' is recognized as a myth by scholars, modern Ukrainian Pagans, for example, do not question their historicity and view themselves as direct Aryan descendants (Lesiv 2013: 29). Shnirelman reports that: 'There are more than a dozen radical political parties and movements in Russia that advocate Neo-Pagan values', along with 'anti-Semitism and racism' (Shnirelman 2002: 205). While more common in Eastern Europe, such individuals and groups are found in other parts of Europe too, and in the United Kingdom and United States (Gardell 2003). They make many eclectic Pagans, more inclined towards left-wing politics, inclusivity and an abhorrence of racism, extremely uncomfortable.

Although it was in Western Europe, specifically Britain, where modern Paganism first became established (Hutton 1999; Pearson 2009),[3] recent research has brought to light flourishing Pagan and Native Faith communities in all parts of Europe, and in the last fifteen years a body of scholarship on diverse groups in post-Soviet contexts has emerged (Aitamurto and Simpson 2013; Lesiv 2013; Strmiska 2005; Shnirelman 2000, 2002, 2007; Gardell 2003; Ivakhiv 2005, 2009; Simpson 2000).

It must be stressed, however, that nationalist and transnationalist expressions of modern Paganism and Native Faith cannot be divided strictly geographically in terms of which part of Europe they inhabit. While those emphasizing the nationalistic aspect of their religious path are more common in Central and Eastern Europe (and, to a degree, Northern Europe), and transnationalist traditions are more common in Western Europe (and in America, Canada, Australia, New Zealand and some other countries), this is a very broad generalization. Nationalist and transnationalist groups may flourish alongside one another – comfortably or uncomfortably – in the same society, as in the Czech Republic (Velkoborská 2015), Sweden (Gregorius 2015) and Hungary (Szilágyi 2015). Moreover, strongly Catholic societies such as Spain, Portugal and Malta provide another scenario for the revival of Paganism, where Roman Catholicism is likely to contribute to the religious ideas and identity of Pagans (Rountree 2010, 2011; Fedele 2013). For these southern European Pagans, this does not amount to bricolage in the sense that elements from plural religious sources are selectively combined to create a single, personally customized faith and religious identity. Rather, Catholic Christianity, as the dominant religion of these societies, is necessarily, at least to some degree, the religion of enculturation, while Paganism may become a religion of choice for a small minority.

Eclectic and Reconstructionist Pagans

Transnationalist and nationalist Paganisms and Native Faiths may appear to correspond, respectively, to Strmiska's 'Eclectic' and 'Reconstructionist' categories of Paganism and Native Faith (Strmiska 2005). Strmiska described Eclectics as being 'more inclined to freely select religious ideas, practices, and even deities from a wide variety of sources, both European and non-European' (Strmiska 2005: 20), whereas Reconstructionists 'aim to reconstruct the ancient religious traditions of a particular ethnic group or a linguistic or geographic area to the highest degree possible' (Strmiska 2005: 19). For Reconstructionists, Strmiska says, ethnic identity is very important, whereas Eclectics may 'distain' such a preoccupation, connecting it with racism (see also Ivakhiv 2009; Aitamurto and Simpson 2013; Shnirelman 2002, 2007). Strmiska suggests that Pagans and followers of Native Faiths can be located along a continuum with Eclectic groups at one pole and Reconstructionist groups at the other. Although he acknowledges (Strmiska 2005: 21) that this model is 'neither as absolute nor as straightforward' as it may appear, nonetheless, it is often invoked in scholarly discussions of Pagan and Native Faith groups. Indeed, two clusters of ideas have come to adhere around the continuum's polar extremes, and a series of dualisms has emerged: Reconstructionism versus Eclecticism, Native Faith versus Paganism, particularism versus universalism, political religion versus apolitical religion, ethnic nationalism versus suspicion of ethnic nationalism, right-wing versus left-wing, East versus West.

Recently, this set of dualisms and the idea that Eclectics are unconcerned with ethnic identity have been challenged (Rountree 2011: 852; Amster 2015; Kraft 2015). This chapter aims to demonstrate through the discussion of several case studies that Eclecticism and Reconstructionism do not necessarily sit at opposite poles on a continuum, that ethnicity may also be important to Eclectic Pagans and that transnationalism and nationalism are not mutually exclusive drivers in contemporary Paganisms and Native Faiths. Rather, they are themes and impulses which may interconnect in complex, important and ever-changing ways for practitioners. In the contemporary globalized, internet-permeated world, this is inevitably so, even where Pagans and Native Faith followers assert the primacy of a uniquely ethnic religion. While a strong connection clearly exists between ethnicity, an inherited attachment to place and nationalism in a number of Central and East European Pagan groups, elsewhere these concepts are less likely to be yoked together, and nationalism – at least a politicized form of nationalism – is not a part of Pagans' emphasis on attachment to a local place.

Moreover, it is worth noting that even where an emphasis on an inherited attachment to place and ethnicity are connected with nationalism, a form of transnationalism may also be identified involving these groups and individuals, whereby various indigenous religious groups come together at festivals, conferences and other gatherings to share ideas, knowledge and rituals. This has been particularly notable with transnational groups of modern shamans. Any resulting eclecticism does not imply a lack of concern for ethnicity or indigenous tradition. Galina Lindquist has described how, in 1993, Michael Harner of the Center for Shamanic Studies in California and some associates joined with Mongush Barakhovich Kenin-Lopsan, a Tyvan poet and playwright, and other Tyvan shamans to organize the First International Conference on

Shamanism in Tyva (an autonomous republic within the Russian Federation, 'Tuva' in Russian) (Lindquist 2011: 76). For a couple of weeks, Harner and fellow shamans (some of whom were anthropologists and psychotherapists) from the United States, Austria, Germany and Switzerland worked together with Tyvan shamans. In 1997, a ten-day gathering of shamans and other indigenous religious specialists was held at a Tibetan Buddhist retreat centre in Savoy in the French Alps to learn from one another's practices.[4] A further example is the Sami shamanic festival, *Isogaisa*, which has been held annually in Norway since 2010, bringing together shamans from all over the world (Fonneland 2015; Kraft 2015). Each of these cases reveals both attachment to a specific indigenous ethnic tradition and a desire to share transnationally. I explore further, below, some other case studies that demonstrate the complex interplay of nationalism and transnationalism among contemporary Pagan and Native Faith groups in Europe and their efforts to construct and assert authentic, religious identities in the context of their changing societies, new political configurations and globalization.

Eclecticism, indigeneity and authenticity

Siv Ellen Kraft has challenged the way in which scholars of contemporary Paganism have tended to juxtapose tradition-bound, indigenous peoples, on the one hand, with innovative, eclectic Pagans, on the other, and then characterize the relationship of the latter towards the former as one of exploitation, romanticization or exotification (Kraft 2015). As a counterpoint to this stereotype, she points out that the rebirth of Sami shamanism in Norway during the late 1990s owed a great deal to US-based Michael Harner's universalist 'Core Shamanism'. It was not until the early twenty-first century that Sami neoshamanism was re-envisioned with 'indigenous' symbols and rituals drawn from the Sami past. This process occurred in the wake of a broader cultural revival among the Sami in the late 1970s and changes to their legal and political status as an indigenous people, and amidst a subsequent period of consciousness-raising among a new generation of Sami. The founder of modern Sami shamanism in Norway, Ailo Gaup, made a journey 'home' in search of his Sami roots and ancient religious knowledge. Instead of finding an indigenous expert he met a Chilean shaman with an African *djembe*-drum who became his guide (Kraft 2015: 27). Thus, from the outset, his pursuit of an indigenous shamanic heritage was diverted by a dislocated indigenous shaman from elsewhere who was already borrowing from another indigenous (African) shamanism. Gaup then made several journeys to California to be trained by Harner. Thus, Kraft argues, until fairly recently it is debatable whether the shamanism practised by Norwegian neoshamans could be called specifically *Sami* shamanism, since it clearly drew on eclectic sources, including some from geographically and culturally distant places and times.

Nonetheless, Kraft shows that a distinctive Sami neoshamanism was pieced together in which indigenous ethnic identity *became* important (Kraft 2015). Sami neoshamans thus confound the idea that Reconstructionist and Eclectic forms of modern Paganism are opposites and that ethnicity is unimportant to eclectic Pagans. Modern Sami shamans consciously drew, and continue to draw, on eclectic cultural resources in constructing their contemporary practice *and* are deeply concerned with issues of ethnicity, cultural continuity and heritage. Moreover, they forge transnational connections with indigenous peoples more widely through such institutions as the Isogaisa festival mentioned above.

Moving to southern Europe, the Maltese modern Pagan community shows similarities to Norway insofar as in its early days the community was highly eclectic, looking particularly to British and, to a degree, US Pagan sources (Rountree 2010, 2011, 2014). Only later, once the community had established itself, did an explicit consideration of the indigenous become important. For the first few seasons of my field research in Malta, which began in 2005, inspiration for Maltese Pagans' ideas and practices came from overseas literature, music, material culture (such as Wiccan tools and Tarot cards) and other resources, their visits to the UK, meeting foreign Pagan visitors to Malta (mostly on Goddess Tours) and, increasingly, the internet. The foreign material was localized through the creative adaptations of local priestesses and practitioners. The only indigenous elements I identified at that time came from blurrings with, and borrowings from, Roman Catholic ideas and practices and from old local customs and inclinations (for example, a preoccupation with divination). Occasionally a small portion of a ritual, such as the invocation of the four directions, would be in the Maltese language, but this did not really catch on because the source texts were in English, and almost all Maltese people speak extremely good English (along with Maltese, it is an official language of the country).

It was not until 2009 that a particular interest in the pre-Christian 'pagan' religions of Malta's past developed within one coven, whose members began making a concerted effort to forge a connection with this past and aspects of the local landscape, seasonal round, archaeological remains and cultural lore. The process of retrieving Malta's pre-Christian religious past, however, did not involve reviving the worship of particular deities known to have once been worshipped there (from the Phoenician, Greek or Roman pantheons). Instead, it entailed inventing – or, they would say, recognizing – a new earth goddess of Malta with a made-up name ('Atilemis'), one they saw as representing a combination of all the female deities who had at some time been worshipped in the islands: I was told that Atilemis was the 'divine female energy of Malta'. They also invented a sea god, Rahab (the Maltese word for 'sea', 'bahar', backwards), to partner her. A painting of Rahab by a coven member showed him as a combination of a Neptune-like figure with the Old Testament God. The idea of establishing an indigenous god and goddess came from Wicca's duotheism: the coven was seeking training and initiation in Alexandrian Wicca from a British high priestess. There was no determination in this coven to bring about the rebirth of a unique, ancient, authentically Maltese religion. It was more a question of creatively synthesizing the local and indigenous with an array of ideas and practices gleaned from international sources. Nationalism seemed to have no role in the coven's goals or activities, yet there was a clear valuing of the indigenous and a strong attachment to local place – the Maltese natural and cultural landscape – along with the foreign.

Followers of modern Hellenic Paganism in Greece,[5] two forms of which are called Ellinais and Hellenismos, conduct research into the ancient roots of their religion but update it to fit their present lives: 'We are, I believe, in the process of moving beyond basic reconstructionism and finding a balance between that approach and innovation, localization, and personal experience' (Winter 2008: 10). In her book explaining Hellenismos, Winter says that in the past there was a distinction between the Greek myths and actual religious practice, as well as numerous variants of the myths and ritual practices. Because of this ancient diversity, whereby 'everyday worship had much more to do with local custom and personal experience than with even the commonly told myths of the gods' (Winter 2008: 18), modern Greek Pagans feel justified in following diverse religious practices. Similarly emphasizing the lack of dogmatism in ancient Greek religion in his *A Beginner's Guide to Hellenismos*, Alexander insists that Hellenismos is 'a sensible religion that embraces the individual and challenges them to be the very best they can be in all aspects of their life without the harsh judgements and dogmatism of some more mainstream religions. Our Gods are not absent. They acknowledge our existence and take an active interest in our lives' (Alexander 2007: 11–12).

Although Greek law recognized Ellinais as an official religion in 2006, and a study of the gods of Olympus is a regular part of school instruction, the gods are deemed by most Greeks – and certainly by the Greek Orthodox Church and the Ministry of Culture – to belong to Greek historical tradition and culture but to have no place in Greek religion today. Similarly, the sites where they were worshipped are today regarded as properly connected with tourism, archaeology and cultural heritage, but not with worshipping the gods for whom they were built. According to sociologist Sofia Peta, modern Greek Pagans 'are reclaiming precisely that space which is held by the Greek-Orthodox church' and 'both want to be considered the genuine expression of Hellenism' (Kourounis 2007). A unique cultural identity is clearly important to Pagan and Orthodox Greeks alike, but the use of symbols associated with that cultural identity – including gods and temple sites – is strongly contested. By resituating those symbols into a religious context, albeit in updated ways, modern Greek Pagans might argue that they are reviving an essentially 'Greek' religion; however, the Greek state and many among the Orthodox majority perceive such claims as 'un-Greek' and ridiculous (Kourounis 2007). The national symbols are agreed upon, but the appropriate context for their usage is not, especially in regard to making claims about cultural or religious authenticity and national identity.

Nationalism, transnationalism and indigeneity

An important factor influencing the shifting boundary between religion and the public sphere in European societies is the current tension between local, cultural or national identities, on the one hand, and wider regional identities and globalization, on the other. Lindquist has claimed that, despite the expectation following the Enlightenment that the arrival of modernity would mean the nation state would become 'one of the primary political and personal identifications of groups and individuals', this premise had to be modified in postmodern times (Lindquist 2011: 69):

> In the second half of the twentieth century, empires disintegrated and nation-states became less significant as identity markers and as symbolic entities of emotional attachment and loyalty for their citizens. In these conditions, people once again resort to ethnicity and religion as cementing forces of their diverse collectivities. Religion becomes, increasingly, the ground for redefining newly emerging polities, nation-states as well as ethnic groups in postcolonial and post-Soviet political formations.

Even as globalization and regionalization faded national borders, and the increase of subcultures and new kinds of identities challenged traditional national identities, simultaneously a new wave of nationalism stirred, especially in post-Socialist countries. In their efforts to forge distinctive new group identities, and amidst pressures from metropolitan and global powers, local political and intellectual elites turned to 'traditional' and 'indigenous' religions to provide the symbolic capital for new nationalisms (Lindquist 2011: 69; Lorentzen 2001). This was true particularly in situations where ethnicity served as a foundation for the nation state: unlike Western Europe, 'east of Western Europe, ethnicity tended to remain the core of the "nation"' (Lindquist 2011: 71). Notably, in such contexts 'ethnicity' and 'nation' did not mean the same as in the West.

According to Kolstoe, in the West 'nation' means 'the sum of all citizens, kept together by common territory, government authority and political history', whereas in Russia and Eastern Europe, where multinational empires survived longer, 'nation' was 'a cultural entity, held together by common language, traditions, folklore, mores and religion' – what in the West might be thought of as an ethnic grouping (Kolstoe 2000: 2). In the East ethnicity is territorial and the basis for nationalism, hence ethno-nationalism.

Reviewing research on religion in post-Socialist societies, Rogers similarly identifies the connection between religion and ethnic and national identities as an important theme (Rogers 2005). On the one hand, there has been a 'resurgence of historic churches … amidst claims to cultural authenticity and with political alliances that aim to re-establish a close connection of the majority church to political power and ideas of national identity' since the end of politically enforced secularism (Ališauskien and Schröder 2012: 3). On the other, historic churches face new challenges: cultural pluralism, consumerism, secularism, the individualization of faith and spirituality and, significantly, 'an understanding of religious identity in terms of culture rather than faith' (Ališauskiene and Schröder 2012: 3). While the historic churches have again become publically visible, their social and political standing in their respective societies has changed since the pre-Soviet period, and there are now other contenders which are also linking culture and religion in ways which capture the public imagination. In such contexts, Pagan and Native Faith groups are emerging and, although numerically small, in some instances have gained political traction in the project of asserting a strong and unique national or local cultural identity based on what are claimed to be ancient indigenous mythologies, cosmologies, rituals, cultural traditions and folklore. Hungary is a case in point. According to Szilágyi (2015: 154)

> An important upswing of religious variety could be observed in Hungary by the end of socialism. The changes involved a double tendency: the destruction of cultural traditions along with the arrival of new religious ideas. This upswing brought with it the expansion of an 'identity market' whose religious dimensions cannot be disregarded. Although secularization theory seems to have been disproved, in the case of some groups religious characteristics have been combined with political orientations. Religious and national identities merge, especially in the post-communist context.

Amidst the emerging religious diversity following the political transition in Hungary, a variety of modern Pagan traditions established themselves (Szilágyi 2011, 2012, 2015; Szilárdi 2009). Some leaned enthusiastically towards the eclectic, transnationalist, Western-oriented Pagan traditions such as Wicca and Goddess Spirituality. Others were committed to the reconstruction of an indigenous Hungarian religion and had a strong attachment to the issue of national identity, often drawing on the figure of the *táltos*, a shaman-like figure from ancient Hungarian religion, possessing magical powers. The sacralization of the nation, ethnicity and 'blood bonds' and the invention of new traditions based on national folklore were all important to the latter groups, representing an ideology broadly in contrast with the globalized mass culture and Western-oriented political and cultural ideologies thought to be threatening the traditional, Hungarian worldview (Szilágyi 2015).

As well as the many small Pagan communities that operate on the periphery of Hungarian religious life, Szilágyi has identified a 'Pagan meta-culture', which has spilled out of the field of religion into the wider culture, particularly into popular culture and right-wing politics. This was closely connected with the rise and successful political performance of radical right-wing movements at the end of the first decade of the 2000s. Although claiming to reconstruct an authentic, indigenous Hungarian religion based on 'true' Hungarian history, language, folklore and other cultural resources, these groups can be shown to be eclectic, he argues, incorporating New Age, Christian and universalist Pagan elements (Szilágyi 2015). For example, the main ethical teaching of one such group, the Yotengrit Church, is: 'You can do anything, but do not harm others'. This is virtually identical to the 'Wiccan Rede', which underpins Wicca's moral system: 'An it harm none, do what ye will' (Valiente 1978: 41).

The Estonian Maausk movement, whose followers are called Maausulised, also emerged amidst a search for cultural roots during the turbulent changes of the mid-1980s to early 1990s. Maausk, an animistic nature religion, stresses continuity between itself and indigenous ethnic traditions, emphasizes its relationship with vernacular languages, is anti-West and hostile to Christianity (seeing it as a subjugation tool of the foreigner) and is closely tied to a developing nationalist discourse (Västrik 2015). Västrik explains that while outsiders might see it as a brand of contemporary Paganism, Maausulised assert their uniqueness and distinguish themselves from transnationalist and Western Paganisms. The movement has links with an earlier ethnic religion, Taara usk, established in the 1920s by intellectuals influenced by Romanticism and Estonian nationalism.[6] Spokespersons of Taara usk thought that Estonian spiritual and cultural independence could be achieved only by establishing a sovereign Estonian religion. Knowing, however, that Estonian religion had ceased to exist during the centuries of foreign rule (from the thirteenth century), they set about creating the principles and practices of this new national religion themselves. Rituals celebrated important events in the human life cycle and national holidays, such as Estonian Independence Day and other days of national significance. Thus an explicitly nationalistic project motivated Taara usk from the outset (Västrik 2015: 134).

Banned by the Soviets in 1940, Taara usk's ideas re-emerged following the Soviet collapse in the form of Maausk, meaning 'the faith of the earth', again driven by intellectuals involved in conservative politics. One of its early leaders was a government minister for several years during the 1990s and another was a founder of the Heritage Protection Club *Tōlet*, in which a group of students from the University of Tartu was active. Hence Maausk's nationalism was, from the beginning, well-integrated with a wider development of Estonian nationalism. Västrik demonstrates that the movement currently enjoys positive local media coverage and considerable local popularity in recent national surveys, is involved in lobbying for heritage protection and wilderness preservation, is active in debates about religious freedom and indigenous rights and works with the University of Tartu in a research project aimed at registering and studying sacred natural sites (Västrik 2015: 145). Presumably, it is because of these types of activities and the movement's nationalist rhetoric that it finds wider support in the current political climate.

Victor Shnirelman, in his review of the growth of Pagan movements in post-Soviet contexts, argues that these movements 'are searching for both a primordial past and a pure ethnic culture, which they view as invaluable resources to overcome the hardship and ideological vacuum of the transitional period' (Shnirelman 2002: 197). Under modernization, he says, the material environment has been 'de-ethnicized'; hence, an authentic ethnic identity is sought in other spheres, such as religion (Shnirelman 2002: 198). One way of achieving this identity is to mine the country's cultural legacy and construct a national religion, which may then be linked with nationalism and may be associated with xenophobic connotations: 'Neo-Pagans' anger is aimed at either a dominant majority – Georgians in Abkhazia, Russians in the Middle Volga River region and the Ukraine – or at those who are viewed as evil alien agents – Jews in ethnic Russian regions' (Shnirelman 2002: 207). In some cases, the politicized ideology may take precedence over the religious dimension.

Just as in southern Europe there are examples of a blending of Catholicism with Paganism, in former Soviet societies Pagan and Native Faith groups may co-opt aspects of Orthodox Christianity (such as the idea of the Trinity) – although in the case of the latter it is likely to be a deliberate attempt to build a bridge between themselves and Orthodoxy, rather than as a result of enculturation. Some Hungarian and Russian Pagans do this; however, as we have seen, Estonians do not. As well as borrowing from Christianity, Pagans and Native Faith followers may draw upon other sources in the construction of their 'genuine' indigenous faith: Hinduism (the idea of reincarnation), Zoroastrianism, occultism, and the beliefs of immigrant groups to their regions.

Even amidst rampant nationalism, Reconstructionist groups morph and splinter, and there are those operating nearby that embrace transnationalist forms of Paganism like Wicca and Goddess Spirituality. Or, they may try to break away from nationalism, working hard to forge a locally meaningful religious path, emphasizing the sacred relationship between themselves and the particular tract of land where they live. The Pagan scene in the Czech Republic is highly diverse, including ethnic Pagan reconstructionists and eclectic Witches, Wiccans, Druids and others. A unique group within this diversity is the Brotherhood of Wolves (*Brothrjus Wulfe*) described by Kamila Velkoborska (2015). The original impulses of the Brotherhood of Wolves' founders were apolitical nationalism, a search for ancient roots, and a spirituality connected with these roots. The group eschews an ethnic or political agenda (despite some members' earlier involvement in White Power groups) and seeks authenticity by creatively combining elements of Germanic religious heritage with an intimate connection with the immediate landscape. Germanic or Old Norse mythology is mixed with stories and legends about forest tribes, wolves and werewolves, along with visions of group members' imagination. Their faith centres on the Great Wolf Fenris of the Eddas and is embodied in a lifestyle revolving around Czechoslovakian Wolfdogs (which most members breed) and an attempt to live as modern hunters and gatherers. Velkoborska describes how the group traces a correlation between the demise of *Canis lupus* in Eurasia and North America, the fate of Fenris in Old Norse mythology and the demise of human intimacy with nature (Velkoborska 2015: 98). Drawing a parallel between their lives with their Wolfdogs and the lives of ancient tribes who lived in harmony with nature and other beings, members of the Brotherhood see the Wolfdog – once wild, now domesticated – as representing their compromised life as Pagans in the modern world.

Conclusion

This chapter has attempted to show that contemporary Pagans and Native Faith followers are part of a growing, dynamic, religious phenomenon, which is a response to the dynamic sociocultural, political and environmental conditions in which individuals and groups currently find themselves. While the emergence of modern Paganisms is a global phenomenon, it is localized in diverse ways – hence Pagan*isms* – and within any national context there may be plural Pagan responses, as several of the cases discussed above attest. The chapter questions the extent to which the polarization of Reconstructionism and Eclecticism, correlating broadly with Eastern and Western Paganisms and Native Faiths, is valid. As knowledge of these movements expands, it seems clear that Reconstructionist and Eclectic groups cannot be divided strictly geographically. It is broadly true that Reconstructionists are found more commonly in Central and Eastern Europe and Eclectic Pagans more commonly in Western Europe (and America, Canada, Australia, New Zealand and some other countries), but the East–West division can be a misleading generalization. Greek Hellenic Pagans, for example, seem just as adamantly committed to reconstructing an authentic and unique ethnic religion as some of the Eastern European groups are; however, their form of religious nationalism does not align with the way in which the Greek state configures nationalism. This is quite different from the case of Estonian Maausk, whose project of reviving a national ethnic religion was, from the beginning, well integrated with a wider development of Estonian nationalism. Unlike the Greek Reconstructionists, who are at loggerheads with the State, Estonian Reconstructionists apparently enjoy considerable popularity, both with the public and with conservative politicians.

Reconstructionist and Eclectic groups and individuals may exist alongside one another – happily or unhappily – as they do in Hungary, Malta and the Czech Republic (and other places not discussed above). Or, the processes of Reconstructionism and Eclecticism may be entwined, as in the cases of Norway and the Czech Republic. It was shown, for example, that modern Sami shamans drew upon eclectic and foreign cultural resources in constructing their contemporary local shamanic practice; this did not compromise their deep concern with their indigenous Sami ethnic and religious heritage. The Brotherhood of Wolves followers draw on their Germanic religious heritage, but create and customize their beliefs and practices for their contemporary lives. The emergence of Paganism in the predominantly Catholic Society of Malta provides another scenario whereby Eclecticism is embraced amidst the enduring importance of an indigenous cultural identity as Roman Catholics.

Although there is a strong connection between ethnicity, attachment to place and nationalism among Central and East European Native Faith followers, post-Soviet societies all have different political histories, and their experiences of communism were diverse (Aitamurto and Simpson 2013). While the centrality of nation and ethnic group may be common to many groups' ideals, these groups are diverse, and nationalism is given different importance and takes a variety of forms. Ethnicity and attachment to place are often important to eclectic Pagans too, but they are less likely to be yoked with a politicized form of nationalism. Maltese Pagans are clearly eclectic and inventive, but this does not indicate an undervaluing of their indigenous traditions or their attachment to the Maltese natural and cultural landscape. Even where Pagans' emphasis on ethnicity and place are strongly connected with politics, a form of transnationalism may also be evident, for example, where indigenous neoshamans come together at festivals and conferences to share ideas, knowledge and rituals. Any eclecticism or borrowing which results from such sharing does not imply a lack of concern for, or commitment to, ethnicity, indigenous tradition or a local place.

Many modern Pagans are interested not only in connecting with their own roots, but may also draw connections between themselves and other indigenous peoples, some of whom may be immigrants living in their societies. Personhood and nationhood, ethnicity and connection to place may be configured in diverse and unconventional ways – so, for example, Gregorius shows that Swedish followers of the Norse deities are also interested in Hinduism and Afro-Caribbean religions like Vodou, and followers of the Norse deities are found throughout the world (Gregorius 2015). Hence, belonging and attachment to place may be configured according to the place one inhabits at a particular time and who one lives with – irrespective of ancestry, place of birth and ethnicity – amidst processes of migration and reterritorialization. Reconstructionism and Eclecticism are valuable tools for thinking about how modern Paganisms and Native Faiths are configured, but they do not belong at opposite ends of a continuum. They intertwine and may change over time, with one process gaining greater or less significance in relation to the other. It is not a question of 'either/or', but 'both/and' in an ever-evolving relationship held together by creativity and invention.

PART TWO

Rethinking the religion–state relationship

8

Religion and state in the twenty-first century: The alternative between *laïcité* and religious freedom

Luca Diotallevi

Sociological studies devoted to church–state relations during the last two decades demonstrate substantial convergence. Previously, even though some theoretical studies (in particular, Luhmann 1977) underlined the need to re-examine the widely accepted understanding of secularization and marginalization of religion as political hegemony over an entire society, there is a general agreement that it was only with the work of Casanova in the early 1990s that a turning point was reached (Casanova 2000[1994]). Casanova recognized the return, even in 'advanced western' societies, of the influence of religion on politics. Since the early 1990s, different theoretical models and labels have been used to reconstruct and interpret this new trend. That notwithstanding, it is clear that there is a wide consensus concerning both the decline of the separatist model and the continuing spread of a model based on relationships of ever-increasing cooperation between church and state. Alfred Stepan, for example, has recently insisted on the need to speak of 'multiple secularisms' (Stepan 2011). The majority of the cases studied by Stepan and others, including non-Western societies, have either not experienced or subsequently repudiated 'separatist secularism' in favour of some form of greater cooperation between state and religious actors, either in the form of 'positive accommodation – positive cooperation – principled distance', or some form of 'establishmentarianism'.

Tariq Modood reconstructs more or less the same process with identical results, contrasting an expansion of those areas influenced by 'moderate secularism' against a decline of those characterized by 'radical secularism' (Modood 2012a). Modood argues not only that the 'U.S. and France are not the best that the West has got to offer', but that their separatist solution is not the dominant/mainstream conception (Modood 2012b: 65). Along similar lines, Madeley, referring to the church–state transformations in Europe between 1980 and 2000, has written: 'Antidisestablishmentarianism, for long I believed to be the longest word – and maybe one of the most obscure – in the English language, can now be seen as a more robust phenomenon than is usually appreciated' (Madeley 2003: 17). This last term is used to refer to a process that shows an inversion of a tendency from the beginning of the twentieth century to around 1970 (Madeley 2009: 178–280; see also Haynes 2010). Findings from a study carried out on a worldwide scale led Fox to conclude not only that 'SRAS [higher level of separation of religion and state] is an exception and GIR [government involvement in religion] is the norm' (Fox 2006: 561) but also that 'modernization is associated with higher GIR'. Furthermore, on a more normative level, Casanova and Stepan insist on the uselessness, if not outright detriment, of secularism to democracy and its development (Casanova 2009: 1058; Stepan 2011).

Criticisms of the prevailing reconstruction

The tendency of continuing close church–state relations can scarcely be called into question, but the same cannot be said for its interpretation. Interpretations based on a series of more or less overlapping category couplings (e.g. radical secularism vs. moderate secularism) have questionable validity. At the very least there are two areas of doubt, one of a formal nature and the other of a 'material' nature.

From a methodological point of view, it is worthwhile to question the usefulness – and perhaps even the logical coherence – of a category when it includes too many disparate cases. This applies, above all, to cases that involve one of the two categories of a binary system. This is the case, for example, for the category of 'moderate secularism'. In line with Fox's data, between 70 per cent and 90 per cent of the cases studied worldwide would be definable by this category (Fox 2006: 545). As Ahdar and Leigh note: even 'several systems of very different natures – mild establishment, pluralism and substantive neutrality – seem to us score highly in that they recognize a measure of interaction and cooperation between government and religious communities is useful' (Ahdar and Leigh 2005: 97; cf. Doe 2011: 39).

The other doubt, however, is even more crucial. In the majority of cases, US separatism and French separatism end up in the same category, and often they alone make up this category (e.g. Stepan 2011: 114; Fox 2006; Jensen 2011: 16). Yet, the dramatic differences between the French and American examples regarding the relations between religious powers and political powers and, in general, the very different conditions under which religious actors have access to public space are well known.

The classic question concerning the possibility of wearing clothes or symbols expressing a religious identity in public more than amply sums up these key differences. The individual behaviour that creates serious problems for a *laïcité* regime creates none for a regime of religious freedom such as that founded on the two religious clauses of the First Amendment to the Constitution of the United States. Further, it expresses one of the conditions for the survival of this latter regime.

Towards theoretical refinement

Treating the French and American types of separation as the same is unsatisfactory, then (Beckford 2004: 31; Modood 2009). The aims of this chapter are (a) to indicate a way in which it might be possible to identify a structural difference between the French and the American regimes. Moreover, bringing into focus the differences between the two separatist regimes can turn out to be useful (b) to work out a more useful arrangement of the content of the present mega-category of 'moderate secularism'. Finally, the aim is (c) to facilitate a reappraisal of the European tradition in the area of church–state relations.

My starting point is the assumption that separation is really an effect and not only a cause. That is, in the analysis of church–state relationships we must return to the question concerning the type of social differentiation in a particular social context and then, within this framework, to the structure of the political system (Madeley 2009: 174–5; see also Jepperson 2002: 67–71). Casanova asks the crucial question: 'how are the boundaries drawn and by whom?' He continues: 'political secularism falls easily into secularist ideology when the political arrogates for itself an absolute, sovereign, almost sacred, almost transcendent character or when the secular arrogates for itself the mantle of rationality and universality, while claiming "religion" to be essentially non-rational, particularistic and intolerant (or illiberal)' (Casanova 2009: 1058).

In effect, when we ask ourselves – as does, for example Jepperson (2002) – whether the organizing principle of a society is corporative or associative and whether the level of institutionalization is elevated or modest (two variables related to the way the political sphere organizes itself and differentiates itself from the rest of society), we can easily observe that the French and American cases appear in very different cells of the matrix.

Therefore, we must look at the dominant forms of social differentiation within these differing contexts in order to better comprehend the how and the why of the different forms of church–state separation. It is in this direction that, among others, Enyedi suggests we pursue our analysis: that it is a matter of recognizing the differing variants and the non-monotonous evolution of secularization, understood as institutional differentiation (Enyedi 2003: 219). Similarly, comparative theorizations of modernization (e.g. Kuru 2007: 572) and public order – and of the role of the judiciary (Richardson 2006, 2014) – point to a promising direction. In order to develop this agenda, I will make use of the theory of social differentiation and the understanding of fundamental rights elaborated by Luhmann (Luhmann 2002, 1990, 1995; see also Beyer 2012; Gorski 2000).

French *laïcité* and US religious freedom: Really so similar?

A good point of departure for our objective is offered by the different ways in which the French *laïcité* and the American religious freedom regimes conceive the relationship between religious freedom and freedom of conscience (see Diotallevi 2010: 80). Briefly stated, in the case of *laïcité* the freedom of religion is just one of the many possible contents of the freedom of conscience; therefore, it is the latter that guarantees the former. On the contrary, under the US regime it is the freedom of religion that is the prime social guarantee for the freedom of conscience. According to *laïcité*, conscience is a space in which the individual can privately maintain his or her own religious preference, the public expression of which, however, remains strictly regulated by the state. Under the US religious freedom regime, it is exactly the public practice of religion that guarantees that political power does not occupy the entire public space: it provides for the expression of political, economic, educational etc. choices and endeavours that are religiously motivated but not religious in themselves. It is this 'free exercise' that prevents the establishment of the state in the specific continental-European meaning of the word (McConnell 2009; Witte and Nichols 2011: 288).

It is not by chance that regimes of *laïcité* and religious freedom define and institutionalize the notion of the autonomy of religious subjects in very different ways. The two regimes differ dramatically regarding the scope

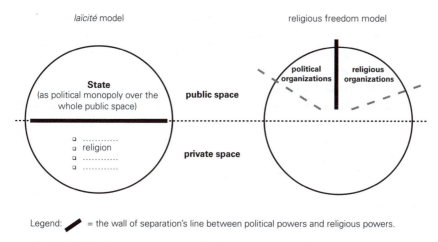

FIGURE 8.1 Laïcité *and religious freedom: Two approaches to separation.*

recognized to the free exercise of religion, which is greater in the US regime. Consequently, each regime has different influences on the conditions of the practice of religious autonomy (Stepan 2001: 217; Ahdar and Leigh 2005: 92; Monsma 2009: 182; Doe 2011: 112–20). In fact, a high stakes game is being played out around the degrees and the forms of recognition of the autonomy of the religious actors. The results of this game will contribute in a decisive way to the difference between regimes of *laïcité* and regimes of religious freedom.

Resorting to a geometric metaphor, it can be said that the two walls of separation, that erected by *laïcitè* and that erected by religious freedom, not only do not overlap, but rather appear to be mutually perpendicular. The *laïcité* wall of separation runs between public space and private space; the religious freedom wall of separation runs across public space. Consequently, while the public space is homogeneous and dominated by political power in the case of *laïcité*, in the case of religious freedom the public space is highly differentiated internally and therefore freed from any hegemony (see Figure 8.1). The *laïcité* regime is a crucial part of the polity of a state society; the religious freedom regime is a crucial element of the polity of a stateless society.

Understanding the difference with Luhmann

The roots of the US regime lie – definitively after the First Amendment, approved in 1791 – in the attribution of constitutional value to two principles that can even appear to be mutually contradictory, as well as asymmetric in their pretensions: disestablishment and free exercise (Monsma 2000: 13,

32–3).[1] We should deal with such a seeming contradiction not as if it were an obstacle to be removed but rather as a highly valuable trace to be analysed.

It is precisely because of the difficulty in interpreting this contradiction that it is useful to appeal to the sociological understanding of the fundamental rights of the individual as elaborated by Luhmann (Luhmann 2002: 57–62, 124, 154; Philippopoulos-Mihailopoulos 2011: 154). From this sociological point of view, the *Grundrechte* (fundamental rights) appear as institutions that no societal subsystem is able to produce *ex novo*, but which many of these functionally specialized subsystems – in the case of fundamental rights, the political and the judicial ones – can accept (as institutions) and maintain by means of a typical and crucial operation: the structural coupling (Luhmann 1997: 778–83, 2005: 325–8; Philippopoulos-Mihailopoulos 2011: 130).

The specific function of fundamental rights is that of guaranteeing and eventually improving the primacy of the functional differentiation of the societal system over every other type of social differentiation. By accepting and supporting fundamental rights, the political system (a) leaves ample room for different social spheres outside it (it limits itself and does not politicize the rest of society) and at the same time protects itself from an excessive influence generated in the non-political social fields. By accepting fundamental rights, the political system also (b) respects the liberty and dignity of individuals (more precisely, it guarantees a social condition for the self-representation of the individual as a single personality [Luhmann 2002: 108]). The societal subsystem does not lose its own self-referentiality and, consequently, a high degree of autonomy, but combines these with a high degree both of social differentiation and of differentiation between social and personal domains.

Sometimes we also speak of two categories of fundamental rights. The function of the first category is often understood in terms of rights to freedom and the second in terms of rights to equality. From a Luhmannian point of view, such a duplicity depends on and reflects the double risk for individual liberty and dignity produced by the differentiation–specialization of each single societal subsystem. In the case of the political subsystem, each single political decision could force the individual to act in a way inadequate to the social differentiation structure, and each single political decision could directly violate the structural instances of a differentiated social order. It is in respect of these two social functions of fundamental rights that Luhmann talks of rights to freedom and of rights to equality (Luhmann 2002: 245).

Given the high degree of complexity and contingency that are allowed and implemented by the primacy of the process of functional differentiation of society, it is clear that a condition of permanent balance between those two risks is not only impossible but also unthinkable. Rather, the conflict between freedom and equality and the reciprocal limits they place on one another plays a positive role. If we understand the disestablishment clause as a right to freedom and the free exercise clause as a right to equality, the history of both the political and also the judicial administration of the two constitutional clauses gains a more evident sociological meaning.

Applying Luhmann's theory, we can interpret the first two clauses of the First Amendment as a fundamental step in the structural coupling between the political system and the judicial system. This institutionalization of religious freedom frames the relationship between the political system and the religious system.[2] Hence, the disestablishment clause must be understood in terms of the right to freedom, and the free exercise clause in terms of the right to equality. The combination of free exercise and disestablishment is what Luhmann calls *Grundrecht*: an institution able to maintain both a level of societal differentiation, first of all between the political and the judicial subsystems (but also with the religious subsystem [cf. Berman 1983: 85–99]) and – at the same time – able to preserve a significant degree of individual liberty and individual dignity also in the religious field and regarding religiously relevant issues (see Luhmann 2002: 244). The apparent contradiction between the principles stated by each of the two clauses depends on a lack of sociological comprehension of tensions and risks produced by the primacy (over other kinds of social differentiation) of the functional differentiation of society and the related increase in differentiation between the social and the personal domains. Taken together, the two clauses carry out the dual function of the institution (*Grundrecht*) of religious liberty. Sociologically speaking, religious liberty, as it is guaranteed in the US regime, is none other than one of the fundamental rights of the individual. In other words, it is one of the institutions that defends and implements the primacy of the functional differentiation of society (over each and every other form of social differentiation) and its stress on the differentiation between the social domain and personal domain.

The hegemony guaranteed to the state in French society with regard to religion (an evident legacy of the Westphalian *cuius regio eius et religio*), is simply impossible and unthinkable in American society.[3] The difference between the French and American cases can therefore be understood in terms of two very different cases of structural couplings between the religious and political sub-systems. In the US religious freedom regime the structural coupling, fixed in the first two clauses of the Bill of Rights, does not only reproduce a different relationship between the political system and the religious system, but it also orients the political system towards a relationship with the judicial system that is very different from that institutionalized in French statism. Speaking in sociological terms, I am referring more or less to the same object to which jurists and political analysts refer to when they distinguish regimes of common law from those of civil law and, more generally, when they distinguish cases characterized by political–judicial regimes of rule of law from regimes of *Etat de droit* or *Rechtsstaat* (e.g. Zolo 2003: 23–6; Costa 2003: 120; Luhmann 2002: 83, note 7).

Therefore, in order to understand the difference between French separatism and US separatism, we should focus not only on the politics–religion relationship, but also on the relations between political and judicial systems, as well as on those between each of these two and the religious system. According to Luhmannian theory, we can treat the two separatisms as particular manifestations of two very different forms (US more radical, French less radical) and two very different degrees (US higher than French) of functional differentiation. In fact, French societal forms and degrees of functional differentiation are, respectively, not radical enough and not high enough to avoid some kind of hegemony and control exercised by the state over religious organizations.

On this basis it also becomes potentially clearer why, within the institutional framework of a primarily functionally differentiated society, a recovery of the influence of religion on politics is not necessarily a case of *de*-differentiation (Jelen 2010; Luhmann 2002: 277–8), nor does it have to be read in terms of a crisis – or the end – of modernity. On the other hand, in *laïcité* regimes, the return of religion into the public sphere is an ambiguous phenomenon. It could turn out to be a driver of social evolution (more developed functional differentiation, more social complexity and more social contingency), but also to be the driver of an opposite process: the *de*-differentiation of society and the loss of the autonomy of politics and of modernization (in Luhmannian terms; cf. Luhmann 1997: 811).

A promising understanding

From the point of view just reconstructed, it therefore appears that the *laïcité* and religious freedom regimes separate church and state very differently. In both cases it is possible to speak of radical separatism and therefore of radical secularism. However, in using the same label, we sidestep a difference; a difference that could turn out to also be very useful in putting some order in the overcrowded category of 'moderate secularism'.

In fact, the goal of religious freedom separatism is to preserve the functional differentiation of society, while that of *laïcité* separatism is to contain it, to reduce it and eventually to block it, defending the primacy of politics over society through the primacy of the state over politics. The former separatism is polyarchic, the latter is monarchic (Stepan 2000; Witte 2000: 45–6). The former is a way of guaranteeing the institutional bases of a stateless society; the latter, those of a state society (Stepan 2011: 215; Jensen 2011: 19). The two regimes imply very different assessments and orientations regarding the degree of autonomy of other societal subsystems from the political subsystem, starting with the economic and scientific ones but, above all, regarding a high degree of autonomy of the judicial system. From this perspective, analyses regarding models of church–state relations (multiple secularities) and those regarding social models (political modernities) converge (Jepperson 2002; Jepperson and Meyer 2000).

Luhmannian analysis helps us to understand that in the end the originality, as well as one of the few key conditions of the religious freedom regime, should be sought in the functional specification process, which does not only differentiate the political system and the religious system but which also differentiates the political system and the judicial system, on the one hand, and the religious system and the judicial system, on the other. A large part of the model of US church–state relations depends on the particular primacy of such a multiple functional differentiation, which ought not to be confused with the claim of attributing a role of mediator to the legal system, as proposed by Ferrari (1999). In fact, a sociologically significant characteristic of the US political system, not found in the political system of the French model, is exactly that of the political recognition and support of those institutions, which guarantee the particular type of differentiation mentioned above. Among these institutions there are those of the fundamental rights of the individual (a mix of rights of equality and freedom) and, first of all, the right of religious freedom as it is recognized and protected not only west of the Atlantic but to the north of the English Channel as well (Santoro 2003: 184–213).

The Luhmannian approach also enables us to better appreciate the British roots of the US model – planted, first of all, in the outcome of the Glorious Revolution (Diotallevi 2010: 141; Zolo 2003: 29). From the same perspective, we are able to avoid confusing the English establishment with that of the Lutheran state churches or of certain forms of the Catholic confessional state (e.g. Hill 2010: 162; Dibdin 1932: 109–12). Likewise, the Luhmannian analytical instruments can produce an explanation of other profiles of the complex difference between *laïcité* regimes and those of religious freedom. In fact, more generally, these two regimes reveal themselves to differ from one another in many aspects: civil law regime versus common law regime (as already mentioned), privatization of religion versus non-privatization of religion, monarchy versus polyarchy, *religion civile* versus civil religion (Diotallevi 2007, 2010: 145). The two regimes shape and determine very different playing fields on which the competition between church and state, and religion and politics, takes place.[4]

Conclusion: Regimes of church–state separation as instances of functional differentiation

Sociologically speaking, the Anglo-American and the French versions of religious liberty are essential elements of two deeply different social polities.

Only the first has a structure that actively supports the primacy of the functional differentiation among societal subsystems. This kind of differentiation between political system and religious system emerges and persists in a context in which other societal subsystems, particularly the judicial system, are analogously specified. This does not occur in the same form and to the same degree in the French regime of *laïcité*.

In both regimes, we can observe some cases of cooperation between state and church, political organizations and religious organizations. However, the label 'cooperation' risks including an excessive number and variety of things. The risk of confusion between radically different kinds of state–church cooperation increases the more cases are subsumed under the umbrella term 'moderate secularism'. However, by means of the Luhmannian approach, it becomes possible to make a distinction between different types of state–church cooperation (cf. Bäckström and Davie 2010: 183) and, consequently, also between at least two different types of 'moderate secularism' (or 'separatism'). While in a highly differentiated society (a stateless society) the cooperation between political and religious organizations is always – or at least can always be – also a competition between social agencies enjoying more or less the same autonomy in the public space, absolutely no kind of competitive cooperation between political organizations and religious organizations can occur in state society, other than within a frame of subordination and social hierarchy shaped by the primacy of the political. Following this analytical path, we can usefully distinguish between those cases of moderate separatism that allow cooperation through subordination and those that allow competitive cooperation. In doing so, the second kind is destined to reveal itself as being much more separatist than the first.

At the end of the day, we could empirically discover that which Rousseau clearly stated theoretically in defining his model of *religion civile* (Rousseau 1974). The greater the separation obtained by means of the primacy of the political, the greater is the need of the political to become also and immediately religious. In the end, in the case of *laïcité* and in similar cases, do we still have separation? Or do we only have an exploitation or a substitution of the religious agencies in their functions by political agencies, that is, through the sacralization of the state or of the party or both?

Finally, from the point of view that I have adopted, it becomes possible to bring into focus two other related issues. On the one hand, the presence of the British variant of the history of European church–state relations makes it impossible to reduce this history to just one model, that of *laïcité*.[5] On the other hand, and for exactly the same reason, the secularizing character of many of the decisions and the policies undertaken by numerous expressions of the European Union can be clearly identified (Doe 2010: 151; Hill 2010; Houston 2010; Scolnicov 2010). These policies tend not to represent, as is insisted, but rather to produce a unified (and in these terms unprecedented) European identity.[6] They try to homogenize the diversity of European traditions in the field of church–state relationship and to do so from a *laïcité* premise. Ironically, or even dramatically, this is happening exactly when *laïcité* itself is becoming a marginal and declining model, and when it increasingly appears to be in crisis.

Acknowledgements

I am very grateful to Silvia Angeletti, Stefano Ceccanti and Giorgio Armillei for their comments.

9

The sacred state: Religion, ritual and power in the United Kingdom

Norman Bonney

Perhaps because of the long reign of Elizabeth, who came to the throne of the United Kingdom of Great Britain and Northern Ireland on 6 February 1952, there is a lack of general appreciation of the persistent religious characteristics of the UK state in what, to many observers, seems to be a more secular age. These features are made most manifest at the commencement of each monarch's reign and were last rehearsed more than six decades ago, but they are exhibited periodically in other events of lesser prominence on various subsequent occasions. They are evident, too, in the daily routine behaviour of UK parliamentarians. In more recent decades, there are, however, signs of a renegotiation of the sacred Christian character of the UK state, which does not challenge the ritual supremacy of the state cult, the Church of England, but which involves symbolic participation by some other religions and Christian denominations in subaltern roles in state ceremonies. While the populace may have become less religious in its everyday attitudes and behaviour, the state remains endowed with significant sacred dimensions, which intermittently call forth wide-scale popular involvement, most manifestly in the ceremonial surrounding the monarchy but also in events such as the official forms of state remembrance for the dead of war.

Proponents of the view that UK society has become increasingly secularized in recent decades (Brown 2009; Bruce 2011) have focused on mass attitudes and everyday personal behaviour and have not considered whether national institutions have adapted to these changing patterns. The perspective adopted in this chapter suggests that there has been remarkable continuity in the religious institutions of the UK state throughout this period of social change and that where there has been change it has been in adaptation to religious diversity and not to secularization. This institutional continuity derives from the embedded role of the Church of England in the very structure of the governance of the state. This embedding has enabled the Church, over the centuries, to resist successive challenges to its position and to continue in the present day as a propagator of a form of official Christianity and to become, during the present reign of Elizabeth, a defender of some other forms of officially recognized, but secondary, Christian denominations and non-Christian religious faiths.

The Church of England as the state cult of the United Kingdom

The monarchy has been a key institution in these patterns of continuity and change. The monarch is Supreme Governor of the Church of England – a body which has an exclusively monopoly of the official relations between the UK state and God. Elizabeth is not the head of the Church. That role is reserved for Jesus Christ. But she is Supreme Governor – a role that was determined by the efforts of Henry VIII in the sixteenth century to assert the supremacy of the crown in religious as well as civil matters over the competing authority of the Church of Rome. Reflecting the hierarchical nature of the Church of England, bishops are appointed by the crown and owe homage to the monarch. Thus according to Canon A7 of the Church, at their investiture they pledge that 'We acknowledge that the Queen's excellent Majesty, acting according to the laws of the realm, is the highest power under God in this kingdom and has supreme authority over all persons in all causes, as well ecclesiastical as civil' (Church of England 2014a). And, since laws are determined by Parliament and administered by the UK government, theoretically as agents of the monarch, it is these bodies that have ultimate authority over the Church. The most significant state acts of the Church, such as the administration of the oaths of the monarch as required by the Coronation Oath Act of 1688; the arrangements for the coronation itself; dramatic events such as the funeral of Diana, Princess of Wales, in 1997; and the form of state commemorations for the dead of war are subject to final decision by the curious curia of the UK cabinet, subject itself, ultimately, to Parliament (Bonney 2013).

What is probably the most famous bible and the source of great literary and religious inspiration is known as the 'authorized version' – 'authorized' since its translation and publication was sanctioned by King James I (VI of Scotland). What was not evident in the considerable official publicity surrounding the 400th anniversary in 2011 was the fact that the translators were instructed in their work not to offer offence to the monarch. While the predecessor English language 'Geneva' bible had forty references to tyrants, the authorized version had none (Bragg 2011: 39–42).

The Church, as the official state cult, is governed by the Queen-in-Parliament, although, in practice, it is granted substantial autonomy. Its internal laws and regulations, or 'measures', as they are known, have to be approved by special procedures in Parliament. In any matter of great concern to the state Parliament may override the Church. Debates in 2013–14 within the Church over whether there may be female bishops have been influenced by debates in Parliament over the matter and could ultimately be resolved by the legislature if changes satisfactory to it are not made. Decisions about the gender of the senior hierarchs of the state cult are thus influenced as much as by political opinion as by theological considerations.

Other manifestations of the politico-religious roles of the state cult are evident in the daily prayers conducted in both houses of Parliament. In the Commons, they are conducted by the Speaker's Chaplain; in the House of Lords, they are conducted by one of the twenty-six bishops who, most unusually by democratic norms, sit by law, as full members of that house. The Speaker's Chaplain has responsibility for the pastoral care of members and staff of the Palace of Westminster and can conduct weddings, marriage blessings and baptisms of members of the Parliament (UK Parliament 2011). There is also a weekly Eucharistic service in one of the chapels of Parliament. St Margaret's Church, beside Westminster Abbey and across the road from the Houses of Parliament, is the church of Parliament, where, for instance, a service of thanksgiving was held at the conclusion of the Second World War in 1945. A contemporary manifestation of this merging of the secular and the religious was the resting of the body of former prime minister Margaret Thatcher in one of the parliamentary chapels the night before her state funeral in 2013 in London's Anglican St Paul's Cathedral, which itself has been the site of many UK state religious ceremonials, such as the thanksgiving services for the coronation of Elizabeth and for her Diamond Jubilee in 2012.

It is necessary at this point to clarify that the constitutional and religious role of the Church of England is not limited to the territory of England. The Church has a constitutional role for the whole of the United Kingdom in that it provides daily prayers and other religious services to the UK Parliament, provides legislators in the House of Lords who legislate for the whole of the United Kingdom and conducts the coronation service of a new monarch of the United Kingdom. It is thus also the Church of the United Kingdom.

The most explicit and elaborated manifestations of the sacred religious character of the UK state occur with a change of monarch, usually through the death of the incumbent. Religious qualifications for succession to the throne of the United Kingdom of Great Britain and Northern Ireland, determined by the Act of Settlement of 1701, continue in operation more than three centuries later. Roman Catholics, and those persons not in communion with the Church of England, may not succeed to the throne because of the incumbent's role as Supreme Governor of the Church of England (UK Monarchy 2014).

The immediate accession to the throne of a new monarch, when the new incumbent acquires all the powers of office, is accompanied by state and religious public declarations involving leading officers of the state cult. Some of these formalities may be eclipsed by extensive mass media coverage of the death and obituaries of the predecessor but among the obligations of the new monarch is an immediate requirement of the Acts of Union of 1707 to swear to 'maintain and preserve the True Protestant religion and Presbyterian church government in Scotland' – in effect qualifying the sovereign's religious role and the sway of the state cult north of the border.

Some months later, either at the opening of the UK Parliament or at the coronation, the monarch is required by the Accession Declaration Act of 1910 to formally reject the ritual, doctrines and authority of the Church of Rome. The wording was changed in the 1910 Act from a seventeenth-century formulation that was much more explicitly antagonistic to that Church, but the monarch still repudiates in a less contentious way the authority of the Pope, the adoration of the Virgin Mary and the doctrine of transubstantiation (the belief that the body and blood of Christ materializes in a communion service). The declaration is, in fact, a relic of the oaths that prohibited Roman Catholics from holding public office until Catholic emancipation in 1829 (Bonney 2013: ch. 2).

The referendum of the people of Scotland on a possible move to national independence on 18 September 2014 might have possibly led to changes in legislation relating to the Scottish oath, although the proponents of independence stated that they wish to retain the monarchy and pledged not to change the legal status of any church or religion. The requirement for the Accession Declaration might come under review following the next succession, but it is a guarantee of a Protestant monarchy and ought not to be a difficult obligation for a government and a monarch determined to maintain the Church of England as the state cult.

The only legal requirement for a coronation of the new monarch is the Coronation Oath Act of 1688, which calls for the Oath to be administered by a bishop of the state church. The monarch performs official duties immediately on succeeding to the throne even before this ritual confirmation of incumbency, which occurs some months and often over a year later. The elaborate rituals of the 'divine service' of the coronation and the accompanying state ceremonials which take such a long time to prepare can be traced back over a millennium. They have been changed over the centuries but include core rituals that mix sacred and secular elements. The most sacred elements are the anointing of the monarch, the taking of communion and the administration of the oaths.

The oaths spell out the essential religious role of the monarchy in UK government. The monarch swears to maintain 'the laws of God and the true profession of the gospel' and the 'Protestant Reformed religion established by law in the United Kingdom'. She or he also pledges to 'maintain and preserve inviolably the settlement of the Church of England and the doctrine, worship, discipline, and government thereof as by law established in England' and 'to preserve the rights and privileges of bishops, clergy and churches'. The coronation oaths are a strong statement of the Protestant Christian character of the UK state, of the privileged and established status of the Church of England, of the religious role of the monarch, and thus of the UK government, that advises her or him as protector and guarantor of these arrangements.

It is open to the UK government and Parliament to vary or dispense with the oaths and the coronation ceremonial. Discussions about these matters may go on behind closed doors, but public debates and statements by the UK government about them are rare and only usually surface, sometimes mutely, at times of succession to the throne. The tendency is to avoid public debate well in advance of the likely succession process, because such debates raise such profound issues about the very character of the UK state, its relationship to religious belief and practice and the nature of the religious settlement enshrined in the Church, the monarchy and Parliament. It seems as though few elected politicians are interested in, or dare raise, the issues involved. And, of course, the province of Northern Ireland is an example of the deep and troubling religious and constitutional conflicts that have arisen over such matters in one part of the kingdom – but, as this discussion demonstrates, they are not conflicts that are solely confined to that province.

The oaths of a new monarch might be considered as a renewal of the contract of the nation with each new monarch and ought to be under review at each succession, but rarely have they risen as major public issues. While there is evidence that the most of the population have little knowledge of the religious role of the monarchy and do not regard it as a sacred institution, nonetheless, the attitude of political elites seems to be that existing arrangements should best be left alone, either because they favour them or because of the profound issues which would arise from changing them. There has, however, been a recent exercise in changing the rules of succession to replace the heretofore prevailing primacy of males over females in the succession by granting precedence by birth order – an exercise that involved getting the consent not only of the UK Parliament but the fifteen other countries of which the monarch is head of state. The experience over this procedure for amending relevant laws provides a precedent for future possible changes of much more significance.

The coming of the next monarch to the throne provides the opportunity for the nation and state to consider whether they wish to continue the existing arrangements of the monarchy in the very changed context of the twenty-first century, and it is possible that the next time they are invoked there will be debate about their continuing suitability. The continuation of a Protestant Christian monarchy, whether the monarchy should have a religious character and, if so, what form it should take could all be issues at stake. Undoubtedly there will be strong inertial forces for the maintenance of the status quo, but if existing arrangements are challenged the UK state could face deep constitutional and religious conflicts (Bonney 2013).

Challenges to the state cult

The notion that there should be an official Christian cult coincident with the state has its origins in the domestic politics and international religious and interstate tensions of the sixteenth century. The Church of England was crafted by Henry VIII and Elizabeth I to be church of the English state, and the perennial political tensions of sixteenth- and seventeenth-century England revolved around the conflict between loyalty to the nation state and its prince or to the international organization that was the Church of Rome, as well as competing views as to the true doctrines and rituals of Christ's church.

The Church of England in those times was totalitarian. The state admitted no deviance from its official doctrines and rituals. State office could only be held by Anglicans. Adhesion to the Church of Rome involved implications of national disloyalty and challenge to the authority of the monarch. Christians with other ideas about church doctrine and organization also encountered state disdain and harassment. Puritans and other sects unable to accept these disciplines left for the Netherlands and North America. Over the centuries, various denominations such as Jews, Quakers and Catholics were able to change the laws that discriminated against them and excluded them from the right to conduct recognized marriage ceremonies or hold public office.

The greatest challenge to the state cult, especially from the eighteenth century onwards, came from the rise of Nonconformity – the Protestant 'dissenting' sects and Methodism. Their rise was propelled by the indus-trialization of the midlands and north, the emergence of large proletarian and bourgeois social classes and the associated growth of the labour movement. Taylor suggested that in the interwar years of the twentieth century, there was a three-fold split of the Christian churches between Anglicanism, Nonconformity and the Roman Catholic Church – the latter being reinforced by Irish immigration (Taylor 1965: 168–70).

The rise and fall of Nonconformity is symbolized in Westminster Methodist Central Hall. In the late nineteenth century, similar, if not quite as grand, buildings were constructed in major city centres by Methodists to attract the working classes with a mixture of serious religion combined with musical items and comfortable seating designed to counter the appeal of the music halls. They were not designed like churches, and they were planned to be welcoming (BBC 2012; Connelly 2014). Westminster's Methodist Central Hall is a grand impressive building situated just across the road as a magnificent physical and symbolic challenge to Westminster Abbey, the central institution of the official state cult. It was opened in 1912 on the centenary of the birth of John Wesley. The poet John Betjeman described the dome of the hall as 'a splendid foil to the towers of Westminster Abbey and the pinnacles of the Houses of Parliament' (Methodist Central Hall 2014). Although the hall was built as the expression of a movement that challenged the power of the state cult, its completion possibly marked the apex of the movement that brought it about. Certainly by the end of the Second World War, and increasingly so thereafter, Methodism, and Nonconformity more generally, became a decreasingly significant force in UK society. As congregations grew smaller and the population less religiously oriented in its everyday behaviour and attitudes, the decline of Methodist central halls symbolized its declining weight and influence. It is reckoned that in the early twenty-first century there are only 300,000 Methodists in the United Kingdom, compared to 70 million worldwide. Religious services are only a small part of the activity in Westminster Central Hall, which itself is eclipsed in public and tourist attention by the abbey across the road. In 1937 and 1953, the Free Churches sought to have a role in the coronation ceremonies, regarding the events as not truly national if they were not included in the ritual. They were present in the congregation – but were not involved in the rites of the Church of England, which the state cult insisted were its unique preserve (Williamson 2007: 249).

The Church of Rome still remains constitutionally suspect in the United Kingdom. Its main UK building – Westminster Cathedral – is completely dissociated from the UK state. It houses the shrine of St John Southworth and others martyred in 1654 – symbolically demonstrating the historic role of the UK state's antagonistic attitude to the Church. While the UK monarchy and senior Anglicans go through the motions of ecumenism and diplomacy with the Church of Rome, there remain important tensions rooted in profound historical conflicts. The Church of Rome does not organize itself on the basis of the UK state. It has separate bishops' conferences in England and Wales, Scotland and all-Ireland – and the affinity of the Church of Rome with republican dissenters remains a source of tension in community conflicts in Northern Ireland. Further, the former Archbishop Keith O'Brien of Edinburgh expressed sympathy for a Scottish breakaway from the United Kingdom in 2006 (Scotsman 2006), and the holding of the installation ceremony of his successor in Edinburgh in September 2013, on the morning of a day which, in the same city, was to see a large rally in favour of independence, was a signal of the Church's sympathy for that cause.

The incumbency of the UK monarchy is still determined by religious criteria that exclude Roman Catholics and those not in communion with the Church of England from occupying the throne. At accession, a new monarch, reflecting the desires of the Scottish negotiators of the Acts of Union of 1707, which created the present parliamentary union with other parts of Britain, has to swear to 'maintain and preserve the True Protestant religion and Presbyterian church government in Scotland'. As well as affirming Protestantism, this oath also preserved the autonomy of self-governing Presbyterian denominations against the historic tendency of monarchs under the union of the crown from 1603 onwards promoting Anglican Episcopalian conformity. The Scots were determined to ensure that bishops did not rule their churches as either Catholic or Anglican agents of a foreign centralizing power. As ever in the UK state, the sacred is buried deep in everyday structures. Politicians stay away from proposing amendments to them, because such steps are feared to unleash conflicting passions and conflicts. While prepared to propose a fundamental change in the political union of Scotland with the rest of the United Kingdom, the Scottish National Party controlling the Scottish government does not propose any changes to the legal status of any church or religion (Scottish Government 2014 Q590).

No cross on the cenotaph[1]

Perhaps the greatest crisis ever experienced by the Church of England since 1689 was the issue of how, in its aftermath, the United Kingdom and Empire should commemorate the immense casualties of the First World War. The

Cenotaph in Whitehall, London, is the site, on a Sunday in early November, of the most sacred annual United Kingdom and Commonwealth state and religious ceremonial for the dead of war. The monument and the ceremony are relatively new innovations in state religion and commemoration, and there is now a standard ritual, but few today appreciate the great controversies surrounding the origins of the much revered monument and the associated ceremonial.

The Cenotaph was designed, originally in wood and plaster form, by Edwin Lutyens, as a temporary construction for the allied Peace Parade of 19 July 1919 following the conclusion of the Versailles Treaty – some eight months after the armistice at 11.00 a.m. on 11 November 1918. By deliberate decision of the war cabinet, it is devoid of religious inscriptions. Some members of the cabinet wanted a giant cross at Admiralty Arch, but Prime Minister Lloyd George prevailed with Lutyens' idea of a secular monument. Troops of United Kingdom and Commonwealth forces, as well as those of allied nations such as France and its colonial forces, and some from Thailand, Japan, Serbia, Italy and elsewhere, marched by the monument and saluted it with its inscription 'The Glorious Dead'.

Because of the immense popular devotion to the monument as a symbol of grief and remembrance, the government quickly decided to make it a permanent construction. By deliberate decision the cabinet agreed, again against advice from Church of England bishops who wanted a cross inscribed on it or even a giant cross atop it, that there should not be any religious inscription because of the religious diversity of the huge numbers of dead of the Allied and Empire forces, which included Sikhs, Muslims, Jews, Hindus and others as well as Christians. It was inaugurated on 11 November 1919 by a simple unveiling ceremony by King George V, accompanied, at his suggestion, by the first two-minute silence.

The basic shape of subsequent ceremonials was, however, determined by a decision of the Church of England, concerned at the mass popularity of what it regarded as a pagan war memorial, to construct a rival focus of national grief and commemoration in the form of the Tomb of the Unknown Warrior in nearby Westminster Abbey. By engineering the appearance of the body of the dead warrior at the Cenotaph on its way to the Abbey at 11.00 a.m. on 11 November the following year, 1920, it managed to incorporate a Christian religious service into the ceremony at the Cenotaph (See also Wolffe 2000: 262–4). This was followed by a Christian service of entombment in Westminster Abbey. The tomb incorporates a Christian inscription, contrary to a decision of the cabinet.

The 11 November 1923 fell on a Sunday, and the Church used that coincidence to arrange for a substitute national ceremony at the Tomb of the Unknown Warrior in place of that at the Cenotaph, coordinated with services at churches around the nation. However, such was the public reaction at the move, and the depth of popular attachment to the Cenotaph, that the Church had to abandon the plan. In the following year, the basic pattern of the familiar ceremonial was performed at the Cenotaph.

Shrinking and hanging on

Since the immediate post-1918 era, the Church of England has withered in many ways, particularly since the 1960s, but it has not disappeared. Institutional continuity, backed by integration into the organs of state, has enabled it to remain as a significant exponent of religious belief in public life. Canada, lacking a national church and failing to appreciate the religious dimensions of its monarchy, even though the religiosity of its people exceeds that of UK citizens, has developed a mostly secular public sphere and discourse with only vague echoes of the big bang of God discernible to scholars deep in the foundational statements of its constitution, in official oaths and in the currency (Bonney 2013: 150–63).

As this contrast illustrates, the very existence of the Church of England, its rootedness in the state, and its occasional prominent public actions preserves formal religious expression in the life of the UK state even though the religious behaviour and belief of the citizenry is greatly attenuated. Whenever citizens have had the opportunity to consider their polity anew from first principles, they have rejected the fusion of state and church represented by the inherited state cult. Scots rejected it in the seventeenth century and in the Acts of Union of 1707; American colonists rebelled against the political authority of the monarch and the religious institutions associated with it. Those states of the United States that had vestiges of establishment had deserted them by the 1830s. The 'dominions' of the UK state – Australia, Canada, New Zealand and South Africa – had no officially established churches because of their very religious diversity.

With devolution in 1999, the newly elected devolved UK parliamentary assemblies in Northern Ireland, Wales and Scotland all decided to abandon the Westminster model of the relationship between the state and religion. The Northern Ireland Legislative Assembly eventually agreed to collective silent contemplation before the start of proceedings; the Welsh National Assembly has no official religious business; the Scottish Parliament has weekly multi-faith prayers in which the Church of Rome is the second most frequent contributor after the Presbyterian Church of Scotland.

In contemporary England, the distance of the population from its official state cult has been clearly demonstrated in recent survey findings by Linda Woodhead (2014). In the 2011 census, 59.3 per cent declared themselves as Christians. Nominal Anglicans, who represent about 30 per cent of the population, and thus about a half of the Christian population, are concentrated among the older half of the population, with only 10 per cent of those people in their twenties identifying this way compared to 45 per cent of those in their seventies. Twenty-five per cent declared no religion, with almost 60 per cent of those in their twenties saying they had none compared to just under 30 per cent in their seventies. Among nominal Anglicans, only 13 per cent (or about 4 per cent of the whole population) could be classified as regular churchgoers. Equally tiny percentages of all people said that they looked to religious institutions or leaders for guidance in their lives. Altogether, 18 per cent thought that the Church was a positive force in society. Of the 14 per cent who thought that it was a negative force in society, the main reasons given were that it was prejudiced against women and gay people and that it was stuffy and out of touch.

Woodhead also cites other measures of the church's declining significance as evident in its falling share of baptisms of live births (65 per cent in 1900; 12 per cent in 2010), declining share of all marriages (65 per cent in 1900; 24 per cent in 2010) and similar declines in the share of funerals (75 per cent until the 1960s; 37 per cent in 2010).

Yet, despite the contemporary tenuousness of the attachment of the population to the rituals, beliefs and authority of the Church of England, its constitutional entrenchment enables it, from time to time, to lead public events that incorporate large sectors of the populace vicariously in national UK ceremonial events (Davie 2007). The coronation of a new monarch, not enacted now for more than six decades; the annual Christmas broadcast of the monarch, which has Christian content and which is transmitted to the country and the Commonwealth; royal weddings such as those of Prince Charles and Lady Diana Spencer and of Prince William to Kate Middleton; funerals such as those of Princess Diana and Margaret Thatcher; the baptism of Prince George, the son of William and Kate; and religious services and wider celebrations to commemorate the Diamond Jubilee of the monarch in 2012 – all these events and more provide occasional opportunities for the Church to rehearse its rituals and institutions, give public prominence to key religious ideas and generate a sense of normalcy about the role of the institution.

Onward Christian soldiers

Although the connection of the state cult to the mass populace is gradually diminishing, if occasionally replenished through public spectacle and national trauma or celebration, it retains an important base in a number of state institutions. Woodhead has referred to the role of the Church of England in a number of significant social institutions – not only the monarchy and Parliament but also in the armed forces, the universities, the judiciary, the prisons, and the private schools (Woodhead 2014).

The armed forces are a good example of this. Paradoxically, while religious affiliations in the general population are low, the armed forces have a high proportion of members declaring religious commitment. In 2008, the British Social Attitudes Survey reported that 43.2 per cent of the population had no religion, but Ministry of Defence statistics indicated that the comparable figure among the armed forces was 11.6 per cent. Furthermore, while the national survey reported that 50 per cent of the population were Christian, and the 2011 census reported the figure for England and Wales to be 59 per cent, the armed forces were reported to be 87 per cent Christian (BRIN 2014).

Clearly, these varying statistics are collected on differing bases and for differing purposes, but they are suggestive of an institutional environment in the armed forces that is supportive and encouraging of Christian religious commitment. Religious information is collected in the armed forces for reasons related to the possible risks of service as much as for routine operational purposes. In contrast, social survey information is collected in a much more open-ended way, in which individuals are free to express their attitudes without profound social constraint. Anecdotally, the author has been informed that forces are informally encouraged to give a Christian or other religious affiliation in their personnel records and identity papers as it is argued that they may receive less punitive treatment if they are seen as religious persons by potential enemy captors.

As argued by British Religion in Numbers, 'religion is quite institutionalized and embedded within the armed services, principally through a strong chaplaincy network (and an Armed Forces Chaplaincy Centre in Hampshire, to train and support the chaplains)' (BRIN 2014). According to the UK Ministry of Defence website, 'spiritual advisors serve with most units offering help and guidance to soldiers at home and overseas. Padres are Christian ministers, but they support soldiers of any faith as well as those who have no religious belief at all' (UK Ministry of Defence 2014b). They are, as it were, commissars of the state cult and are deemed to have special qualities to counsel soldiers of all denominations.

A Church of England paper (2014b) reports that there were 464 paid professional chaplains in the UK armed forces from what is known as 'the sending churches' – all of which were Christian (Church of England 2014b). Almost two-thirds of these were Church of England; 142 were Church of Scotland or Free Churches and 37 were Roman Catholic. The Church of England retains its dominance of the armed forces chaplaincies but has conceded places to other Christian churches including the Roman Catholic Church – representing a new quasi-establishment in the armed forces. It has been estimated that the Ministry of Defence salary bill for chaplains was £22 million in 2011 (National Secular Society 2014a). The salaried Christian chaplaincy of the armed forces is now supplemented by ancillary *civilian* support representatives from other faith traditions.

Other public institutions also provide salaried employment for chaplains. The National Health Service, universities and prisons are very important in this respect. According to a study by the National Secular Society, £29 million of healthcare money was used to fund the salaries of chaplains in the health service in England in 2009/10 (National Secular Society 2014b).

The infrastructure of the UK state is thus permeated by a network of salaried chaplaincies that purvey the Christian mission in many official and other institutional contexts. The chaplaincies are dominated by the Church of England, with concessionary participation granted to the Church of Scotland, the historic Free Churches and the Roman Catholic Church. Other faith traditions are beginning to make inroads into this Christian monopoly but on a secondary basis with few paid posts.

Interfaith initiatives: A new establishment?

In recent years, in recognition of the increasing diversity of religion in the United Kingdom, representatives of 'world religions' have been in attendance in a formal religious delegation that lays wreaths as part of the official remembrance ceremony at the Cenotaph. The formal state recognition of Buddhists, Jews, Jains, Hindus, Muslims and Zoroastrians at the Cenotaph ceremony has also been evident, most notably at the commencement of the Queen's Diamond Jubilee celebrations in 2012, when the first official event took place in Lambeth Palace, the residence of the Archbishop of Canterbury. Here, the monarch was introduced to representatives of these denominations and inspected sacred objects of each faith.

There have been numerous other official interfaith initiatives. The heir to the throne, Prince Charles, has frequently made known his sympathy for what he regards as the common spirituality of all religions. However, whatever official recognition is accorded to diverse faiths, this does not threaten the pre-eminence of the state cult. At the ceremony at the Cenotaph, there is a prominent Church of England procession led by a celebrant bearing high a gold or bronze cross, and a bishop utters a prayer invoking the 'Lord Jesus Christ'. The representatives of other faiths seem to accept the state recognition they are granted on such occasions by being in a religious delegation and laying a wreath, but in doing so they submit themselves as secondary participants to the ritual supremacy of the state cult.

Other denominations are excluded from these forms of official state recognition and the Church of England (2014b) plays a key role in defining the boundaries of official religious recognition. It specifically excludes 'alternative spiritualities', 'new religious movements', pagans, Jehovah's Witness,

Mormons and numerous other religious groups from involvement in interfaith networks that are supported with government funds and, through the offices of the Chaplain-General, it regulates admission to, and exclusion from, the official religious delegation at the Cenotaph ceremony.

Conclusion

The Church of England remains an important UK institution, since it is embedded in the constitutional architecture. The monarch is its Supreme Governor, and the Church has an exclusive link between the UK state and God through Jesus Christ. While the population has become largely religiously indifferent in its everyday behaviour and less involved in the routine activities of the state cult, nonetheless much of the population becomes vicariously or more deeply involved in occasional state religious activities such as royal weddings, baptisms and Jubilee events. Even while public interest in religion is diminishing, salaried chaplaincies in public institutions provide an important social and financial base for the state cult. When a new monarch comes to the throne, the Church plays a significant part in the constitutional and religious confirmation of the new reign. Such events expose the religious nature of the UK constitution and provide potential opportunities for democratic review of these arrangements – particularly the entrenched status of the established Church of England.

In recent decades, increasing secularization of popular attitudes and behaviour has been accompanied by increased religious diversity, and the state has looked to the Church to be the prime adviser and broker of its relationships with other religious denominations. Its advice has been important in separating out certain religious denominations, often seen as 'world religions', as a diverse secondary religious establishment that receives some official state recognition in ceremony and access to executive policy advice circles. However, these latter denominations have been less successful in penetrating the chaplaincies of the armed forces and other public institutions that are dominated by the state cult and its close Christian cousins. Excluded entirely from this charmed circle are those citizens from numerous other denominations, such as Mormons, Jehovah's Witnesses, humanists, pagans and others, who are officially deemed less worthy of official respect, recognition, and inclusion. They are the religious pariahs of the United Kingdom.

10

Social class and Christianity: Imagining sovereignty and Scottish independence

Paul Gilfillan

On 18 September 2014, the Scots faced the choice of voting in favour of creating a sovereign Scottish state of their own or choosing to remain in a political union with England, and in light of the 2011 census where 54 per cent of the Scottish population defined themselves as Christians, how Christians voted in the Referendum was decisive, so that an empirical inquiry into whether Scottish Christians have a preferential constitutional form for their nation (Schmitt 1996, 2005) is of some significance.[1] As a sociologist wishing to engage with the 'signs of the times' I wanted to explore this question, and in March and April 2013 I conducted sixteen in-depth semi-structured interviews with members of the Catholic Church and the Church of Scotland in the Fife village of Cardenden, taking the Independence Referendum as an opportunity to inquire into a series of questions:

- What, if any, are the alignments between social class, Christianity and the constitutional debate?

- Do Christians see any theological significance in the Independence Referendum?

- Is there a specifically Christian answer to the political problem of deciding the constitutional form of the nation?

- Insofar as history involves a relationship between God and humanity, do Christians have a particular historical consciousness that informs their answer to the referendum question, *should Scotland be an independent country?*

- Do Christians imagine (national) *sovereignty* in a particular way?

- Do Catholics understand themselves as the 'cradle' of the nation, and do Scottish Presbyterians have a particular sense of being 'custodians' of the nation?

Catholic informants

In March 2013, I interviewed Mhairi (lab technician, born 1952), Nora (housewife, born 1940) and Ronnie (housewife, born December 1943) together as we sat in the local church hall after Sunday Mass, and I began by asking them whether the referendum held any religious or spiritual significance for them.

Mhairi: Well, aye. Ah do think there is because, basically it's goin back tae aa these laws aboot when people can have their bairns aborted an things like that. These have all come from the government – what's legal, what isnae legal.

Me: Where is God operative in Scotland today?

Mhairi: Jist basically in oor churches.

Nora: Naw, God's everywhere.

Ronnie: He's in the people but the people are no respondin tae Him.

Nora: Ah sat wane night, it wis quite sad, Ah wis sayin ma prayers in the hoose. Ah wis sittin sayin the rosary an Ah wis greetin [crying] because it wis so sad, cause Ah got tae that stage where Ah said 'God, what's happenin in the world?' The way things is gaun, the wiy things are birlin, and they're aa gaun tae damnation. And it's so sad. Ah go back tae ma mammy who said, 'Och it's a hard joab savin souls, so jist save yer ain.' Everything seems tae be bad.

Me: It sounds like if Ah asked if the Devil was operative in history you'd be able to …

Mhairi: Yes he is! Where there's power there's evil.

Nora: Ah think he's in power.

Me: Does it make any sense tae say yer a Scottish Christian as opposed tae just sayin yer a Christian?

Mhairi: Naw. It doesnae matter.

Ronnie: Nut, Ah dinnae think so. Cause it's a world-wide faith.

Nora: Well, Mary Queen e Scots got her head chopped off cause e it! Doon there!

Me: If ye have a different belief dae ye have a different politics?

Mhairi: Well Ah wid say so.

Ronnie: Ah think so.

Mhairi: You could be a Protestant an be quite happy wi abortion. Or same sex marriages.

Me: Mhairi, you said earlier you're against independence. Is it because of economics?

Mhairi: I'd still be against the idea even if we were financially no worse off. Ah don't know really. Ah jist feel who have we got tae back us up if the government doon in London washed their hands e us? What wid happen tae us then? Let's face it, what the heck have we got here? There's no an awfi lot. An the price e electricity, what would happen wi benefits? Are they benefits aa gonnae be cut like they're getting cut noo left, right an centre fir people that's disabled? Ah heard they'd take aa oor bus passes away. Ah heard that. On the television. Ah'm very dubious about independence. Just tae say we are independent, tae say 'We've done it!'

Ronnie: Is Wales independent?

Me: No.

Mhairi: So why is Wales not independent?

Nora: Do you know that Scotland is the only country that's no got independence? Let's face it, aa the British colonies noo are oan their ain – we're the only wane that's no.

The next informant I interviewed was Mary, a retired teacher (born 1933). During the interview I asked Mary whether Catholics have a particular view on Scottish independence.

Mary: I really don't know. Apart from our previous archbishop [Cardinal O'Brien] who was friendly with Alex Salmond.

Me: Has the referendum any spiritual or religious significance?

Mary: I suppose in a way it does. But I mean unless someone started to stop us Catholics going to church, Ah mean if anyone wanted that then the other party would get my vote every time.

Me: Does being Scottish, in some way, shape or inform your being a Catholic or is it incidental?

Mary: I suppose your Christian faith does sort of kind of rule you or push you in a certain direction, but if you have grown up with that faith you really don't know if other people have those same thoughts.

Me: Is God operative in Scotland today?

Mary: Well a Christian could say that. But it is difficult to bring God into everyday matters. But there must be some sort of effect. But more than that I don't know.

I next interviewed Cathie, a retired office worker (born 1930) and I began by asking the referendum question, should Scotland be an independent country?

Cathie: Ah think Ah'd vote fir Scotland. Ah really do because Ah love ma country.

Me: Is there any spiritual or religious significance to the 2014 referendum?

Cathie: Ah believe everybody should have their own country. Nobody should belong tae anybody else's country.

Me: Does your faith impact upon how you vote?

Cathie: Well, no really. If they were sayin things Ah didnae like then Ah'd say 'Oh Ah'm no voting fir thame.' Ken if they're gonnae dae this or dae that.

Me: Does it make sense to say you are a Scottish Catholic as opposed to just a Catholic?

Cathie: Ah don't know. Ah'd need tae think. Ah like the queen. An Ah wonder how it'd work if we were separated. Ah widane mind bein separated. Ah'd like tae hae oor ain wee country tae oursel. Ah really would.

Next, I interviewed retired tradesman Andy (born 1937), and again I began by asking should Scotland be an independent country?

Andy: Naw. Ah don't think so.

Me: Should politics and religion mix?

Andy: Politics is based on religion! See that chess board over there, ye have the king and the bishop beside him, advisin the king on what to do. That's where aa the laws were brought from. Politics and the Church are still connected Ah think. But they're trying tae separate Christian principles from politics.

Me: Does you faith have a bearing on how you vote?

Andy: Oh of course, yes! Ah'm tryin tae see how our faith will survive with the politicians of today.

Me: Does it make any sense to say you are a Scottish Christian?

Andy: No it doesn't. Because Christianity is universal. It's a world thing.

Me: Is there any religious or spiritual significance to the independence referendum?

Andy: No. Ah don't think so. Actually Ah'm jist trying to understand the question.

Me: The Christian God is an historical God. He acts in history. Does he act in Scottish history?

Andy: No. Ah don't think so. Ah widnae blame God for what happens in history.

Me: So you don't think God acts in history?

Andy: No. History is made by the action of individuals. God makes the rules and if people don't abide by the rules, they make the history, not God.

Me: Is God's presence in history finished?

Andy: No.

Me: Where is God at work in Scotland today?

Andy: Ah don't think He is actually to be honest with ye. Scotland has lost its spiritual dimension. Ah think Scotland is now a secular nation. Ye see aa the churches closing. In fifty years' time my church will be closed. Cause there's no kids nowadays. No young people. Bit when it comes to politics Ah'll tell ye this: Salmond is the most brilliant politician, the most devious person I have listened to in my life.

Me: You don't respect Salmond. Who do you respect?

Andy: Well Ah respected the old lady that wis the Tory person for Scotland. Ah liked her, instead e the lesbian fae Fife [Ruth Davidson, Conservative Member of the Scottish Parliament (MSP)] which is an aberration e nature. This is what's comin in now. Ah don't have anybody tae vote fir nooadays casue they're aa the same, so Ah'm a lost person politically.

Finally, I reproduce extracts from an interview conducted with Margaret, another retired teacher. Having established that Margaret was sceptical about Scottish independence, I asked her to expand on her views.

Margaret: Ah don't think we have any group of people in Scotland that can actually provide us with a government, that can give us a self-governing country. Ah think they're gonnae make a mess of it and were gonnae end up being almost third world. Ah've no confidence in any of them, no confidence in Scottish Labour, am not confident in anybody. Ah think as a country, as a union, we should as a whole country all of us, Wales, we should all be fighting to get Westminster changed. And have proper representation. Cause Westminster never ever represented Scotland.

Me: I'm confused Margaret. You're talking nationalism on the one hand and then on the other you're not wanting anything to do with it.

Margaret: Ah jist don't have any confidence in any of the people that are in parliament. If we become independent, Salmond and his crew, they're twisted, they don't think things through.

Me: Give me an example of their incompetence.

Margaret: Well, for example, the euro thing. But there's so many other things. Ah don't know enough about it but Ah don't think we have the financial capability to be independent.

Me: Upon what basis do you think that?

Margaret: What resources do we have? The oil's there but that is the only thing we have. An tourism. Ah think well end up being quite poor. A poor country.

Me: Why will we become poorer?

Margaret: Well first of all, do we have the resources? Ah have not read it and Ah have tae say Ah have not gone into any detail, am quite lazy about it. Ah suppose in a way have formed an opinion without really investigatin as deeply as I might do if I was formin an opinion about something else. Am maybe talking through a hole in ma head. I don't believe that we have the resources in Scotland to be totally and completely financially independent. We don't have the jobs. We don't have the industry here. And Ah think some of the industry especially the American ones will go. Ah don't think they'll stay with us once we become independent. And again, from what Ah do read in newspapers and what Ah hear on the news and the telly or whatever, nobody's provided any proof that those resources or the industry is gonnae be brought to Scotland. A lot of the American firms have moved out already.

Me: Which ones?

Margaret: Don't ask me.

Me: Ah don't mean to put ye on the spot.

Margaret: Well ye are putting me on the spot. But there have been. Ah'll come back to ye on that. Ah read these things. Vaguely.

Me: Do Catholics have a particular view?

Margaret: No.

Me: Is there any spiritual or religious significance to the independence referendum?

Margaret: I'm not sure what you mean by that.

Paul: That there are non-natural forces at work in human history. That above and beyond natural, social and cultural realities there is a specifically supernatural action in the world.

Margaret: Ah haven't thought about that.

Me: Is God operative in Scotland today?

Margaret: Ah don't know. Ah would only say Ah hope so and Ah think so but I have no proof to say that. It's just a personal internal thing. But Ah'm not certain that as a community, as a country we think like that.

Me: Does it make sense to say you're a Scottish Christian rather than just
a Christian?

Margaret: Ah don't identity myself as a Scottish Catholic. I identify myself
as Scottish and a Catholic.

Protestant informants

The first interview with a Church of Scotland member was with Theresa (born
1947), an office-bearer in the local church, and took place in her home after
we watched the breaking news from the Vatican that a new pope had been
elected. After a while enjoying the spectacle and excitement of Pope Francis
addressing the gathered crowds in St Peter's Square, I began by asking
Theresa whether the Church of Scotland had a particular view on Scottish
independence.

Theresa: The people in the church don't discuss it at all. It might be the higher
up ones do. Ah vote the way Ah vote regardless of whether I'm
a church member or not and Ah think that's how most people do.

Me: Interviewing Catholics they tell me their church is quite involved in
politics. For example, the recent move to have legislation to allow
euthanasia. The bishops said you have to oppose this. Life is sacred
etcetera and you need to write to your MSP. Does the Church of
Scotland have anything like that?

Theresa: No. There is never anything political brought up from the pulpit
or even at the Kirk session. We'd never be told how to vote or
anything or to go against anything. You know, something that was
prominent in the news. Definitely not. Even hinted at. They are
two separate entities, politics and the Church of Scotland.

Me: Does your faith impact upon how you vote?

Theresa: Oh no. I never think about them linked together at all.

My next interview with members of the local Church of Scotland congregation
was with a man and wife, Sonia and Michael (the latter a retired Church of
Scotland minister), both born in 1945, and I began by asking whether the Church
of Scotland had a particular view on politics or the upcoming referendum.

Michael: The issue of homosexuality has been ongoing in the Church of
Scotland. It's like women ministers. Ah mean it's gonnae come
and the whole thing about Christianity is that you should accept
a person for who they are. And therefore we should accept
homosexuals for who they are.

Sonia: The bedroom tax. Ah see the Presbytery has got something oot on that.

Me: What about the constitution?

Michael: If Ah wis preachin Ah'd say you've got tae use yer vote and think of others and the country and it'd be left at that. It's left tae individuals.

Me: Does faith and politics mix?

Sonia: In oor politics we should be caring for those less fortunate than ourselves. That's faith.

Me: Do you believe there is any theological significance to the referendum, that Christians view the referendum any differently than people of no faith?

Sonia: No. They'll have their own individual views on it.

Me: My idea was whether the Church of Scotland has a special care for the nation. That the church not only is charged with handing on the faith, but the Scottish church is charged with the fate of the nation as well.

Michael: Ah wid say that by getting independence the Church of Scotland has a greater chance of making its views known.

Sonia: But then Ah also think if we had an independent Scotland the Church of Scotland has a great input, but so does the Catholic Church because that has been a strong part of Scotland as well. Ah mean the Church of Scotland has only been from the Reformation but the Roman Catholic Church goes right back.

Process, continuity and change

Some ten months after my initial interviews I happened to learn through a chance conversation with Mhairi in early 2014 that she had changed her mind from being firmly against independence to being firmly in favour of independence and, intriguingly, as I chatted with Mhairi about her new views, I noted she did not advert to having been of the opposite view ten months previously. As we chatted it dawned upon me that Mhairi did not advert to any change of view because she had no recollection of what her views were some ten months ago, and so was not aware of having changed her mind. When I asked why she was voting 'Yes' in the referendum, she told me it was to avoid the impending 'austerity measures' of the Conservative Westminster government, and so from her point of view there was no change to account for as her original concerns in 2013 about austerity cuts and changes in welfare funding had remained the same, with the only change being that she now viewed independence as the better means of protecting these interests and priorities.

In light of my conversation with Mhairi, I decided to contact the rest of my Catholic informants again to see if any more had changed their mind, and

I discovered that Margaret, Nora and Ronnie had also changed their views from being against independence to being in favour, with Mhairi, Nora and Margaret even attending a local public meeting organized by the local Yes Cardenden group which was addressed by the former MSP Tommy Sheridan on 2 June 2014 in the local Church of Scotland church hall.[2] Among my Catholic informants, then, in 2013 only two out of eight were in favour of independence, while a year or so later in 2014, six out of eight were now in favour of independence.[3]

In contrast to Mhairi, in my second interview with Ronnie it was clear that she was very conscious of having changed her views, and integral to her conversion was her recognition of and her desire to see her fellow Scots break from a condition of psychological-cum-symbolic domination.

Ronnie: Ah think am definitely wi the yes.

Me: Really? What made you change your mind?

Ronnie: Well, jist different things, what wis on the ither night, it wis an English boy that wis daen it on the telly an he wis talkin tae aa the people in England that were Scottish, an in aa the high places in England, an they were sort e sayin 'Oh Scotland widnae be able to make it,' ye know, an Ah wis gettin fair annoyed at this. They've made their money and are livin in England noo, an they aa hid sort e Scottish blood in them, an Ah thought you're mair worried that you'll lose money than yer worried aboot Scotland, ye know? A really didnae let anybody influence me, Ah just prayed aboot it, an thought aboot it, an Ah thought tae masel, we're no gonnae grow as a country … and there was a thing on aboot Glasgow the other night an, it was a Sikh boy, a comedian, an he wis talkin tae somebody an she wis saying ken the Scottish people we're down on ourselves ken, the attitude is make a joke, but there's always an underlyin thing we're no worthy, well we're never gonnae be worthy if we dinnae stand up! An ye see Norway and Switzerland an aa these wee countries and they're no much bigger than us. Ah think likes e aa the poor people, the people that are unemployed, it's a wee bit e a sick attitude among a lot e people in Scotland Ah think, an Ah think that until we're on our own they're no gonnae step up to the mark, and they're no gonna be made tae look at theirsels, and we have tae help oorsels noo, we cannae rely on, an Ah'm talking aboot the hail e Scotland … an if we are independent there will be mair asked e people, and that's what Scotland needs, instead e this downin oursels, so maybe we'll have a better identity Ah suppose, an aa oor resources that we've got.

Me: Some Catholics I interview do not have this view of Scotland being able to be financially independent.

Ronnie: Well, let's face it, Cardenden's minds are completely closed. I remember when years ago one e the nurses doon there at the health centre said to me, 'You will never grow til ye move oot e Cardenden.' Cause it's like, there's a big fence roond Cardenden, an Ah says ye ken yer right. Ah went away tae live in Dunfermline an got married and went aa oer the world on pilgrimages and when Ah came back to live in Cardenden years later Ah couldnae identify wi the people. Ah came back and am really strugglin in the parish because Ah think the people in the parish are closed-minded. A lot e folk are terrified e change, but Ah still have this urge tae gane forward, and Ah then thought aboot the apostles and what were they faced wi. Fir they went intae villages, they hid tae walk through it and the wanes that followed them wanted tae be changed and taught. An it's the same wi this Scotland thing. There'll be a lot e people no wanting tae change, so we hiv tae keep walkin forward. An Ah mean maist folk roond here the furthest their imagination gets is a week in Benidorm. Let's face it.

Similarly, when talking again with Margaret, who attended the local Yes Cardenden meeting in June 2014, I noted an enthusiasm for independence that wasn't there in the first interview in March 2013, which had included the following exchange:

Margaret: I'm nationalistic but don't agree with the party [the Scottish National Party (SNP)].
Me: So you're in favour of independence?
Margaret: Hmmm, not sure. I'm in favour of independence but I don't think we have any means of being able to do it. ... Westminster provides us with nothing, they don't give us any opportunity, and I can't see anything that can possibly come from them that'll help us either. I think people are gonnae choose because they cannot provide anything for Scotland, they have ignored Scotland but that's not the reason to choose independence. To choose independence I think you need to have a much better, stronger political party than we have.
Me: So you are not in favour of independence?
Margaret: Ah don't know whether to vote for independence or not.

Again, I found it interesting that, when chatting with Margaret some sixteen months later in June 2014, she was not only clearly voting 'Yes' but was making a point of trying to persuade friends and family members and was adamant to me that she had always been 'Yes,' but did recognize that she had been unsure about the SNP's ability to deliver independence. Margaret was not clear that sixteen months earlier she had been very unsure about how to vote, and in explaining this it seems clear that, once again, if there is change there is also continuity, as when I first interviewed Margaret it was clear that her political 'unionism' or faith in Westminster rule was already near breaking point.

Finally, when talking with Nora about her movement from 'No' to 'Yes', her simple reply was: 'Well, Ah'm thinkin. We're aa thinkin about it.' In trying to explain the shift, Nora also mentioned friends and younger family members who were pro-independent as being influential and, again, from the original interview with Nora, it seems clear her previous de facto 'unionism' was weak as her historical consciousness meant she knew about Mary Queen of Scots and the historical legacy of British colonies seceding from the United Kingdom, so that for Nora, Scotland was the only colony of Britain/England that had yet to become independent. Already, then, it was clear that a pro-independence view was always a real possibility, and we can see how for Nora her 'new' position does not involve any great semantic sea change from her point of view.

That four of my elderly female informants shifted to being in favour of independence was interesting in light of the consistent findings of opinion polls that the elderly and older women in particular are the social groups least favourable to independence (Survation 2014, Table 13). In explaining this change, it seems that the experience of undergoing the 'referendum process' itself and the inevitable media attention it generated and the many thousands of conversations and social interactions concerning the question of independence had been pivotal in engaging people and clarifying their thinking and coming to a view. Certainly, given the shift among my Catholic informants, it is clear that their views are decentred realities, and over time and through social interaction some informants have changed their view and, perhaps surprisingly, the final view arrived at was not the view they started with.

Deus absconditus: A Godless history?

While considerations of space allow only short excerpts from some of the interviews, a clear twofold conclusion I took from interviewing was that, in terms of religion or theology, my informants do not see their God at work in their parish or national lives, while in terms of politics and the present historical moment, informants upon the basis of my first interviews in 2013 could be characterized by a certain alienation from the 'cut and thrust' of the times they were living through, as they seemed estranged from the constitutional ferment which they were 'objectively' living through (with exceptions such as Michael and Sonia). It seems clear that while the normal democratic process means my informants are familiar with having to decide between the different social policies of political parties, they are much less familiar with having to address the question as to whether 'society' should be located within a Scottish nation state or the multinational British state, and nonplussed by having to address the question whether 'the nation' or the 'national question' has any religious or spiritual significance for their lives as Christians.

In terms of integrating their Catholic and class identities, for example, informants were alive to the task of reconciling or aligning their views on society and politics with their faith, and saw the politicization of class (via left-wing voting) as very much aligned with their Catholicism. However, even the Catholics in favour of independence both in 2013 and in 2014 did not give me any indication that effecting the alignment of the nation or its constitutional form with their faith was an exigence of their 'being Christian,' so that their politicization of the nation or national identity was not the result of feeling pressure to do so from their Catholicism. What did emerge, quite clearly, is that most informants have a weak theological consciousness and a weak political and historical consciousness, and these weaknesses are in alignment with each other, with the result that in 2013 the constitutional crisis was not being lived through in what could be described as a profound way where informants' deepest identities were being brought to bear upon the great question of the day. It seems clear, then, that there is no specifically Christian motivation to be concerned with the nation or engage with the Independence Referendum, as if the question of the relation between transcendence and the present historic moment has little existential purchase upon them.

It seems clear that a consequence of Scotland having been a stateless nation for so long has been the emergence of a *stateless Christianity*, or a non-national form of Christianity, as the majority of my elderly informants have a de-historicized God and have 'invented' a Christianity that is de-historicized, de-nationalized, depoliticized and privatized as they have no narrative of God at work in their country or its history or its present and are content with a vague nod in the direction of God being at work in hearts and minds, as when Margaret advised, 'It's just a personal, internal thing' when commenting on her less-than-convincing belief that God is operative in history. It also seems clear that my informants have no specifically Catholic or Protestant historical or national consciousness that is any different from that of Scots of no faith, as the Catholics I interviewed certainly did not represent themselves to me as caught up in the work of evangelization that has made them more consci- entious or politicized them as a result of having brought them into contact and conflict with social and economic and cultural realities.

When interviewing retired construction worker Jim (born 1940) and asking whether the referendum had any spiritual or religious significance, his answer was: 'Well it's never been mentioned,' and asking if it made sense to say he was a Scottish Christian as opposed to just being a Christian, his answer was: 'Well in these times yer jist a Catholic. Ah don't think it makes any difference now if yer a German or a Scottish or an Irish Catholic.'

Rather than any politicization of religion or a religious-based politicization of the 'social structure' or 'the nation,' it seems clear that the supernatural has been privatized and is hidden from informants' view. When asking informants whether it made sense to describe themselves as a Scottish Catholic in order to uncover whether informants accord their nation any theonomic or soteriological value, whether God uses nations to mediate or work out the 'salvation of souls' of members of nation states, for example, the answer I received was a clear 'no.' Furthermore, if language and consciousness were all of reality, the data from these working-class Catholics would make us conclude they do not come to the love of Christ or the supernatural via their 'secondary natures' (Bauman 1976) or their ownmost *dasein* i.e. their contextualized being-in-the-world.

To take the example of Andy, it seems the fideism that he and many of his generation have imbibed from their pre-Vatican II supernaturalistic Catholicism dictates his seeing the political form of Catholicism as a universal one-world government insofar as during the interview he concedes no reality to the *Scottish* Catholic Church, and thereby avoids the exigencies of 'particularity' such as class, nation and history, which do not appear in his language. Insofar as his universalism dissolves all such problematics the nationality issue cannot arise, and so the task of aligning his Catholic identity and his national identity cannot arise, while the political issue and the class and the historical issue also cannot arise insofar as all such 'secondary natures' are submerged in a blanket universalism. The end result is that Andy's Catholicism does not exert pressure upon him to constitute a series of tensions and tasks of imagining the relation between transcendence, history, politics and social class as integral to him working out his salvation as a Christian, and the question of the soteriological value of the nation and the pressing issue of identifying where God is operative in history similarly cannot arise – in fact is flatly denied by Andy! – as it is liquidated or dissolved by his universalism. Thanks to his universalism, Andy has a very weak historical or national consciousness, so there is no sense in which Catholicism is the cradle of the Scottish nation. Whereas the pro-independence Cathy can tell me: 'Ah love ma country,' for Jim and Margaret who advised, 'Ah don't identify myself as a Scottish Catholic,' their Catholicism is not the cradle of the nation.

If a research question was whether the ongoing constitutional crisis in Scotland was a stimulus to avoid a form of Christianity characterized by a supernaturalism/fideism that turns away from 'the world,' another question was whether the social class of informants entered into how they imagined their 'being Christian;' whether class mediates or even constitutes informants' experience or understanding of their salvation in Christ. For example, then, I wished to explore whether working class Christians would be especially aware that their faith is not majestically beyond or transcendent to social conditions but is criticized, tested and given mundane ballast by social conditions or the class system that forms part of their experience, so that to keep 'being Catholic' or 'being Protestant' meaningful and relevant to their living-in-society they would feel obliged to reconcile or align these two forces or realities in their lives.

If the question of the theonomic value of 'the nation' is a blood relative of the question of whether informants afford any theological value to membership of a particular social class and whether informants think God uses membership of social classes to mediate his gift of salvation to people who live their lives immersed in social classes, *at the level of discourse* it is clear that my informants accorded no theonomic significance to 'secondary natures' such as class and nation. For these Christians, *secondary natures* can either be engaged with or left alone but are not integral to the task of becoming Christian. At the level of awareness and discourse, then, it seems 'being Scottish' and 'being working class' are irrelevant to or unaligned with 'being Christian,' so that rather than coming to Christ via their ownmost *dasein,* they perhaps come to Christ or are saved despite their *dasein*, with the latter being free to be 'disorganized' or misaligned with their Christian faith, so that this provincial Catholic consciousness remains immersed in a mixture of educational disadvantage and clerical supernaturalism that is estranged from the task of aligning faith with territory, history, class and nation.

Despite these findings from my interviews, however, at the level of political practice there is evidence that an alignment of class, Christianity and the constitutional option of independence is occurring. The 2011 Scottish Election study, for example, found that 44 per cent of Church of Scotland members voted SNP (with 26 per cent of members voting Labour) and this represents something of a revolution in Protestant voting if we look back to the 1950s (Carman et al. 2011). Similarly, since the establishment of the Holyrood parliament in 1999, Catholics have moved from being as likely as any other social group to vote SNP to positively preferring to vote SNP. The 2007 Scottish Election Study, for example, found that 30 per cent of Catholics voted for the SNP, while the 2011 Scottish Election Study found that 43 per cent of Catholics voted for the SNP, so that in 2011 the SNP became the preferred party among Scottish Catholics for the first time ever. *In terms of practice and behaviour*, then, there is empirical evidence that an alignment is occurring among Catholics and Protestants among younger generations but without any consciousness that this alignment is taking place among an older generation, as none of the Catholics or Protestants I interviewed gave any indication of being part of an historic shift to the SNP.[4]

Conclusion

While my informants have a clear sense of having a 'date with destiny' in the 2014 referendum it seems clear that it is a purely natural or social affair that does not emerge from their Christianity, and this suggests it is sociological forces (and not membership of the historic Scottish churches) that operationalizes an otherwise inert (certainly depoliticized) national identity; that it is social, historical and political events that have come into play since the 1970s that are the agents behind the rise of Scottish nationalism among all Scots – Christians or otherwise – and that membership of churches has been more or less marginal to the rise of Scottish nationalism.

Interestingly, as I chatted to one of the local Yes Cardenden activists who had booked the hall, she told me how she had extended an invitation to the members of the local congregation and then made a point of telling me how the woman she had spoken to had 'firmly' advised that no one from their Church would attend such an event, meaning that as a matter of principle they would not attend a meeting to listen to Tommy Sheridan.

The two Catholic informants originally in favour of independence in 2013 were still intending to vote 'Yes' a year later, while the two Catholic men (Andy and Jim) who were against independence remained so when I interviewed them again in August 2014. Interestingly, with the help of a member of the Yes Cardenden group who is also a long-term member of the local Church of Scotland congregation, I learnt that none of my Church of Scotland informants had changed their views, so that there was no movement towards 'Yes' among my elderly Church of Scotland informants.

On the day of the referendum itself a Yes Cardenden activist (Dave Clark) manning the polling station at Denend School quickly sensed that old people were 'doing their bit' to stop Scottish independence and joked: 'Ah'm not ageist but Ah wish all these old age pensioner bastards had died in their sleep last night!' Dave's judgement regarding a generational split was borne out by a poll of 2,047 voters conducted on 18 and 19 September which found that, in every age cohort under fifty-five years old, most respondents had voted Yes, while among voters aged fifty-five to sixty-four and sixty-five+ only 43 per cent and 27 per cent, respectively, had voted for independence. See www.LordAshcroftPolls.com. On the existence of what I term *the 1945 generation* and an ethnographic description of its long-standing antipathy towards the return of Scottish sovereignty see Gilfillan (2014).

11

National piety: Religious equality, freedom of religion and national identity in Finnish political discourse

Titus Hjelm

In 2005, two Green[1] MPs, Rosa Meriläinen and Irina Krohn, submitted a Members' initiative to enact a law in the Finnish parliament, with an aim to 'strengthen the freedom of religion and religious equality of citizens' (LA 157/2005 vp).[2] The initiative proposed changes to the constitution, criminal law, two education acts and several other laws, the purpose of which was to balance the privileged position that the Evangelical Lutheran Church of Finland enjoys. Although the initiative never made it to voting stage because of the election of a new parliament in 2007 (initiatives do not carry over to the next parliament in the Finnish system), the preliminary debate in the plenary session provides a case for examining whether 'God is back' on the micro-, everyday, level of parliamentary practice.

The purpose of the chapter is threefold: First, empirically, I will analyse the interconnectedness of discourses of freedom of religion, religious equality and national identity and the ideological consequences of this interconnection in a national context where a church – or more accurately, two churches[3] – receive preferential treatment (e.g. the Nordic countries, Greece, Germany, Ireland etc.; see Fox 2008: 114). Secondly, methodologically, I wish to contribute to the broader sociology of religious pluralism, where arguments about 'political secularization' tend to be based on policies and policy outcomes rather than the policymaking process itself (e.g. Monsma and Soper 2009; Michel and Pace 2011; Barbalet, Possamai and Turner 2011; Anderson 2009; Gustafsson 2003). The consequence of these standard approaches is that we do not know what the actual arguments and rhetoric for and against these policy initiatives are and, most importantly, whether questions of church and religion are discussed as 'religious' matters in the first place. From a discursive perspective, the political discourse can be secular even if the outcome of the political debate is not – and vice versa. The kind of micro-level discursive approach to religion and politics that I'm advocating here is indispensable if we understand contemporary parliamentary politics as 'government by speaking' or 'government by discussion' (Palonen 2008: 82; e.g. van Dijk 1997). Finally, this chapter represents a contribution to *critical* sociology of religion that pays serious attention to social inequality, including religious inequality, and which, as I have argued elsewhere (Hjelm 2013), is currently under-represented in the sub-discipline.

My primary data source for a critical discourse analysis (CDA) of the discourses of the parliamentary debate is a transcript of the preliminary discussion in the Finnish parliament on 15 February 2006.[4] The discussion includes twenty speeches of various lengths by eight MPs. In addition, I will refer to the original initiative (*lakialoite*) text, but mainly for the purposes of cross-referencing MP Krohn's responses in the discussion, where she reiterates the main points of the initiative. The aim of a CDA approach is, in a very condensed form, to pay attention to the 'naturalisation of inequality and neutralisation of dissent' (Richardson 2007: 6) through the use of discourse.[5]

Four different discourses – ways of speaking – emerge from the debate: inequality of religions; the 'completeness' of the freedom of religion in Finland; the justified hegemony of the 'folk' church; the church as a value base in a pluralizing world.[6] I argue that the discursive struggle between the different positions is a struggle between 'minimalist' and 'maximalist' definitions of freedom of religion (cf. Lincoln 2003: 5). I also argue that the issue of religious equality in Finland is a case of 'national piety': an issue that (a) when discussed, problematically conflates discourses of religious equality, freedom of religion and national identity, and (b) is rather *not discussed at all* in the political arena, mostly because, I argue, of a 'folk church' ideology. These factors effectively reproduce the status quo and function ideologically by doing so.

The social and political context of the LA 157/2005 vp initiative

Like the other Nordic countries (Denmark, Iceland, Norway and Sweden), Finland has a strong national Lutheran church. Although independent Finland became officially religiously neutral with the implementation of the Freedom of Religion Act of 1922, the Evangelical Lutheran Church of Finland retained a special legal status, which in international comparison warrants the title 'state church' (Chaves and Cann 1992; Christensen 1995; Heikkilä et al. 2005: 527; Robbers 2005; Fox 2008: 115) – despite the widespread apologetic claim that 'the state church is changing into a folk church', as if the latter somehow negates the former (Sihvo 1991: 21; Seppo 1998, 2003). In addition to its legal status, the church is, for example, financed by a 'church tax' collected by the state from the members of the church, plus a share of the corporation tax (*yhteisövero*).[7] Despite a recent update of the Freedom of Religion Act (in 2003), the status of the Lutheran Church remained unchanged (Hjelm 2012). In fact, because the Lutheran Church's status is defined separately, the LA 157/2005 vp initiative suggested changes to a number of laws, including the constitution, but not the Freedom of Religion Act itself. The proposal was not all about the Lutheran Church, although that ended up being the gist of the preliminary debate analysed here. The proposed changes to the Education Acts, which suggested either common religious studies to all students (after the Swedish model) or moving the content of religion classes to other existing curricula (e.g. history, philosophy), would have affected all religious communities that have an approved curriculum for teaching their own religion in state schools. Similarly, the proposal to change all marriages into civil marriages would have affected all those religious communities that have the right to marry couples (although not their right to bless marriage after civil registration). Overall, although minor amendments have been made to laws pertaining to church–state relations throughout the years, the LA 157/2005 vp initiative represents the most comprehensive challenge to the state church system since the drafting of the constitution and the original Freedom of Religion Act in the immediate years after Finland's independence in 1917. It can be easily characterized as a radical initiative in the Finnish context.[8] As such, one could have thought that the initiative would have been widely discussed in the media and hotly debated in parliament, ending in a dramatic vote.

None of this happened. Instead, as Rosa Meriläinen wrote in a personal communication to me, 'the initiative went to initiative heaven, that is, nothing happened to it' (email to author, 14 December 2009). In order to understand the nigh-on non-existent impact that the initiative eventually had, I need to briefly discuss the legislative process in Finland.

Legislative proposals in Finland are presented to parliament in the form of Government bills or Members' initiatives.[9] Any individual member of parliament can propose an initiative proposing the enactment of a law. As these initiatives may be proposed at any time, they are a highly popular form of activity for parliamentarians as they allow them to demonstrate to the electorate their areas of interest and that they are working to advance various causes. Each year, between 150 and 200 initiatives are submitted. However, only a very small proportion of these are actually accepted, and even fewer become law. The majority are rejected or not dealt with at all beyond the preliminary debate.

Initiatives for the enactment of a law are first presented to parliament in a preliminary debate in a plenary session. During the plenary debate, no decisions are taken on the substance of the proposal; it is largely a technical procedure to determine as to which one of the parliament's subject-specific special committees the initiative should be referred to. Only after the relevant special committee has produced a report on the initiative can it go forward to be handled in plenary session. Most initiatives fail to make it further than this initial committee stage, and many are 'left on the table' at the committees, which effectively voids them if the process is not finished by the tenure of the current parliament, as initiatives don't carry on to the next – as was eventually the case with LA 157/2005 vp.

The plenary session discourse is, however, interesting regardless of the *outcome* of this case. Pekonen argues that 'public talk in plenary sessions is not primarily addressed to other parliamentarians ... the main audience is the general public, the media and the voters' (Pekonen 2008: 213). Although from some MPs' point of view the hard work of parliament is conducted in the 'professional' parliamentary committees (Pekonen 2008: 214; cf. Wodak 2008: 16), the plenary is a forum for articulating broader politics in addition to individual policies. These articulations – discourses – are, in turn, a reflection of broader social positions.

Inequality of religions and the role of the state

The 'justifications' section of the LA 157/2005 vp initiative outlines its rationale by describing what the (signatories think the) current state of affairs in Finland is:

> Freedom of religion includes three principles: the right to practice religion, the right to not participate in the practice of religion, and that the public

authorities have to treat all religions and worldviews equally. Except for the last, these principles are fulfilled in Finland reasonably well.[10]

The gist of the initiative is, then, to show – in categorical language typical of legislation – how religions are currently unequal in Finland because of the privileged status of the Lutheran and Orthodox Churches. Hence, the aim of the initiative is to '*strengthen* freedom of religion and the religious equality of citizens' (emphasis added).

The preliminary debate on 15 February 2006 opens with a lengthy response to the initiative, which I will discuss in the next sections. Yet MP Krohn, who ended up being the only one espousing this discourse (the other signatory, MP Meriläinen, was absent from the plenary) then spends her first response (and most of the two others) in further explaining the rationale of the initiative. The gist of it is, Krohn says

> Our initiative really comes from the principle that freedom of religion includes three elements: the right to practice one's religion, the right to not practice one, and a third element, that the public authorities treat all religions equally. In Finland, these first two elements have been applied really well and this last element, that is, the attitude or position of the public authorities towards religions is not equal. That is the spirit, if you will, of this initiative. The spirit is not against religions, including Christianity, but instead the aim is to draw attention to the fact that at the moment the state takes a stand on which god and which conception of god is right, if you will, and I think this may have hazardous consequences.

Here, Krohn repeats the gist of the initiative, but – compared to the initiative itself – in a defensive language, which is explained by the fact that this is a response to a long critique of the initiative discussed in the next section. Krohn uses 'hedging' (Fairclough 1992: 142) throughout the reply: the two first elements of freedom of religion are said to apply 'really well' (as opposed to 'reasonably well' in the initiative) and the spirit of the initiative is said not to be against religions.

In addition to the construction of the religious situation in Finland as unequal, there are two further points that set Krohn's discourse apart from that of all the other MPs, and which become the focus of the subsequent discussion. Her narrative emphasizes that equality is best achieved by following *international* examples and making religion a *private* matter. The 'justifications' section of the initiative text starts with the words: 'In the European tradition religion is a private matter that the state should respect and protect'. This invokes an international precedent for the case, but also assumes – rather problematically – (a) that there is a common 'European tradition' of religion and (b) that in this tradition religion is a private matter. In the discussion itself, she offers many examples of international precedents and privatization: the proposed changes to the Education Acts are already implemented 'in a couple of other Nordic countries'; 'in America, the American state, or the United States, does not have religion, but it believes in god'; and, perhaps most importantly, 'in France already a hundred years ago, because there were such bitter quarrels between Protestants and Catholics, they took the situation (*tilanne*)[11] [sic] that the public authorities are neutral in their relation to religions, and are secular'. Also, mid-February 2006 saw the Danish Muhammad cartoon crisis (which was invoked by several MPs) spreading to Finland when *Suomen Sisu*, a far-right organization, published the controversial cartoons on its website. Interestingly, considering that religious pluralization in Finland and Europe in general is mostly a matter of accommodating growing Muslim populations, Krohn raises the 'Europeanness' of this initiative (which, to her credit, is in line with the opening words of the initiative):

> It has been also highlighted in the publicity on this initiative that we, together with others, as an European constitutional state, have issued a challenge to Islamic states, in some of which, one can say, a very theocratic model of governance exists, in which the church and the state are very close to each other.

In sum, strengthening freedom of religion through religious equality is a matter of privatizing religion in the LA 157/2005 vp. The representation of the unequal situation is mostly devoid of actors – naturalizing the representation as something given – but Krohn, more than any other MP, emphasizes that it is 'our' (the MPs') responsibility to make this change. The categorical language of the initiative itself is balanced by Krohn's hedging in the actual debate, where she says that 'it *might* be better for all of us that the position of religion is a matter of a person's private life', or 'it *may* be that this initiative is not the best possible' (emphases added). On a less textual level, Krohn uses footing to boost her rhetoric in two opposite ways. On the one hand, as noted above, this is not a personal issue for her, not an anti-religious issue, but a matter of updating Finland's legislation to conform with international standards. On the other hand, she evokes personal language that could be taken directly from a 'strict separationist' argument in the American discourse on church–state relations (e.g. Davis 2011). Krohn talks about how her grandfather left the church 'because in his opinion spiritual life belongs to the private sphere and the state should not be used as a *crutch* in such an important thing as relationship with god' (emphasis added). She repeats that '[I] would wish that we could trust that Christianity and this religion truly carries itself without us public authorities making such, as I said, crutches'.

That argument, however, did not carry the day in the parliament that February 2006.

'Complete' freedom of religion

The opening response to LA 157/2005 vp was made by the Christian Democrat leader, Päivi Räsänen, an outspoken evangelical Christian known for her active participation in all matters related to religion in the Parliament. Her response is by far the longest and, based on the style and comparison with the other turns in the debate, the only one prepared in advance. She tackles all the proposed amendments and presents all of the main discourses discussed here in her first response, but in this section I will concentrate on the argued 'completeness' of the freedom of religion in Finland. This discourse is a 'factual' counter discourse to the 'inequality of religions' discourse of the initiative, that is, it tries to show that the premises of the initiative are false when it comes to freedom of religion in Finland. I quote the beginning of Räsänen's turn at length:

> Dear Mister Speaker! MPs Meriläinen and Krohn are proposing a long list of measures in this initiative, which could in different ways weaken the influence of the Church, churches, and Christian cultural heritage in Finnish society. … The objective of this initiative is right as such, however. That is, … to strengthen the freedom of religion and the citizens' religious equality, but I think it is done in quite the wrong way in this initiative. … Pekka Hallberg, president of the supreme administrative court, has stated about the connection between state and church that since its birth, our republican Constitution included a fundamental change to the relations between church and state. Our Constitution was based on the principle of the freedom of religion and did not acknowledge the significance of the Lutheran faith as state ideology anymore. … Elsewhere, Martin Scheinin has stated in the book *Perusoikeudet* ('Basic Rights') that our implementation of the legal status of the Lutheran and Orthodox churches is not against the Freedom of Religion Act.

In Räsänen's contextualization, the point of the initiative is to '*weaken* the influence of the Church, churches, and Christian cultural heritage' (emphasis added) – quite different from the preamble to the initiative, which claims (see above) to '*strengthen* freedom of religion and the religious equality of citizens' (emphasis added). Although Räsänen positions herself as a supporter of freedom of religion and religious equality in the next two sentences, the contextualization is a negative one (anti-church and anti-Christian) because of the way the initiative purports to drive freedom of religion and religious equality by privatizing religion. She goes on (in the first and subsequent responses) to expand on the issue of 'Christian cultural heritage' (see below), but first lays down the constitutional and legal 'facts'.

By referring to two legal experts, Räsänen distances herself from the issue ('footing', see Goffman 1981; Potter 1996: 122) and represents the constitutional and legal situation with the voice of outside authority. The message is that, from this perspective, a 'complete' freedom of religion already exists: the Lutheran Church is not privileged, because it is not a state church (any more) and because 'our implementation of the legal status of the Lutheran and Orthodox churches is not against the Freedom of Religion Act'.

In terms of freedom of religion, the two stances can be summarized as 'maximalist' and 'minimalist': the signatories of the initiative clearly explicate that although the freedom to practice religion and the freedom not to practice religion are mostly well established in Finland, the freedom of religion can't be complete as long as some religious communities are privileged in law and in the constitution. From the minimalist – Räsänen was the only one of the MPs to employ this type of 'factual' discourse – point of view, as long as the state does not require adherence to a particular religion, freedom of religion is complete. The justification for the 'complete' freedom position in the speeches of the MPs opposing the initiative is provided by the discourse of the 'folk' church, which practically takes over the discussion after Räsänen's first response.

'Folk' church, democracy and Christian heritage

If the inequality discourse and the opposite 'complete' freedom of religion discourse are mostly about constructing the 'facts' of the Finnish situation (the 'ideational' function of discourse; Fairclough 1992: 64), the discourses on the 'folk' church and values – although intertwined with the ideational function of discourse – can be characterized as fulfilling both the 'identity' and 'relational' functions (Fairclough 1992: 64). That is, they are less about defining what the legislative situation is like than defining what Finnish society is like and what it should be like. Päivi Räsänen sums up the idea in her long opening response: 'The state is not denominational in itself, even though the Lutheran Church and also the Orthodox Church have the status of folk church'. The term 'folk church' gained widespread credence in academic and public discourse especially after the passing of the 1922 Freedom of Religion Act, which was considered to have severed the church–state connection for good (e.g. Juva

1960). As such, its use in the LA 157/2005 vp debate continues an established tradition. The 'folk' status of the church is constructed in three distinct ways: symbolically, through an appeal to democracy and by equating 'Finnish values' with the values of the church. With regard to the first, I quote Räsänen again:

Quickly going through this list, it seems like just about the only things that are forgotten is a proposal to abandon the flag with the blue cross, and changing religious holidays into working days. In my opinion, the best part of this bill is its short list of signatories.

There are at least two things going on here. First, Räsänen draws a connection between the status of the church and the national symbol, the Finnish flag. Second, she uses populist rhetoric that implies people would need to work more days in a year if the initiative was to pass – a point significant even for people indifferent to the status of the church. The reason she is able to presuppose that the church and flag go hand in hand for many, if not all, MPs is the idea of 'home, religion and fatherland' (*koti, uskonto ja isänmaa*) which, according to Virkkunen 'were the central Finnish values between the world wars' (Virkkunen 1981: 207). The saying was popularized by the Finnish arch-hero Marshal Mannerheim's widely publicized speech on his assumption of the command of the Finnish forces when hostilities with the Soviet Union broke out in late 1939, where he said that 'we fight for home, religion and fatherland' (Virkkunen 1981: 207). This discourse, although diminished after the Second World War, is deeply ingrained in Finnish public discourse, and Räsänen is able to intertextually (Fairclough 1992: 101–36) exploit it in her defence of the church.

In addition to symbolic rhetoric, the idea of a 'folk' church is constructed by Räsänen and others also by what could be called the 'democratic' argument. In her opening response, Räsänen says that 'in legislative work, it is justified to take into consideration the prevailing religious circumstances (*olot*). It is justified for a religious community's legal status to reflect the community's real status in society, and *this is how democracy works*' (emphasis added). She goes on to point out that '84 per cent of Finns belong to the church and of them 73 per cent have never considered leaving the church. The juridical status of the Lutheran church reflects the religious situation in the country and its religious-cultural history'. Finally, she repeats the argument in her closing statement: 'Based simply on the *principles of democracy*, it is quite right that the influence of Christian values, Christian cultural heritage is visible' (emphasis added).

Although the 'folk' church discourse is only one and not necessarily the most significant in Räsänen's repertoire, it is the one that sets the tone for the much of the rest of the discussion. So we have, for example, Lauri Oinonen, a Centre Party MP and Lutheran minister from rural Multia,[12] arguing that

Therefore, the laws are in harmony with the fact that citizens, who are both citizens of the state, inhabitants of municipalities and mostly members of the Evangelical Lutheran Church, can live with a legislation which is in harmony with itself.

Centre Party colleague Simo Rundgren, also a Lutheran minister, from Kolari in Lapland, puts the same thing bluntly when defending religious education in state-funded schools: 'About 85 per cent of Finns belong to the Lutheran church. ... This is just the way our will is'.

The third way in which the status of the church as a 'folk' church is justified equates 'Finnish values' with a Christian heritage in general and the Lutheran Church (to a lesser degree with the Orthodox Church) in particular. Esa Lahtela, a Social Democrat from rural Kitee, who closes his first response by saying that the initiative should be thrown into the dustbin, argues

First of all, the whole Finnish society is in any case built on this Christian value base. From that one could of course immediately say that when in Rome, do as the Romans do (*maassa maan tavalla*), which means that certain foundations have existed. Our legislation is built on a particular value base and it draws its strength from these values, which come from Biblical doctrines, Christian doctrine.

In an age of global immigration, the idea of 'when in Rome ...' is controversial, to say the least. But, perhaps more interestingly, for Lahtela, legislation 'is built' on Christian values, but in this case no one is doing the building. The human actions, the debates and struggles that created the legislation in the first place, disappear, and the putative Christian value base is naturalized as an essential characteristic of Finnish society, which, in turn, supports the 'folk' church discourse. This is in stark contrast to, for example, the seemingly endless debates in the United States about the 'original intent' of the Founding Fathers regarding the second amendment (e.g. Davis 2000; McGraw 2003).

Social Democrat MP Kalevi Olin, from Jyväskylä in central Finland, echoes the sentiment:

That equality is realized is surely a modern aspiration, but, dear mister Speaker, according to research the success of Finnish society, for example in working life, is based on exactly the Protestant ethic, especially in agricultural society, but also in industrial, on work ethic and in this case it is worth asking whether there is reason to abandon this kind of Lutheran viewpoint.

For Olin, the matter is not simply taking the essentially Christian culture at face value. Instead, this is so 'according to research' (or 'studies'). The issue is, therefore, not a matter of personal preference but something that is scientifically backed.

Perhaps the most significant blow to the initiative comes from Krohn's Green colleague Erkki Pulliainen, from the northern city of Oulu, who again repeats the fundamental role that Christian heritage has for the Finns:

> Values belong to Finnish society as a very important element. Those particular values, specifically Christian values, whether they are realized (*toteutuivatpa ne*) in the Evangelical-Lutheran church or the Orthodox church, are very important things. They are downright ultimate things.

Pulliainen also does what the others do less explicitly when arguing about the Christian value heritage, that is, he equates the value base with the two 'folk' churches (where the values are *realized*). By doing so, his and the others' responses switch the focus of discussion from a question of religious equality to a question of national identity.

Pluralism and the Church as a value base

Issues of national identity are also at stake in the fourth type of discourse that I have named the 'pluralism' discourse. This discourse is also concerned with values, but whereas the naturalization of the 'folk church' as the cultural carrier of putatively essential Finnish values is a backward-looking discourse, the pluralism discourse looks forward in a situation of increasing religious diversity.

MP Räsänen again hints at this discourse by stating in her opening speech that 'it has to be admitted that the way in which religions and worldviews really have an important cultural significance is brought up with distinction in this initiative'. Yet, whereas the initiative argued that 'strengthening religious equality increases trust in the public authorities, improves social harmony, helps the adjustment of immigrants into our country and increases the attraction of Finland in the eyes of foreign professionals' (LA 157/2005 vp), Räsänen sees things differently. Just the previous day, the public prosecutor in Finland had decided to open up an investigation into *Suomen Sisu* after the organization published the controversial Danish Mohammed cartoons on its website. Now Räsänen asks, 'in the eyes of what kind of foreign professionals would the attraction of Finland be increased' if the initiative's proposal to get rid of blasphemy laws would be accepted.

The pan-Nordic (or rather, pan-European) crisis over the cartoons works as a springboard for elaborations that go beyond the legislation at issue. Again, beyond Räsänen's initial remark above, the discourse does not even directly address the initiative's legislative points but, rather, is an answer to an assumed attack against the 'folk' church. This time, however, the point is not so much about retaining essential cultural values, but arguing that Finns need Christian values – which are 'realized' in the church – in order to cope with religious diversity. So, for example, Centre Party MP Rundgren says that

> First I would now say here that the more the world is globalised, internationalised, and we meet with a variety of cultures, the bigger challenge it is for us to take care of this worldview and religious education and upbringing in our own country. The knowledge of our own roots, our own tradition, the knowledge of our own religion is in my opinion the best way toward building peace, toward creating a climate of tolerance and agreement in the whole world.

The same theme had already been taken up by another Centre Party MP Oinonen:

> I think that, contrary to what is presented in the bill, the Christian vision of life in Finland should be strengthened. For example, it has been said by Muslims that if Finns were more Christian and better Christians, then it would be better for Muslims to live in this country. I hope that they live well also now, and so I believe they also feel, but they feel that if the people of this country were more Christian, then that would be good for everyone else as well.

Notably, no individual Muslim or a Muslim organization comes forth in Oinonen's passive formulation. The broader point that the more the Finns are anchored in Christian values, the better they are equipped to deal with religious diversity and to be tolerant is repeated by others, including Krohn's Green League colleague Erkki Pulliainen. The presupposition, which is constructed by masking the actor and (in Oinonen's case) by distancing the speaker from the opinion, is that more religion equals more religious tolerance. Because, as the 'folk' church discourse made clear, being Christian in Finland more or less equals being Lutheran, retaining the role of the church is supported both explicitly and implicitly.

National piety: The hegemony of absence

In the above, I have identified four discourses in the preliminary debate on the LA 157/2005 vp initiative. The analysis shows that while the purpose of the bill was, as Krohn also reminds her fellow MPs in her second response, to discuss 'where the place of religion and faith is relation to public authority', the debate soon branches into fundamental issues of national identity. The legislative struggle is fought between the signatories' original inequality discourse and the 'complete' freedom of religion discourse of MP Räsänen, especially. Räsänen's 'minimalist' discourse might as well be called a *liberal* definition, because according to it, freedom of religion is 'complete' when it guarantees religious freedom to the *individual* – an argument that Seppo explicitly makes – regardless of unequal treatment of religious communities (Seppo 2003). This of course leads to long-standing debates about multiculturalism and the rights of individuals versus the rights of communities.

Those debates are not, however, at the heart of the discussion on the LA 157/2005 vp initiative. Instead, the legislative details of the initiative play second fiddle to what is interpreted by most of the discussants as an attack against the church and, by extension, against Finnishness. This, in turn, is seen as a hopeless cause, as witnessed by the condescending remarks towards MP Krohn by the other MPs. Päivi Räsänen says that 'MP Krohn has many wise ideas and also some good political aims, and I even feel a little bit sorry for you for having to defend this initiative by yourself, without any support from the floor'. Indeed, MP Tarja Cronberg, the then leader of the Greens, emphasizes in her response that this was not a party initiative. Finally, the speaker had to remind MP Rundgren that it is against the parliamentary code of conduct to use the singular 'you' (*sinä*) or refer to other MPs using their first names, after Rundgren had referred to Krohn as 'sinä, Irina'. One wonders whether that would have happened had MP Krohn been a man.

The variety and type of discourses, and what plausible political choices are enabled by those discourses, is one aspect of the analysis; but the *absence* of any type of discourse on behalf of the vast majority of Finnish MPs is another. This has two important implications. First, methodologically, the context matters: it is not only what is said that matters, but also what is *not* said. Second, empirically speaking, what emerges from the legislative discourse in this case is what I call – following American essayist Joan Didion – 'national piety' (Didion 2003: 24):

> We have come in this country to tolerate many ... fixed opinions, or national pieties, each with its own baffles of invective and counterinvective, of euphemism and downright misstatement, its own screen that slides into place whenever actual discussion threatens to surface.

Although speaking of public discourse in post-9/11 America, Didion's words ring true for the issue of religious equality in Finnish parliamentary discourse in the early twenty-first century. National piety, as used here, refers to both active and passive support for the status quo. This should be differentiated from 'civil religion', however. In the Finnish context, Bellah's original formulation of a non-denominational civil religion has been interpreted so that the Lutheran Church becomes an inseparable part of Finnish civil religion (Bellah 1967; e.g. Sunback 1984). Whether that assessment is correct or not is a sociological question. 'National piety', by contrast, is the ideological discourse – and silence – that legitimates the privileged status of the Lutheran Church.[13]

The crushing opposition to the initiative and, even more importantly, the silence of the majority of the MPs on the subject indicates that there is an overwhelming consensus about the fact that if legislation on religious equality or freedom of religion threatens the church–state status quo, it is a topic that should be left alone in parliamentary discussion. In other words, the bill was 'clammed up dead' as the Finnish saying goes.

Analytically, there might be good reasons 'to separate the issue of religious freedom from the church–state relationship rather than using it as an indicator' (Minkenberg 2003: 198). Empirically, however, neat boundaries between the two are muddled, as the LA 157/2005 case shows. It is the task of critical sociology of religion to interrogate situations where the analytical separation is muddled in an ideological way – as in the current case where the hegemonic political discourse in Finland represents a state church and a 'folk' church as separate entities and by doing so uses the latter to reproduce the former.

Further, if we only look at the outcomes of parliamentary discourse, that is, the constitution and current law, we miss a point about 'political secularization' that is not obvious from a macro perspective. This is the secularization of the political discourse itself. As I have argued above, the 'folk' church discourse may be used to reproduce an 'active state religion' (Fox 2008: 114–16), but the ways in which this is accomplished are overwhelmingly secular: we find constitutional and legal arguments, appeals to tradition and common values – national identity – but little in terms of explicit religious discourse (cf. Bruce 2011: 171). In the Finnish case, 'national piety' enables the continued privileged position of the Lutheran and Orthodox Churches, but a religious revival in politics it is not.

Acknowledgements

A longer version of this chapter was published in *Religion*, 44(1) (Hjelm 2014a). Used with kind permission of Taylor and Francis.

12

Religion, democracy and the challenge of the Arab Spring

Ian Morrison

According to popular narrative, anti-government protests in Tunisia following the self-immolation and consequent death of fruit seller Mohamed Bouazizi inspired a series of uprisings across the Middle East and North Africa (MENA) in 2011. These uprisings, which have come to be known as the Arab Spring, led to the ousting of rulers in Egypt, Libya, Tunisia and Yemen, civil war in Syria, and unprecedented anti-government protests in several other states. Initially, the Western response to the Arab Spring was a celebration of the fall of autocracy, the rise of democracy and the awakening of the Arab people. However, as the participation of Islamist figures, organizations and parties in these uprisings began to become evident, the Arab Spring was increasingly greeted with apprehension and reservation by Western observers.

The focus of this chapter will be an exposition and critique of early Western reactions to the Arab Spring. As evident in the coverage of the uprisings within the Anglo-American media, the anxiety often provoked by these uprisings and the subsequent attempts at democratization is a result of a perception that 'the democratic face of the revolutions may serve to hide its "true" Islamist nature or ... the masses, unable or unwilling to recognize the distinction between religious and political spheres, will hijack the fledgling democracies by electing Islamist governments' (Morrison 2014: 328). As such, the dilemma that is posed by the plurality of Western reactions is whether democratization, through permitting the election of groups with anti-democratic agendas, will lead to an opening for, or a closure of, democracy. The Arab Spring is an event for which a response is demanded from all of us who wish to be invested in questions of politics, democracy and religion. As such, we need to ask: how do we orient ourselves towards these events? How do we develop a politico-ethical response to the election (or potential election) of Islamist governments? Or, in basic terms, how do we respond to the Arab Spring?

In order to begin to address these questions, this chapter engages in an exposition and critique of responses to the Arab Spring within Anglo-American media commentary during the initial stages of the uprisings. First, I suggest that these reactions do not, in fact, answer the call for a response. Instead, they offer the writers alibis to excuse themselves or make themselves absent from the scene of true engagement with the issues outlined above. Second, I argue that the two sides of what appears as a debate regarding democracy and the Arab Spring both serve to efface democracy. In conclusion, an alternative approach to developing a response to these events, and, in particular, the presence of religious subjects and demands within the post-Arab Spring political sphere is offered.

It is possible to situate the bulk of early reactions to the Arab Spring in Western media and policy circles within two competing camps. Consistent with many contemporary debates concerning the relationship between religion, secularism and democracy, responses to the uprisings in the Middle East and North Africa cannot easily or accurately be distinguished based on their adherence to the traditional ideological categories of Left and Right. Rather, the two camps can be distinguished based on the level of enthusiasm expressed with regard to the uprisings and the related prospects for, and desirability of, democratization in the MENA, with each camp containing figures and sentiments usually associated with both the Right and the Left. The first camp – which I will refer to as the optimistic response – champions the uprisings and exhibits optimism with regard to the prospect (if not the necessity) of democratization in the region. In contrast, voices within the second camp – which I will refer to as the pessimistic response – warn that the Arab Spring will lead to an 'Islamic' or 'Western winter' (Khanfar 2011; Napolitano 2012; Phillips 2012).

The pessimistic response

The pessimistic camp argues that the potential rise of Islamist governments requires an abandonment of democracy (until some unspecified future date when the election of Islamists is no longer possible) in order to protect democracy. The democracy to be protected is either democracy in the West or some eventual form of 'true' democracy in the Arab world. Within the discourse of the pessimistic camp, concerns with the Arab Spring are related to a twofold threat posed by the collapse of authoritarian regimes in the MENA. This purported threat relates first, to revolutionary and post-revolutionary instability and the consequent potential for a descent into anarchy. Exemplary of this position is Bret Stephens's description of post-Mubarak Egypt as 'the early stages of Thomas Hobbes's bellum omnium contra omnes' (Stephens 2011). The image of chaos that he depicts, of an Egyptian war of all against all, is one of 'officials who will not stand up to the Islamist mob. Furious Coptic youth who no longer accept the cautious dictates of their elders. Conscript soldiers not afraid to disobey their orders. A "free" media that traffics in incitement. …' This purported anarchy, resulting from the collapse of authoritarian regimes, was said to have produced a rise in crime, violence and sectarianism.

The greatest concern for many pessimists, however, is not the immediate consequences of instability for the lives of the people of the MENA region but that such a situation may be of advantage to extremist Islamist groups. They suggest that a post-revolutionary security vacuum with no authority capable of restricting the formation and activity of radical jihadist groups will transform the MENA into 'an ungovernable staging ground for terrorism and sabotage' (Stephens 2011). Indeed, since the toppling of authoritarian regimes in Egypt, Tunisia and Libya, such groups have engaged in a number of attacks on military, political and secular institutions and figures. Moreover, they have come to play a prominent role in the Syrian civil war. The pessimists' fear is that the security vacuum created by the uprisings will allow these groups to become not only a threat to the states in which they are based but to Israel and the West. They argue that post-revolutionary disorder will provide violent Islamist groups the opportunity to train, spread their values in an uninhibited manner and launch attacks within the MENA region and on Western targets. As such, pessimists view the instability resulting from the events of the Arab Spring as a threat to the potential future establishment of democracy in the MENA region, as well as to Western democracies.

The second threat to democracy identified is also related to Islamism. However, unlike the first set of concerns, it does not focus on the risks posed by post-revolutionary disorder but on those posed by the establishment of regimes of electoral democracy. Pessimists often invoke the case of the 1979 revolution in Iran to argue that the initially democratic revolutions of the Arab Spring will be hijacked by anti-democratic Islamists. Just as Khomeini and his supporters used the democratic mechanism of a referendum to legitimate the establishment of the theocratic Islamic Republic, pessimists argue that elections will allow for the institution of repressive, anti-democratic Islamic regimes.

Describing the initial stages of the Egyptian Revolution in the *Daily Mail* on 31 January 2011, John Bradley, a purported expert on Egyptian politics and society, asserted that 'frighteningly, this is exactly what happened in Iran in 1979' (Bradley 2011a). Just as Khomeini was able to make use of 'the uncertainty and chaos' that followed the Shah's departure to hijack an initially populist uprising that 'saw intellectuals, academics, feminists, the middle classes all demonstrating on the streets of Tehran', 'Egypt could easily go the same way, only more quickly and more dramatically'. According to Bradley, the uprising in Egypt 'is an even worse scenario for the anxiously watching West', not only because the Muslim Brotherhood is the only organized opposition force, but also due to 'the bloody history of Islamist terrorism in Egypt' and the probable escape of 'dangerous Islamist terrorists' from the Wadi Natrun prison (Bradley 2011a). Consequently, he dramatically asserts, 'there is a real risk that Egypt, one of the birthplaces of civilisation and a home to an Arab society with a long tradition of pluralism and tolerance, could well find itself ruled by a harsh, Iranian-style theocracy. Indeed, it may be too late to stop it' (Bradley 2011a).

While it may not be surprising for such fear-mongering about the Islamist threat to appear in the pages of an arch-conservative tabloid such as the *Daily Mail*, similar fears that the uprisings of the Arab Spring would have a similar outcome to the Iranian Revolution were also voiced by the editors of the centre-left newspaper *The Independent*. The leading article of the edition published on 2 February 2011 asserted that although Islamists had, to that point, maintained a low profile in the Egyptian Revolution, 'if the Brotherhood ... chooses to assert itself the consequences will be dramatic. An Iranian-style theocracy cannot be ruled out' (*The Independent* 2011). Consequently, the article asserts that

This is a moment of great optimism for millions of oppressed people across the Arab world. But it would be wrong to ignore the reality that ... it is also a moment of potential danger. It is a time to hope for the best, but also prepare for the worst.

As Islamists were both the most organized opposition groups in the many of the states of the MENA region prior to the 2011 uprisings and were respected by a significant portion of the population due to their provision of social services and lack of association with corruption, the pessimist camp feared that the establishment of electoral democracy would inevitably lead to the formation of Islamist governments. Confirming these fears, Islamist parties, such as Ennahda in Tunisia and the Muslim Brotherhood's Freedom and Justice Party (FJP), were victorious in a series of early post-revolutionary elections. Despite the moderate, pro-democratic rhetoric of these groups – particularly that expressed in messages presented to Western audiences – the pessimistic responses asserted that 'a troubling spirit of extremism lurks in the background of the Arab Spring' (Takeyh 2011). According to critics of the Arab Spring, such as Ray Takeyh, the apparent moderation of Islamist movements is inauthentic, 'born of compulsion, not some kind of intellectual evolution.' 'Relieved of the constraints of Arab police states,' he argues that Islamists will be 'free to advance their illiberal, anti-Western agendas' (Takeyh 2011).

The true face of these supposedly moderate Islamist parties is said to be evident, first, in the measures they introduced after successfully forming post-revolution governments. Pointing to statements by figures in Egypt's FJP concerning a desire to ban bikinis and alcohol in Red Sea resorts, John Bradley (2011b) argues that an Egypt ruled by such a party would soon come to resemble Saudi Arabia. He suggests that shift away from cosmopolitanism towards radical conservatism is already evident in states 'historically renowned for their openness,' such as Tunisia and Morocco, which 'are becoming more repressive as the Islamists take control' (Bradley 2011b).

Second, pessimists argue that the true nature of parties such as Ennahda and the FJP is readily apparent within their guiding principles, particularly the long-held goal of the establishment of an Islamic state based on fundamentalist interpretations of sharia (Bradley 2011b; Takeyh 2011). To downplay such elements of the dogma undergirding these movements would be to 'denigrat[e] their commitment to their ideology' (Takeyh 2011). Given the purported ideological commitment of Islamists, pessimists argue that the participation of these groups in the political process is a (Takeyh 2011)

> menace to an inexperienced democratic order. Their deputies are extremely likely to press discriminatory legislation; their religious leaders will stimulate passions against women's rights groups and nongovernmental organizations; and their militias will threaten secular politicians and civil society leaders who do not conform to their template.

The seemingly anti-democratic values and goals of supposedly moderate Islamist parties has led pessimists to view their participation in the Arab Spring uprisings and their demand for free elections as part of 'a long game' to achieve the creation of an Islamic state (Bradley 2011a) rather than as representative of a true commitment to liberal democracy. In this sense, within the pessimistic reaction the establishment of democratic regimes appears not as an end-in-itself for Islamist movements, but as a Trojan horse making possible the establishment of theocratic regimes.

The concern voiced by pessimists with regard to the involvement of Islamists in democratic politics is not, however, only related to what the election of Islamist governments would mean for democracy in the MENA region but also to the consequences of such an event for Western democracies. Pessimists argue that Islamist governments will inevitably renege on treaties signed with Israel (Bradley 2011c; Rubin 2011). Through doing so, and by providing Islamism with a platform through which to further spread its ideology, Islamist regimes appear as a danger to regional and extra-regional instability

Presented with these risks associated with the participation of Islamists in the democratic political sphere, pessimists assert the need to delay the establishment of democracy in the MENA region for two reasons. First, they suggest that due to the anti-democratic nature of the groups likely to be elected, democratization will not result in the establishment of enduring democratic states. Second, the election of Islamist governments will pose a threat to Israel and the West, and, therefore, to already-established democracies. Consequently, pessimists argue that democracy must be temporarily abandoned in order to protect democracy. As the fall of authoritarian regimes poses a threat to democracy, they assert that the Arab Spring should be greeted with caution rather than celebration.

The optimistic response

While sometimes acknowledging the threat to democracy posed by radical Islamist movements, the second set of responses to the Arab Spring views the uprisings in the MENA region as a positive development and asserts that the establishment of electoral democracy must be supported rather than restricted. This alternative discourse – evident in the statements of a diversity of figures associated with neoconservatism, liberal internationalism, the Left and those referred to in foreign policy circles as idealists – advocates the value of democracy as a good in-in-itself, the only means to truly combat radicalism, or both.

Within this discourse, optimism with regard to the Arab Spring is evident in the celebration of the uprisings themselves and the toppling of dictators as well as in the depiction of the democratic legitimacy of elected Islamist governments. Thus, the optimistic response tends to equate elections with democracy, and, consequently, responding to the questions of democracy and the Arab Spring often simply involves determining the fairness or validity of elections. As such, the legitimacy of any new regime is based on the result of elections. Reza Aslan, for example, depicts the Islamist presence in the post-Arab Spring political sphere as reflective of popular will. Writing about post-Gadhafi Libya, he argues that, 'the country is predominantly Muslim and it can be expected that, given the freedom of an option, the majority of the population will opt for a far greater role for religion in government ... that in and of itself is not a bad thing' (Aslan 2011).

Within this discourse, then, Islamist governments are deemed to be legitimate democratic rulers if the elections in which they were victorious were conducted in a fair manner and illegitimate only if they are determined to have been unfair. This is evident in arguments, such as those made by Haroon Siddiqui, that describe the opposition to the presidency of Mohamed Morsi as guided by an 'undemocratic nature' (Siddiqui 2012a). According to Siddiqui, calls for the removal of Morsi as president of Egypt amounted to 'the educated, mostly urban elite who are undergoing conniptions about the sudden political and social rise of the rural illiterate hordes' attempting to 'sabotage' an elected government (Siddiqui 2012b).

Unlike within the pessimistic response, optimists do not consider the participation of Islamist groups in the political sphere a danger to democracy. As Aslan asserts, 'the prospect of any of [the Arab Spring] countries transforming into another Islamic Republic of Iran is almost nil' (Aslan 2011). In contrast to such fears of theocratic forces undermining democracy, optimists suggest that promoting the involvement of Islamist groups in a democratic political process will foster further democratization and political stability.

Some, such as the neoconservative Ruel Marc Gerecht, argue that moderate Islamist groups, and the population of the MENA at large, have genuinely adopted democratic values and principles (Gerecht 2011). In contrast to the oft-voiced notion that Islam and democracy are incompatible, he argues that 'democracy for the faithful has become a means for society to affirm its most cherished Islamic values' (Gerecht 2011). Rather than merely a notion connoting the freedom of the believer to worship, Gerecht asserts that 'today, in Egypt and elsewhere, hurriya [freedom] cannot be understood without reference to free men and women voting' (Gerecht 2011). This 'momentous marriage of Islamism and democratic ideas' means that 'men and women of devout faith, who cherish (if not always rigorously follow) Shariah law [have] increasingly embraced the convulsive idea that only elected political leadership was legitimate' (Gerecht 2011).

Others, such as Reza Aslan, suggest that Islamist demands for the introduction of sharia are misunderstood, resulting in an exaggeration of the threat it poses to democracy (Aslan 2011). Aslan argues, first, that the most powerful Islamist groups, including the Muslim Brotherhood and Ennahda, have clearly and repeatedly stated that they are opposed to the implementation of a conservative interpretation of sharia (Aslan 2011). Moreover, he states that demands for sharia may represent a rejection of autocratic rule rather than a wish for the institution of a theocratic regime. As such, 'sharia is merely code for "rule of law" ... something written down and codified that can be relied upon by all citizens' (Aslan 2011). Understood in this way, sharia is merely a 'form of identity', or a set of values and norms in opposition to those of corrupt, dictatorial regimes (Aslan 2011).

The most recurrent arguments found within responses that downplay the threat of political Islamism invoke what Siddiqui labels the 'magic of democracy' (Siddiqui 2012a). According to these arguments, elections are a force for moderation. In order to appeal to a wide enough segment of the population, parties who wish to be elected must moderate their positions or else be defeated and marginalized (Siddiqui 2012a; Beaumont 2011; Guéhenno 2011). It is argued that by entering into electoral politics Islamist groups are forced to moderate their positions. Moreover, the participation of Islamists in the political sphere is considered a means of marginalizing radical Islam, as electoral democracy provides a non-violent means to achieve social transformation. To establish this, proponents of this position point to the significant decline in support for Al Qaeda and similar violent Islamist groups throughout the Arab world owing to a sense of agency brought about by the Arab Spring and the subsequent establishment of electoral democracy (Beaumont 2011).

Consistent with these arguments, optimists assert that continuing to support autocratic regimes or repressing emerging democracies risks radicalizing not only moderate Islamist groups but also other moderate segments of the population (Kagan 2011). In contrast to the previously outlined fear that, in a repeat of the 1979 revolution in Iran, radical forces will hijack the Arab Spring uprisings, optimists contend that it is the West's support of dictators and resistance to democratization that permits the rise of figures such as the Ayatollah Ruhollah Khomeini. Supporting dictators, then, risks a rise in both anti-Western sentiment and the belief that violence is the only means to achieve social change.

It is in relation to such arguments about the moderating influence of elections and the risks associated with opposing democratization that Robert Kagan argues the ostensibly clear distinction between pragmatic and idealist responses to the Arab Spring breaks down (Kagan 2011). Many of those associated with the optimistic position support the establishment of electoral democracy in the MENA region, not only on the basis of the moral value they attach to the democratization of these states but also because they contend that it would serve to protect already-established democracies. First, by promoting moderation and marginalizing radical groups, democratization would create greater security not only in the MENA region but also globally. Second, consistent with the refrain voiced by liberal and neo-conservative interventionists, many optimists argue that democratization promotes peace, as democracies apparently do not go to war with other democracies. Therefore, within the optimistic reaction to the Arab Spring, elections appear not only as the embodiment of democratic principles but also as a mechanism necessary for the protection of democracy.

The failure to respond

Reactions to the Arab Spring and the prospects for subsequent democratization in the MENA within the Western media during the early period of the Arab Spring, then, can be said to have taken two forms. The first – the pessimistic response – calls for an abdication of democracy in the MENA in order to protect the prospect of future democratization in the region as well as already-established democracy elsewhere. As the election of Islamist governments is viewed as a means to institute theocratic regimes and as a threat to Israel and Western democracies, democratization must be opposed. In contrast, the second – the optimistic response – argues both that elections are the institutional manifestation of democratic principles and that the establishment of electoral democracy in the states of the MENA region is vital to safeguard global democracy.

It would seem, then, that the pessimistic and optimistic camps each offer a particular response to the uprisings of the Arab Spring and democratization in the MENA region. However, despite their different reactions to the Arab Spring, each of these apparent responses amounts to a refusal to respond. By approaching the Arab Spring with predetermined definitions of democracy, political subjectivity and the relation between Islamism and democracy, they fail to contend with the singularity of these events. Instead of offering responses for which the responder is singularly responsible, both sets of reactions to the Arab Spring simply refer to an equation establishing the relationship between Islamism and democracy. In this way, the responder is made absent. They are not responsible for their decision, as it has already been made by the pre-existing equations and definitions.

What both the pessimistic and optimistic reactions actually describe is a non-relation between Islamism and democracy. Within each discourse, any contact between Islamism and democracy is depicted as inevitably resulting in the annihilation of one of the participants. Consequently, any encounter between Islamism and democracy is rendered impossible and unthinkable, as one of the constituents does not survive an initial contact.

This inability to truly respond to questions of democracy emerging from the Arab Spring is most readily discernible within the discourse of the pessimistic camp. For pessimists, Islamism and democracy are defined as essentially irreconcilable phenomena. Islamism is seen as a corrosive force working towards the negation of democracy. Consequently, any encounter of Islamism and democracy is constructed as one of negation, with democracy negated by contact with the essentially anti-democratic force of Islamism. As the nature of the relation between the two phenomena is predetermined as one of negation, a relation of pure externality must be maintained in order to immunize democracy from contamination by the essentially anti-democratic force of Islamism. As a result, any consideration of Islamism within the democratic political sphere is unthinkable, as contact between Islamism and democracy will lead to the destruction of democracy.

In order to safeguard democracy, pessimists argue that contact with Islamism must be prevented. To do so requires excluding Islamists from the democratic political sphere. Within this pessimistic discourse, then, the democratic political sphere must be protected from the influence of Islamists, through either continuing to support secular authoritarian regimes or enacting measures that ensure that Islamists governments will not be elected. By precluding any contact between Islamism and democracy, this discourse avoids all questions related to the participation of Islamists in the post-Arab Spring political sphere.

In contrast to the pessimistic position, the optimistic discourse seems to welcome and even promote the participation of Islamists in the democratic political sphere. However, it too portrays a relation of negation between Islamism and democracy. As previously outlined, optimists argue that Islamists have already ceased, or will immediately cease, to be Islamists upon entry into electoral politics, as either (a) they are already democratic subjects who have fully and authentically internalized liberal democratic values – that they are already *liberal* Islamists, with their liberalism overriding any of the questions Islamism poses for liberal democracy; (b) their seemingly theocratic goals are 'merely' anti-authoritarian markers of identity reflecting demands for freedom and the rule of law; or (c) through the 'magic of democracy', Islamists will be transformed into moderate political actors.

According to positions (a) and (b), those Islamists willing to participate in democratic politics already resemble subjects proper to the liberal political sphere. As a consequence, no encounter between Islamism and democracy can occur. Any specificity of Islamist politics or subjectivity is denied, as Islamists who desire to engage in democratic politics are already liberal democratic subjects in a disguised form. Similarly, position (c) denies the possibility of any exchange between Islamism and democracy. Unlike pessimistic accounts, which argue that any encounter between Islamism and democracy would result in the annihilation of the latter, this position requires that the result of such an encounter would be the negation of Islamism. Upon entry into the democratic political sphere, the specificity of Islamist politics and subjectivity would vanish as a consequence of the moderating and liberalizing force of electoral politics. As such, the optimistic position tends to equate elections and democracy, as the subjects who participate in elections are already, or will immediately become, democratic political subjects.

By presenting the encounter of Islamism and democracy as a non-relation, and therefore unthinkable, both pessimistic and optimistic discourses are unable to engage in the difficult, yet necessary interrogation of the meaning and consequences for democracy posed by the presence of Islamism – in the form of Islamist parties, demands or subjects – in the post-Arab Spring political sphere. As such, they are unable to provide a response to the events of the Arab Spring. Instead, they merely provide alibis of the incommensurability of Islam and democracy.

The Arab Spring and 'the scandal of democracy'

Not only do both sides of this apparent debate fail to respond to the events of the Arab Spring, the reactions they do provide serve to efface democracy. While pessimists and optimists assert that they are speaking in favour of, and attempting to defend, democracy, they are fundamentally anti-political and undemocratic. Both of these camps can be seen as part of a long-standing 'vicious circle' (Rancière 2001: §3) within social and political thought that attempts to efface what Jacques Rancière refers to as 'the scandal of democracy' (Rancière 2005: 40).

As Rancière outlines in his various studies of the history of political philosophy, from Plato onwards politics has been defined anthropologically, as 'a mode of being proper to those who those who in turn possess the characteristics proper to it' (Morrison 2013: 890). In other words, political subjects are always predetermined by their possession of the particular characteristics necessary for ruling. In this way, social and political thought always posits the existence of a particular subject proper to the political and defines politics as the 'deployment of the properties of a type of man ...' (Rancière 2001: §28). It is this identification of politics as at once a particular relationship and form of subjectivity that forms the vicious circle of political philosophy.

The vicious circle that Rancière identifies is historically manifest in two forms of rule, each of which posits the existence of a particular subject proper to the realm of politics. Within the first of these, what Rancière refers to as the 'archipolitics' of Platonic philosophy, this takes the form of conferring each individual a social role – as ruler or one who is ruled – according to their natural capacities. Politics is the domain proper to rulers, those endowed with the skills and virtue necessary to understand the common good (Rancière 1995: 65–71).

In contrast, the subject of 'parapolitics' (Rancière 1995: 70–81) is one 'who has the capacity to agree to and abide by the principles necessary for achieving the common good' (Morrison 2013: 890). This political subject, capable of conducting him- or herself according to a social contract or the rules of public discourse, is 'defined by the capacity to bracket individual needs, desires, interests or beliefs in the accordance with the dictates of the public/political sphere' (Morrison 2013: 891).

The above-outlined Western reactions to the Arab Spring are grounded in a parapolitical understanding of politics. In the discourse of both pessimists and optimists, democratic politics appears as an institutionalized form of governance, comprised of particular norms and subjects capable of abiding by those norms. This is perhaps most easily discernible in the assertion of the incommensurability of Islamism and democracy present in the pessimistic position. Islamists, apparently unwilling to set aside their religious goals and values, are declared to be unable to abide by democratic norms. As such, the pessimistic response asserts that they must be excluded from the political sphere.

Despite welcoming the participation of Islamists in the political sphere, the optimistic reaction also remains within the bounds of parapolitics. As previously discussed, the justification for the participation of Islamists in the political sphere is that they are, or will imminently be transformed into, subjects proper to the democratic political sphere. Thus, within Western reactions to the Arab Spring, the inclusion or exclusion of Islamists from the post-revolutionary political sphere is determined by a capacity to abide by the rules and embody the values proper to this sphere.

Referring to Aristotle's definitions of politics and democracy, Rancière argues that archipolitical and parapolitical understandings of politics are both anti-political and anti-democratic. In Book III of *Politics*, Aristotle, by defining the citizen as 'he who partakes in the fact of ruling and being ruled' (Rancière 2001: §1), disrupts the traditional distinction between those who exercise power and those who are subject to it. Within Aristotle's formulation, the subject of politics is never predetermined on the basis particular capacities, but is defined only by this 'knot of subject and relation' (Rancière 2001: §4). It is this knot that political philosophy has perpetually attempted to undo by defining politics as the activity proper to subjects possessing particular characteristics. As such, Rancière is able to argue that the history of philosophy since Plato is the history of an ongoing attempt to efface politics. It is within this tradition of anti-politics that the parapolitical reactions to the Arab Spring are located.

It is in reference to a second of Aristotle's statements regarding politics that Rancière argues that the vicious circle of political philosophy is not only anti-political but also anti-democratic. In Book I of *Politics*, Aristotle distinguishes politics – as the ruling of equals – from all other forms of rule

(Rancière 2001: §1). In combination with the relational definition of political subjectivity, this second definition of politics marks 'a specific rupture in the logic of *arche*' (Rancière 2001: Thesis 3). Not only is there no distinction between the ruler and those who are ruled, but also, as the ruling of equals, there are no capacities proper to those permitted to rule. For Rancière, then, politics is understood as the activity of equals partaking in ruling and being ruled. As such, politics is equated with democracy, 'that state of exception where no oppositions can function, where there is no pre-determined principle of role allocation" (Rancière 2001: §9). It is the absence of a qualification for ruling that Rancière refers to as the 'scandal' – 'the scandal for the well-to-do people unable to accept that their birth, their age, or their science has to bow before the law of chance' (Rancière 2005: 40) – that political philosophy seeks to efface.

Unlike within the Western reactions to the Arab Spring, for Rancière democracy cannot be defined as a particular political regime or as the activity of subjects possessing particular characteristics. According to Rancière, the subject of politics, the *demos*, is not marked by any positive property but only by the empty property of freedom, what he refers to as the qualification of those without qualification (Rancière 1995: 8). The political subject, then, is never merely a part of society or a definite collectivity but always subject to a miscount. The *demos* is a designation open to constant interpretation. Political subjectivities are 'surplus names', names that call into question who is to be included in their count (Rancière 2004: 302). The *demos*, then, as a democratic subject marked only by the equality of freedom, 'is identified with the community as a whole, while at the same time always exceeding any attempt to delineate the boundaries proper to the community' (Morrison 2013: 894).

In contrast to what Rancière refers to as police – the ongoing 'partition of the sensible whose principle is the absence of a void and of a supplement' (Rancière 2001: Thesis 7) – 'politics exists as a deviation from the normal order of things' (2001: §18). It is the rare occurrence when subjects defy the given definition of a community by supplementing it, by refusing the identification of the people with a particular population, race, nation or way of being (Morrison 2013: 894). Politics, as 'the part of those who have no-part' (Rancière 2001: Thesis 5), is opposed to the vision of society of police, one in which all have a part. Police seeks to partition society into distinct spheres and eliminate any void or overlap on the map of society by articulating the realm of each phenomenon and form of subjectivity. The primary aim of doing so is to isolate the political realm and subject from all other social spheres and forms of subjectivity (Rancière 2004: 305). Such a partition of society permits the depoliticization of subjects through establishing a clear distinction, and making impossible any overlap, between the public life of equals in which rights can be claimed and the private realm, 'from which only groans or cries expressing suffering, hunger, or anger could emerge, but not actual speeches demonstrating a shared *aesthesis*' (Rancière 2001, Thesis 8). In constituting and drawing boundaries between the subjects and their corresponding social spheres, police is not only able to dictate who is capable of speaking but also what demands are able to be voiced (Tanke 2001: 45).

In contrast to these police processes, politics generates what Rancière terms a *dissensus* (Rancière 2001: Thesis 8). By destabilizing categories, identities and the boundaries of the community, it aims to 'distance the sensible from itself' (Rancière 2001:Thesis 8). Politics is not a set of institutional procedures. Rather, it is the process of 'overturning police identities' (Tanke 2011: 64–5, 70). Through the 'production through a series of actions of a body and a capacity for enunciation not previously identifiable within a given field of experience, whose identification is thus part of the reconfiguration of the field of experience' (Rancière 1995: 35), politics opposes police. This, however, does not involve the establishment of a new consensus through accommodating the *demos* within a particular order (May 2009: 112–13). Nor does it mean that a political event will not result in some form of accommodation and the institution of a new police regime. Accommodation, however, is never the aim of politics: it 'is not where politics lies' (May 2009: 113). Politics, therefore, it is not simply defined by demands for equal treatment, inclusion or recognition. Rather, politics involves the creation of dissensus through actions grounded in a presupposition of equality.

Conclusion

Rancière's conceptions of democracy, police and the vicious circle of political philosophy not only provide us with the analytical tools with which to critique Western reactions to the Arab Spring. They also provide us with the means to begin to enter into the sort of politico-ethical engagement with these events that both pessimistic and optimistic reactions avoid. Rather than evading an engagement with questions of democracy and the Arab Spring through offering predetermined notions of democracy as a particular institutional form with a corresponding map of society distinguishing political and non-political subjects (including Islamists) defined by their possession of particular capacities and characteristics, Rancière's political philosophy allows us to respond to the events of the Arab Spring and their relationship to democracy. As such, rather than fleeing the scene of the encounter of Islamism and electoral politics, we can ask whether the actions and demands of the various parties involved in the Arab Spring are those of politics or police, and, thus, democratic or anti-democratic: Do they reinforce the categories of the police through attempting to attain consensus or seek dissensus through exceeding the identifications of political and non-political accorded them by the police order? Are they enacting political subjectivity in the name of equality or attempting to inscribe an alternative police order? It is only through contending with such questions that we can begin to develop a response to the events of the Arab Spring rather than abdicating responsibility through alibis provided to us by the vicious circle of political philosophy.

PART THREE

Religion and social action

13

Social welfare provision and Islamic social movements in the Middle East and North Africa (MENA): A viable form of social action?

Rana Jawad

This chapter critically examines the role of contemporary Islamic social movements in social welfare and social justice issues in the Middle East and North Africa (MENA) region. Such movements, which include the Muslim Brotherhood (Egypt, Jordan), Hamas (Palestine) and Hezbollah (Lebanon), have become a prominent part of academic debate in the last three decades – a debate that frames them primarily as political movements that use social welfare services instrumentally to gain political support from local deprived populations. This chapter will part with this mainstream analysis by shedding new light on the political and social dynamics that surround these movements, thereby proposing that their social welfare role may also be considered as promoting civic engagement and social justice for the poor and vulnerable. The chapter will categorize the different types of religiously inspired social welfare and development action offered by the non-state sector in the MENA region in order to make two key arguments:

(1) Religion has played a historical role in the development of the public sphere in MENA. Institutions such as *waqf* and *zakat* have been instrumental in developing notions of the common good and public services including health, education and economic development. Today, most religious actors choose to operate as non-governmental organizations (NGOs) drawing upon religious precepts of fellowship and responding to human need. However, religion also operates through the state apparatus in many MENA countries, as in Iran and Saudi Arabia. The chapter explores the varieties of institutional mechanisms through which religion interacts with social welfare and development by discussing a typology of religious development action developed by the author.

(2) The research evidence on the extent to which religion is a force for transformative social change in the MENA region is not conclusive. The ethos of charity continues to prevail, and civil conflict interrupts development work as religious organizations respond to emergency humanitarian needs. Thus, the extent to which religion can promote a substantive discourse of development in the MENA region has yet to be realized. In the meantime, most MENA states work closely with international development institutions to implement socio-economic policies or social safety-net programs which, at best, produce piecemeal solutions to the critical social challenges the region faces.

The role of religious actors, values and institutions in shaping public policy interventions, in terms of both policy formulation processes and outcomes for end users, has become much more prominent in development studies and social policy in the last decade. This flourishing academic literature has, so far, paid little attention to the MENA region, in part, perhaps, as a result of the hegemony of political science in Middle Eastern studies and the dominant concerns with issues of international security and geopolitics. Yet, the study of development, social welfare and social justice issues has never been more urgent in the MENA region as now, and no doubt it is made so by the civil unrest that has swept across MENA countries starting with Tunisia in 2011.

To a large extent, therefore, the task ahead for scholars is not a small one. It is twofold: a new generation of social scientists outside the discipline of political science need to consider the MENA region in their academic work and to explore the social and developmental issues this region faces. Further, these social scientists should consider in more depth the intersection between religion and development in the MENA region. To this end, this chapter draws upon extensive research I have conducted on the social and development policies in the region (Jawad 2009; see also Bonner et al. 2003; Heyneman et al. 2004; Moghadam and Karshenas 2006).

The research on which this chapter is based covers public interventions by state agencies, international development agencies and indigenous NGOs.

The focus is on Muslim (Shi'a and Sunni) organizations, although it should also be acknowledged that Christian welfare NGOs are also active in the Arab and wider MENA region. The chapter begins with some basic conceptual discussion to set the scene for critically evaluating the relationship between religion and development in the MENA region. This entails a consideration of how modern international development policies and practices have been shaped in the MENA region and what, in comparison, the history of religious interventions in the public sphere has entailed. In some respects, we may say that these are parallel universes.

The 2002 Arab Human Development Report (AHDR) famously described the Arab region as rich but underdeveloped. To a large extent, this is reflected in the trajectory of development initiatives in the MENA region, which have been couched in uneven processes of nation-building, continued conflicts over identity politics and a lack of effective engagement with processes of economic globalization. Thus, the MENA region is marked by 'exceptionalism', not only because it has not successfully integrated into the world economy but also because it is the home of 'political Islam'.

The influence of religion on processes of social change and development action in the MENA region can be partly understood in relation to the relative success or failure in the countries of the MENA to establish legitimate modern secular states that are responsive to the needs of their citizens. Instead, this is a region plagued since the time of independence of its nation-states by a disjuncture between state and society, a situation that has been both reinforced and exacerbated by the rise of political Islam and the entry of Islamic movements into the political epicentre following the uprisings of Tunisia in 2011. Against this backdrop of political upheaval at the macro level, the MENA region boasts a vibrant non-state sector where religiously inspired philanthropic, charitable and civic actors engage in a vast array of both development and humanitarian relief work, depending on whether there is war or peace.

Social welfare policy in MENA: Historical developments

Global forces have played a key role in the shaping of the modern Middle East, the definition of its social problems and avenues to their policy solutions: from European economic domination in the seventeenth century, to colonization and mandate rule, to modern-day global economic integration (El-Ghonemy 1998). Since the 1980s, the region has also been subjected to the pressures of economic reform in the context of a globalizing economic world order and structural adjustment programmes led mainly by international development agencies such as the International Monetary Fund and the World Bank. These factors have resulted in public policy becoming dominated by the interests of elites made up of tribal, religious or ethnic leaders and wealthy merchants whose privileged status during mandate rule and afterwards marginalized the interest of a primarily rural agricultural population (El-Ghonemy 1998). The increasing market-orientation of Arab economies and the privatization programmes they underwent under the influence of globalization and international development actors has further diminished the role of the state as main provider of social services and employer in the public sector.

Commentators argue that states in Arab countries have failed or are failing to develop effective democratic institutions that can ensure representative government and political participation for all citizens (Moghadam and Karshenas et al. 2006; El-Ghonemy 1998; Henry and Springborg 2001; Clark 2003). Whether heavily centralized and coercive (such as Egypt and Saudi Arabia) or weak and dysfunctional (such as Sudan and Lebanon), states are blocked from functioning effectively by corruption. State social provisioning is especially affected because of several factors, namely (1) the misallocation of resources and the prioritization of military spending over other important social policy sectors such as health and education; (2) the narrow economic focus of public policy, which links social progress to economic prosperity; (3) the dominance of minority factions in Arab countries dating back to the colonial era; (4) political insecurity and military conflict including, of course, the Arab–Israeli conflict; (5) high levels of state indebtedness, which have taken away funds from social welfare services; (6) the introduction of structural adjustment programmes and the increasing privatization programmes, which have reduced the role of the state further as provider of social services and public sector jobs (El-Ghonemy 1998; Karshenas and Moghadam 2006; Bayat 2006). The resulting social ills of unemployment, wealth polarization and even undernourishment need to be addressed through the reform of public policy and state legislation.

The most comprehensive employment-based social security schemes are enjoyed by urban public sector workers, with the best forms of protection going to the army and security forces. At the heart of this residual social policy approach lies an emphasis on economic development in public policy and a corresponding lack of importance accorded to the social sphere. A significant example of this residual approach is highlighted by the Egypt case study in Bayat where, since the 1990s, the state has not been able to cut back on key consumer subsidies due to the outbreak of violent public protest (Bayat 2006). Ironically, this is one social right accorded to Arab citizens that has proved difficult to retract. Related to this is the characterization of Arab states as 'rentier'. The oil windfall in the region which occurred in the mid-twentieth century is depicted as a curse by El-Ghonemy, since it has weakened the structures of social citizenship and the need to develop the productive capacity of the local population, because of over-reliance on foreign labour (El-Ghonemy 1998).

The uprisings of the Arab Spring have made these issues much more urgent. If issues of social justice and social welfare were not a concern for governments and development agencies in the region a few years ago, they are now. Momentum has grown among international development agencies to begin to engage with issues of social protection in the MENA countries and with what suitable social policy responses might look like.

The United Nations Economic and Social Council for Western Asia for example has published five reports over the course of the last few years that seek to define social policy in a suitable way for the MENA countries and explore options for future action. In this view, development policy is not only about the enhancement of state social protection systems, but, for some countries, it may be the case that a mixed economy of welfare model is being proposed whereby civil society actors are called upon to play a role in social welfare and social protection more generally. In accordance with this new trend, governments in the region have also been seeking to draw up social vision statements that reflect the rights and obligations of their citizens towards their states. To a large extent, however, these remain vision statements. In Lebanon for example, a National Social Strategy was produced in 2011 as a product of collaboration between a private research organization, the United Nations Development Programme and the Ministry of Social Affairs, but the population at large is unaware of this endeavour, although local NGOs were consulted. In some ways, this lack of governmental engagement with issues of social welfare is historically rooted.

It is partly explained by the dominance of religious actors and institutions in the social welfare sphere. Islamic and Christian forms of social action have dominated the Arab region for centuries. Under Islamic rule, religious institutions such as the *waqf* (religious endowments) flourished and were seen to contribute in fundamental ways to public life and economic development. The city of Istanbul, Turkey, is particularly noted in this regard. *Waqf* institutions were also means by which women could own property and invest capital in the public sphere. During colonization, many of the *waqf* institutions and practices were destroyed by European colonizers who sought to seize profitable land and assets. Public life and political institutions gradually became overtaken by more modern forms of government that reflected the tendencies and interests of urban elites.

Public policies aimed at social development outcomes increasingly became politicized and used instrumentally by the state to gain power and political legitimacy (Jawad 2009). Some authors argue that this is a historical factor; for example, the introduction of social benefits to workers and employment guarantees to university graduates in Iran and Egypt in the 1950s and 1960s was motivated by the need to win the support of the working classes in the postcolonial states and was not based on policy objectives of expanding social citizenship (Bayat 2006). Today, social benefits are channelled through clientelist networks, which link ruling governments to their supporters. Hence, the long-running social policy challenges facing the Arab countries in terms of social welfare provisioning are less about the long-term structures of democratic participation and a share in decision-making by society and more about the urgent measures of wealth redistribution, income transfers, provision of basic needs and ensuring the basic support systems of survival (Karshenas and Moghadam 2006).

Today, the region demonstrates diverse socio-economic profiles, with per-capita income levels ranging from over $25,000 (US) to below $1,000 (US). The first Arab Human Development Report described the Arab region in particular as being 'richer than it is developed', with its oil-driven economic policies resulting in substantial social and economic volatility (UN 2002). There is also limited availability of poverty statistics. The region has made some progress in reducing absolute poverty levels in the last two decades. Extreme poverty is especially acute in the low-income Arab countries, affecting around a third of the population. A distinctive demographic feature with important development policy implications is the region's 'youth bulge', with around 60 per cent of the population under the age of twenty-five years. However, poverty is a multidimensional phenomenon (UN 2009). There are, therefore, a variety of social problems with which Arab countries today are grappling, namely, unemployment, particularly among the youth; population growth; adult illiteracy; high school dropout rates; lack of access to universal health care; and social, income and gender disparities (UN 2009).

Thus, the key characterization of the Arab region has therefore been one of a detachment between state and society (Henry and Springborg 2001), and this has come to a head with the current uprisings. The sense of social unrest is exacerbated further by the common notion within society that the state should take more responsibility for the welfare of citizens and that the latter have the right to be provided with state social services. Discord between state and societal groups over the public sphere is most acutely expressed in Arab countries by the rise of Islamic groups, which are providing vital public and social services and are thus challenging the state, not only as a provider of welfare but as a modern secular institution of government (Jawad 2009). Some of these groups are well-known political groups such as the Muslim

Brotherhood (Egypt) and Hamas (Palestinian Territories), but others are more local and less political, such as the Islah Charitable Society in Yemen or the Mustafa Mahmood Health Clinic in Egypt (Clarke 2003).

Social justice in Islam

Islam (like Judaism and Christianity) exercises tremendous influence on social and political institutions in the Arab world and even makes its way directly into government social vision statements, as in the cases of Qatar and Saudi Arabia. Islamic values and traditions also have a direct influence on social welfare programmes and inheritance laws, as well as family planning. In this sense, Islam is sometimes considered to perpetuate wealth and gender inequalities, although perspectives differ, with researchers arguing that women do have rights to property and to work and have a say in family planning (Bowen 2004).

Islamic doctrine makes specific provisions for welfare through a variety of practices and institutions. Bonner discusses in historical terms the principles of 'return of wealth' (radd or ruju') to the poor and maslaha 'amma (public welfare) through obligatory Islamic practices – the waqf (religious endowments) and zakat (an obligatory 2.5 per cent tax levied on assets) (Bonner 2003:13). Zakat has acted as an important source of poverty alleviation for the poor, and waqf played a key role in the socio-economic development of the Middle East in the last few centuries prior to colonization (Heyneman 2004). Islamic principles have also entered particular public policy areas such as health, finance and economy and human rights legislation (Heyneman 2004). In the health sector for example, some countries such as Iran have been able to improve primary care thanks to the influence of Islamic principles in Iran after the revolution (Underwood 2004). In contrast to the zakat, which may be seen more as a tool of social assistance and wealth redistribution, waqf has played a much more important role in the development of MENA societies. Singer and Dallal discuss in depth the range of economic, social, political and cultural impacts that the waqf institution has produced, though this changed as state institutions began to take over the management of religious endowments from the nineteenth century onwards, and later through colonization (Singer 2003; Dallal 2004).

Islamic values are also important as an activating force for social groups and movements in society to engage in public and social service provisioning. In Egypt, Yemen and Jordan for example, Islamic movements or Islamic charity organizations use social welfare to challenge the basis of the secular modern state or to protect the political status of the professional classes through the provision of employment opportunities and social networks, or both (Clarke 2003; Wiktorowicz et al. 2003). In the case of political Islamic groups, Wiktorowicz et al. depict organizations such as Hamas in Palestine as social movements that have developed locally and are now supported by a comprehensive institutional basis of which the provision of social welfare and public services is a vital component (Wiktorowicz et al. 2003). In these cases, Islam is depicted as the only remaining platform for political contestation and struggle for social justice in the Middle East (El-Ghonemy 1998). As has been demonstrated so far in Tunisia, Morocco and Egypt, Islamic political parties such as Al Nhada and the Muslim Brothers were able to gain control of government following elections – though the tide turned against the Muslims Brothers in Egypt when President Morsi's government was toppled by the military.

The relevance of religion to social welfare in the MENA region

Today, governments and international development agencies are becoming more interested in social justice issues in the MENA region (particularly in the Arab and Muslim-populated countries). Ten years ago, this was a very different story. No one spoke of the need to protect citizens in the MENA region (except, perhaps, for some of the UN AHDRs), and government officials did not really know what social policies aimed at enhancing development social welfare would look like. But since the mid-2000s, we have an explosion of new terms such as social protection, social security, social assistance, social solidarity, social integration and new welfare mix, which headline reports and conference events. But are we any closer towards understanding how social policy systems work in the MENA region and crucially, what the way forward might be now that the Arab Spring has brought issues of social justice and social welfare in the MENA to the fore?

Muslim groups, no matter how notoriously linked they are to armed military struggle, have extensive social welfare networks in the countries they operate in, which are well-organized and successfully solve the daily social and economic problems that everyday people face. Indeed, it is impossible to devise policies that can support social integration and social security in the MENA region without taking into account the place and role of religious groups.

Hence, when we compare the types of services that are provided by religious NGOs in the MENA region, regardless of what political affiliation that organization might have, we find that all of these organizations have a similar social welfare ethos that prioritizes vulnerable groups such as orphans, the elderly and female-headed households. Indeed, they all operate on a social assistance basis, be this of an in-kind or in-cash nature. Take the case of Emdad and Caritas in Lebanon for example: Emdad is part of the family of Hezbollah-led welfare associations, but it offers social assistance to some of the poorest segments of society, which tend to be of the Shi'a denomination. Caritas is also a very prominent welfare and development organization with a Catholic orientation and provides the same kinds of social assistance and family support services as Emdad. These types of services are the most widespread and underpin the social assistance ethos that dominates much of the work that religious NGOs do in the MENA region.

Another key area of activity of religious NGOs in the MENA region is micro-credit and small enterprise loans. All religious groups operate with the ethos of fostering autonomy among their service users, though the extent to which they achieve this is not always proven. Many NGOs set up credit unions or offer direct loans to their beneficiaries in an attempt to help keep families together and, in cases where the father is absent, to support the mother in finding a new source of income. Some of the larger Islamic groups such the Jihad Al Binaa, which is affiliated to Hezbollah, invests in major rural development projects supporting farmers and subsidizing them in remote rural parts of Lebanon.

The research on which this chapter is based has helped to develop a typology of religious action in the social welfare and development spheres (Jawad 2009): it illustrates various forms in which religion influences state and non-state structures in development activity in the MENA region. There are five 'types', some of which overlap. The make-up of these types depends on the circumstances that led to the establishment of the religious NGOs. The types are summarized in Table 13.1 and described in more detail below.

Table 13.1 Types of religious welfare providers in the MENA region

Type	Characteristics
Religious order	Clergy-led, e.g. Caritas
Elite family	Elite-funded, e.g. Dar Al-Aytam
Popular political movement	Populist Islamic mass organizations, e.g. Hamas, Hezbollah
International humanitarian relief organization	International NGOs originating from the region, e.g. Deniz Feneri
The para-state organization	Welfare arms of the state, e.g. Emdad Iran

The first type of religious development organization is entirely clergy-led, for example Caritas, in Lebanon. We may call this type 'The Religious Order'. This organization is part and parcel of a religious body, such as the Catholic Church or a religious order. It may employ lay individuals, but the managerial cadre is reserved for clerics who carry out the social services themselves. This is in line with Christian social activism around the world and is characterized by the monastic character of some Christian traditions, where the clergy decide to leave the seclusion of the Church to engage in social life and help those less fortunate.

A second type, 'The Elite Family', is directly linked to the elite families of particular communities such as the case of Dar Al-Aytam in Lebanon, which was set up by prominent Beirut families, or Al-Maadi Community Foundation in Cairo, Egypt (Lethem-Ibrahim and Sherif 2008). In the case of Dar Al-Aytam, the Beirut families established an Islamic orphanage to care for orphans and widows living in the capital city and its suburbs. Some organizations are a joint endeavour between religious and political elites. The charitable activity of upper-class families in the Middle East has a long history and is closely linked to public action (Lethem-Ibrahim and Sherif 2008). In Egypt, in 1882, the first feminist movement mobilized in this way under the name of the 'Women's Educational Society'. The 1940s and 1950s, which witnessed waves of anti-colonial movements in the region, often involved aristocratic families. In Turkey today, it is common for prominent families to set up charitable public institutions such as schools and universities, otherwise translated from the Islamic concept of *waqf* (religious endowment) into English as 'social foundations'.

The third type, 'The Popular Political Movement', is perhaps the most revolutionary and, indeed, the most politicized. It is the one under which Hezbollah in Lebanon falls. This type can also be found in Egypt, Morocco and the Palestinian Territories in the example of movements with a clear Islamic ideology, such as the Muslim Brotherhood, Justice and Development Charity Movement and Hamas. It is important to pause here and consider the literature on Islamic social movements. Makris, and Sutton and Vertigans, make a distinction between 'radical Islamic movements' such as Al Qaeda and 'mass organizations' such as Hamas, the Muslim Brotherhood and Hezbollah (Makris 2007; Sutton and Vertigans 2005). This chapter goes some way in demonstrating how important a development perspective is for understanding the character of Islamic groups, particularly those falling under the category of 'mass organizations'.

As argued in Jawad, this chapter uses the term 'Popular Political Movement' (type 3) to denote the 'mass organizations' referred to above, since a key facet of their identity is their populist character expressed through their discourses on anti-imperialism (usually American) and social justice and their active involvement in development action (Jawad 2009). Salamey and Pearson, in analysing the particular case of Hezbollah, speak of a populist proletarian movement that is part of an anti-imperialist international alliance (Salamey and Pearson 2007). This, they argue, takes better account of the particular political discourse adopted by Hezbollah. Here, the populist pro-poor discourse feeds into one of resistance, not just against neocolonial dominance but also against poverty and ignorance.

A fourth type of religious development organization exists and is especially evident in Iran and Turkey. This is 'The International Humanitarian Relief Organization'. Organizations such as Insani Yardim Vakfi and Deniz Feneri in Turkey have become well known for their international relief efforts to emergency situations around the world. They also provide aid within Turkey. It is noteworthy that the religious NGOs that were researched for this chapter can sometimes work with each other in practice. As part of its international relief efforts, Deniz Feneri, for example, has offered financial aid to Emdad Lebanon. This links more broadly to an international Islamic identity that these organizations adhere to. Emdad Iran is also beginning to cross international borders, though it primarily denotes a fifth type of Islamic development organization, particular to a theocratic state (see below).

This fifth type we may call 'The Para-State Organization' following Saeidi's classification, which is based on the Persian name for welfare institutions, *boniyad* (Saeidi 2004). The general public perception in Iran is that Emdad is the welfare arm of the state. This view differs from that of the organization itself, since its staff members see it as a 'holy organization' set up by Imam Khomeini to serve the people. Indeed, the populist association emerges again here, with staff members arguing that the local population are more likely to donate to and support an NGO that they trust (Jawad 2009). As Saeidi argues, Emdad is part of a large array of development and social welfare institutions in Iran that offer a variety of services (Saeidi 2004). He argues that, since 1979, development policy in Iran has, in some cases, increasingly been used as a tool of social control and political legitimization. In this sense, the formal apparatus of government in Iran is an administrative structure, since development organizations such as Emdad respond directly to the supreme leaders.

Conclusion

The chapter has provided an overview of the role of religion in social welfare and development in the MENA region. This is a region that has long been considered as lagging behind on social and economic indicators and one that has occupied political and academic debate more over concerns with terrorism and political Islam than social welfare and development. This makes the argument presented in this chapter, that religion in the MENA region, and Islam in particular, can be a force for development and civic flourishing, an important departure from conventional scholarship.

MENA states continue to prioritize economic growth as their main development strategy, but the greater visibility that issues of poverty and social justice now have has meant that government policy can no longer turn a blind eye to social development and welfare concerns. NGOs that have a religious character are also striving to bring about long-term social and economic development through, for example, rural development projects and micro-credit programmes, but these programmes are outweighed by social assistance services focused on family allowances and emergency relief to families who have lost their main breadwinner. This social safety-net approach helps to not only bring about strong bonds of solidarity with the poor but also to encourage dependency.

It may also be argued that for many religious NGOs in the MENA, there is an overriding moral concern to protect destitute families from criminal or sexually deviant behaviour, as defined by the religious teachings followed by the religious organizations that provide the welfare support. Hence, these NGOs place a lot of emphasis on moral and spiritual education among their service users. Religious NGOs therefore perform a difficult balancing act. They are more likely be involved in poverty relief activities than they are in economic and social transformation. Having said this, religious NGOs have a strong sense of civic duty and service provision, and, in some cases, their beneficiaries later become volunteers. They are also able to work at grassroots level in a way in which many MENA governments cannot due to weak institutional and governance capacities.

Governments and global development agencies will do well in the formulation of new development policies, if they take serious account of the experience of religious NGOs in social action. But beyond this, religion also informs the salient moral values that underpin particular conceptualizations of the good society in the MENA region. An example discussed in this chapter is how the family remains central in religious thinking on well-being. What we find in MENA countries is that both state agencies and religious organizations target services to vulnerable groups such as orphans or female-headed households because they have no male breadwinner. So for policy purposes we can only understand patterns of development and social welfare organization in the MENA region by making the link to religion. For better or worse, this is a force that the MENA region should not be ashamed of but should enter into dialogue with.

14

Understanding definitions and experiences of care and caring among Hindu and Muslim older people: The role of ethnicity and religion

Akile Ahmet and Christina Victor

Informal or family care is fundamental to any community care policy. Its relevance for older people and those with long-term physical or mental disabilities in the United Kingdom is well established. It underpins the policy goal of enabling older people to live at home for as long as possible, with 70 per cent of adults expecting that their family will provide such care (Wanless 2006). Despite almost four decades of empirical research into caring, the observation (Atkins and Rollings 1992) that the large-scale studies of carers in the United Kingdom did not 'give … information about the number and circumstances of informal carers from black and ethnic minority groups' remains robust. Surveys rarely include sufficient sample sizes to enable explicit analysis of caring within and between minority communities. However, we would argue that there is not only limited understanding of the relationship between ethnicity and caring but that existing literature does not take into account the importance of religion in how care is understood and conceptualized among the key ethnic minority communities in the United Kingdom. In this chapter, we start to address this evidence gap by considering how the role of religion in care and caring is understood among four of our ethnic minority samples: Indian, Bangladeshi, Pakistani and Somalian (taken from our Black African sample). Our empirical evidence is drawn from a mixed methods study consisting of (a) a large (1,200 participants) quantitative survey of care provision among six ethnic groups – Black African, Black Caribbean, Bangladeshi, Chinese, Pakistani and Indian – and two age groups: forty to sixty-four and sixty-five+; and (b) sixty in-depth qualitative interviews conducted across England and Wales (see Burholt et al. forthcoming). In the first part of our chapter, we define who we consider to be informal carers. In the second part, we consider the current literature on ethnic minority carers and make a case for the need to explore religion within this area of investigation. We then present our empirical data, focusing upon the role of religion in the narratives of care provided by the participants in our in-depth interviews.

What is informal care?

Walker et al. conceptualize informal care as being part of a wider definition of family care, 'when one or more family members give aid or assistance as part of the "normal" everyday' (Walker et al. 1995: 201). They also argue that family care for older people begins when ageing family members require assistance because of a limiting long-term illness. This is not, however, a sharply delineated process. Nolan has developed a model of the transition from 'normal' family relationships to providing 'informal' care (Nolan 2002). However, it is important to note that, as well as older people, children and younger and mid-life adults with mental or physical disabilities may require care from their families. In this context, care is broadly conceptualized as both 'caring for' (i.e. providing help with activities of daily living, personal care and other forms of direct practical support) and 'caring about' (providing emotional and material and practical help as required) (see Phillips 2007). Walker et al. consider two different types of caring: 'instrumental activities to daily living' and 'assistance of daily living activities' (Walker et al. 1995). Similarly, Matthew and Rosner identify five types of what they refer to as 'helping patterns': routine help; back-up help; circumscribed help; sporadic help; and dislocation, which occurs when an adult child cannot be counted on to help his or her ageing family member (Matthew and Rosner 1988). It is important to understand that for researchers, policy makers and practitioners there is not yet a uniform definition of informal carers, and all debates about variations in rates of caring between groups defined by age, class, gender or ethnicity need to be contextualized by this caveat.

In Britain, the landmark 1985 survey of informal care provision and the characteristics of those receiving and giving care reported that 14 per cent of the adult population of Great Britain provided informal care to a dependent person (of any age) either living with them or living in another household. This survey has been repeated on a number of occasions (1990, 1995, 2000 and 2009/10), and a question on informal caring was included in both the 2001 and 2011 censuses. According to these surveys, the prevalence of 'caring' has remained roughly constant (see Table 14.1). However, caring is not equally distributed across the population but is associated with both gender (being higher among women than men) and age, with those in the forty-five to sixty-four age group being most likely to self-define themselves as carers. As argued earlier, informal caring is a complex concept, which is inevitably simplified in the use of these survey questions that aim to capture the 'prevalence' of caring. Thus, the degree to which these differences in terms of age and gender reflect different interpretations of a single question is unclear.

Table 14.1 below shows the prevalence of care across gender and age using data obtained from the General Household Survey (GHS).

'Informal carers' within the GHS were defined as 'people who provide unpaid care for family members, neighbours or others who are sick, disabled or elderly (ONS 2006). Also, some people have extra (family) responsibilities, because they look after someone who has long-term physical or mental health problems, disability or problems related to old age.[1] Respondents were also asked to classify the amount of time per week they provided care, ranging from 'low caring responsibilities' (1–19 hours a week) to 'heavy

Table 14.1 Number of carers across gender and age

	1985	1990	1995	2000	2009 census	2009/10	2011 census
Male	12	13	11	14	11	10	9
Female	15	17	14	18	14	14	12
Age 16–29	7	8	6	8			
Age 30–44	14	15	10	13			
Age 45–64	20	24	20	24	20	17	14
Age 65+	13	13	13	13	12	14	
All	14	15	13	16	13	12	11

Source: Data from the General Household Survey, www.ons.gov.uk.

caring responsibilities (50 hours or more per week – equivalent to 7 hours per day). The 2011 census showed that 10.3 per cent (5.8 million people) of the population provided some level of unpaid care, ranging from 1 to 50+ hours per week (see Table 14.2). The proportion of people providing unpaid care and the amount of care provided varied greatly among ethnic groups. British (11.1 per cent), Irish (11.0 per cent) and Gypsy or Irish Traveller (10.7 per cent) were among the highest providers of unpaid care in England and Wales. White and Black African (4.9 per cent), Chinese (5.3 per cent), White and Asian (5.3 per cent) and Other White (5.3 per cent) ethnic groups were among the lowest providers of unpaid care.

These variations demonstrated in Table 14.2 may reflect a range of different factors. For example, the Bangladeshi population is very young with a median age of thirty-three years, so the 'need' for care may be less in this population. However, these differences may also reflect differences in how caring is defined and interpreted across ethnic groups. We sought to explore these differences in understandings of care within different ethnic groups in order to examine whether ethnicity has an impact on how care is experienced and conceptualized. In what follows, we will discuss the literature surrounding black and ethnic minority older people and care, explore the literature on ethnicity and religion and argue why we are focusing on religion.

Race, ethnicity and religion

Religion is often subsumed into findings of race and ethnicity; therefore, it is important to briefly examine the definitions of race and ethnicity and how religion should be differentiated. Speaking of race, Anoop Nayak argues that (Nayak 2006: 414)

> There is an inherent paradigmatic tension in socially constructionist approaches to race. This involves the tendency to view race as socially constituted on one hand, yet to continually impart ontological value to it on the other, with the effect that race can take a reified status.

Early thinking and research on race prioritized race as biological (see for example, Meer 2014 for a review), which was the foundation of scientific racism. The very existence of race is fundamentally connected to the need for categorization. Naomi Zack explains that the epistemology of race is the process of 'sorting' people into different groups and it is the criteria of racial membership of an identity which is the ontology of race (Zack 2002).

Table 14.2 2011 census data on caring

	1–19 hours unpaid care	20–49 hours unpaid care	50 or more hours unpaid care	Total unpaid care (1 to 50+ hours)
White: English/Welsh/Scottish/ Northern Irish/British	7.1	1.4	2.6	11.1
White: Irish	6.7	1.4	2.9	11.0
White: Gypsy or Irish Traveller	4.4	1.9	4.4	10.7
Black: African/Caribbean/Black British Caribbean	6.4	1.5	1.9	9.8
Asian/Asian British Indian	5.9	2.0	1.9	9.7
Asian/Asian British Pakistani	4.8	1.9	2.4	9.1
Asian/Asian British Bangladeshi	4.7	1.8	2.3	8.8
Other ethnic group: Any other ethnic group	4.4	1.5	1.8	7.7
Asian/Asian British Other Asian	3.9	1.5	1.5	6.9
Black/African/Caribbean/Black British: Other Black	4.2	1.2	1.4	6.9
Mixed/multiple ethnic group: White and Black Caribbean	3.8	1.0	1.2	6.1
Mixed/multiple ethnic: Other Mixed	4.0	0.9	1.1	6.0
Other ethnic group: Arab	3.0	1.3	1.8	6.0
Black/African/Caribbean/Black British African	3.1	1.3	1.2	5.6
White: Other White	3.2	0.9	1.2	5.3
Mixed/multiple ethnic group: White and Asian	3.6	0.8	0.9	5.3
Asian/Asian British: Chinese	3.4	0.8	1.0	5.3
Mixed/multiple ethnic group: White and Black African	3.1	0.8	0.9	4.9

Source: Data from www.ons.gov.uk.

Bhopal has suggested that 'ethnicity is replacing the scientifically limited and somewhat discredited term race in the scientific literature' (Bhopal 2004: 445). Ethnicity, as Nobles argues, 'cannot be defined by criterion like origin, whether it is defined by place of birth or descent, since it results from a combination of multiple criteria, having equally to do with origin, place of residence, social networks, migratory path and so forth' (Nobles 2002: 47). Mahtani more specifically argues that (Mahtani forthcoming)

> Ethnicity is a relational term and employed differently in different contexts. Social distinctions made on the basis of national, linguistic, or caste criteria are thought to mark differences in ethnicity, and thus, ethnic boundaries, like racial boundaries, are invented. This means that almost anyone who is singled out as 'ethnic' can be given a whole range of 'ethnic labels' that can be declared, or rendered, socially relevant or irrelevant.

It is important not to place 'religion' into the ethnicity category but to consider it as a separate identity, as Beckford et al. write (Beckford et al. 2007: 8):

> While there are often clear areas of overlap between aspects of religion and aspects of ethnicity, it is important that the dimension of 'religion' should not be completely collapsed into that of 'ethnicity' nor vice versa. Rather, their complex relationship needs to be borne in mind and teased out in each specific context under consideration.

The literature on ageing and ethnicity is cross-disciplinary in nature, but to date there has been limited engagement or research from British scholars on what has been termed *ethnogerontology*, the study of ageing among black and ethnic minority adults. Within the United Kingdom, the primary focus of research has been ethnicity and health, where the black and ethnic minority populations demonstrate significant health inequalities when compared with the general population (see Bhopal 2002, 2003; Nazroo 2000). For example, among the South Asian populations there is a greater prevalence of chronic heart disease compared to the general population (see Katbmana et al. 2002). Hence, we may hypothesize that the ageing black and ethnic minority will present significant needs for care. Sharon Wray argues that there has been a lack of attention to the interconnection between ethnicity and variations in the timing of key life occurrences and this has led to an over simplified accounts of mid-life, as a prolonged extension of 'youth' (Wray 2007: 40). Mid- and later life are universalized with little credence being given of alternative perspectives on ageing and later life. Similarly, Burton et al. highlighted the importance of a need for 'cross-cultural gerontology' (Burton et al. 1992). Sandra Torres, in her research, explored what she termed a culturally relevant framework for successful ageing indicating the need to explore diversity and ageing (Torres 1999).

Dowd and Bengston suggest that ethnic minorities face what is termed the 'double jeopardy' of being aged and ethnic, and the consequence of their ageing experiences can be doubly negative (Dowd and Bengston 1978). Apart from predominantly single-group studies with a focus on people from Pakistan, Bangladesh and India (as discussed above), little is known about the nature and experience of informal care among black and ethnic minority communities. More specifically, there is a need for more comparative studies looking across ethnic groups and looking within groups by focusing upon variations by gender and generation. It is also necessary to consider the role of racism in how informal care is assumed and whether formal service provisions are culturally appropriate.

Our research findings

There has also been a failure to consider the religious dimension among ethnic minorities and the delivery of family-based care. In Ahmed et al.'s study of Bangladeshi women, religion was an important factor, as the strong sense of duty to provide care derived from their religious belief (Ahmed et al. 2008: 66):

> Most respondents in their study expressed a strong sense of duty to provide the care. This sense of duty derived from strong religious (Islamic) beliefs and appeared to place constraints on seeking outside support. This was particularly the case when they were caring for someone who had become infirm due to old age. This kind of care creeps up on the individual and they gradually find themselves doing more and more, and often do not identify themselves as a carer and see themselves as a wife doing her duty. There was a sense of duty about providing care. Most of the women in the study ascribed their position in life to be the skill of God.

Similarly Ahmed and Jones, in their study on Bangladeshi carers in London, found that their caring role was a manifestation of a sense of duty derived from their Islamic faith (Ahmed and Jones 2008). The majority of these studies have noted that South Asian participants have perceived their caring role as an Islamic duty. However, none of these studies have explicitly considered religion, rather it has been emergent theme as researchers focused upon cultural norms and values rather than looking at their derivation from faith-based duties. Religion and spirituality has been subsumed under research on the end of life care rather than informal care (see Nelson-Becker et al. 2013).

In our research, we aimed to consider the role of religion in the narratives of care provided by the sixty participants in our in-depth interviews. Interviews were semi-structured in nature, using an interview guide based upon existing literature, the results of our quantitative survey and pilot interviews. Interviews were conducted in English or in the language of participants' choice. Interviews were translated (if necessary) and transcribed verbatim and coded using Nvivo software with a grounded theory approach. Table 14.3 summarizes the caring responsibilities and religion of our participants.

Studies opting for a comparative approach across the key minority groups in the United Kingdom are rare and focus upon quality of life (see Bajekal et al.

Table 14.3 Summary of respondents and their caring responsibilities

	Black African	Black Caribbean	Chinese	Bangladeshi	Pakistani	Indian
Religion						
Christian	6	10	5		1	
Muslim	4		1	10	9	
Buddhist						
Hindu						9
Sikh						1
Caring						
Cares for older relative			2	2	1	2
Cares for partner		2	1	1	3	1
Cares for adult child		1		2	12	1
Cares for grandchild	2	2	2	4	1	1
Other relative	1					
Receives care from family	4	1	2	2	3	1

2004; Bowling 2009), loneliness/social exclusion (Victor et al. 2012), social support (Butt and Moriarty 2004) or the experiences of specific groups such as women (Maynard et al. 2008; Wray 2007) or black and ethnic minority service users with rare long-term neurological conditions (Hoppittet et al. 2011). Research in Britain focusing upon South Asian older people is more common than that focusing upon Black Caribbean, Black African or Chinese communities. Victor has considered the role of physical activity in the daily life of older people (aged 50+) from the Bangladeshi and Pakistani communities. In the same population, Victor et al. have stressed the importance of care and caring as a resource for old age and later life and demonstrated the strong expectations that older people have of their adult children's 'duty' to provide them with care (Victor et al. forthcoming). Focusing upon inter and intra-generational patterns of care, Victor and Zubair demonstrate the interaction of gender and generation (Victor and Zubair forthcoming). Older men expected their wives to provide care for them in the event of illness and disability, while both older men and women looked to their children; older women rarely looked to their husbands. In this study, there were again clear examples of the provision of care stemming from religious faith. The participant below described how she had cared for her husband and the important religious element of providing such care:

> I provided care for my husband for nearly 10 years. He died two years ago after a stroke. He could not move without help. I looked after him, lifting him, changing clothes, bathing him, and helping him to the toilet ... I enjoyed it because he was my husband. Allah said if you take care of our husband you earn God's reward ... lifting him over a period has given me a bad back. ... He did not want a nurse looking after him ... he only wanted me to do everything, also I did not want another woman to look after my husband, so I did what made him happy. When he died we were all close to him. That is my peace (Zenab, Muslim).

In our qualitative interviews, we asked participants about informal care and what caring meant to them. The answers given by our participants varied between ethnic groups (this is discussed in a forthcoming paper). However, in the narratives of our Muslim and Hindu participants, the role of religion became central to why they provided informal care and why they would care in the future:

> Our religion encourages people to care for each other and you are supposed to help your family in the first place ... the religious views are also what makes people help as well because sometimes they think that if they help

when the time comes and they need help they will have some help given to them (Surji, Muslim).

Surji is identifying that in the Muslim religion, care is encouraged as part of everyday practice, specifically within the family. Another participant similarly reported

I am Muslim ... in Islam looking after family is very important, so it help to keep me wanting to care for family because I also rewarded for it. ... In Somalia looking after family is very important as it is only thing you can truly trust (Abdul, Muslim).

Similarly, another participant suggested:

In the Somali tradition we look after our families and if anyone is in difficulty we help them ... this is something we don't have to even think about ... we come from a cultural background where family and kinship is first. Being a Muslim also means that we help each other ... doesn't matter if Christian, Muslim or Jew we still have to help when someone is in trouble or needs help (Saba, Muslim).

Central to all of the above narratives is care, family and religion. They all stressed the importance of religion teachings in relation to care within their families and beyond. Likewise, our Hindu participants echoed a similar narrative:

When I provide support to my friend, it's completely my choice ... in my culture and religion we believe that when you help others without any selfishness you have a peaceful death ... and you can have an entry in heaven (Oorja, Hindu).

Within the microspaces of the home, our Muslim and Hindu participants carried out their caring responsibilities based on their religious beliefs. These were 'private lived experiences' of religions. According to Ammerman, Weber's theory of theodicy is one way to consider the role of religion to the response of care (Ammerman 2007). Theodicy is defined as the religious response to suffering (see Musick 2000). Ammerman suggests that informal carers within the Muslim community employ their religious beliefs to shape and inform, cope and make meaning from the caring role (Ammerman 2007; see Buckman 2011). The above narratives suggest that the private practices of religion inform how care is perceived and carried out within South Asian and Somali families. Although we presented an official definition of informal care to our participants, they provided us with a narrative of personal and religious obligation and duty of care enacted within the family unit.

Duty and obligation of care

Ajrouch and Fakhoury have considered the 'Islamic perspective on aging' and have argued that 'Islamic scripture states unequivocally the expectation that older adults shall be cared for with patience, empathy, and kindness. Parents are to be honoured and respected, placed second only to God' (Ajrouch and Fakhoury 2013: 354). The concept of duty was recurring throughout the Somali and South Asian interviewees, including those that did not mention religion explicitly.

> It's my duty to do so. Parents are the angels that has been sent by Allah ... and doing something for them is a chance given by Allah (Saj, Muslim).

> Our Prophet Muhammed (Peace be Upon Him) made it clear that we must care for our neighbours, our families, strangers and even animals. Once a woman was in a desert and extremely thirsty. She has a small handful of water left and she as she was about to sip it, she heard a dog cry out in pain from lack of water. She proceeded to give water to the thirsty dog rather than quenching her own need. The Prophet said, that her sacrifice for the animal would render her a place in Heaven. That is what care is about – it is totally selfless (Abdul, Muslim).

> It is our religious duty to care ... you know you are encouraged to visit the sick in hospital ... give to poor people ... even feed poor people ... like its Ramadan now and if you miss a fast you can either make up for it or pay for meals for poor people ... our religion shows it to be very important to be caring and this is how true Muslims are. If I saw anyone who needed my help I would help them because I feel empathy for them but also I am also seeing it as a religious duty and hoping for some blessings from this ... there is a story of a lady who was at a well and she was thirsty she was about to have water when she noticed a cat who was also thirsty ... she got the cat and gave it water first ... she was blessed because of that with heaven ... that is the true Muslim! (Zahra, Muslim).

> We are warned about our responsibilities and caring is taken very very seriously in Islam (Ali, Muslim).

An Indian Hindu participant stated the following:

> Because there is nobody else here who can care for her ... I don't want my kids to leave everything and be a full-time carer. And she's my wife. ...

In our culture husband and wife are part of each other and wife is called 'Ardhangini' (half part of husband's body). ... Today she is in pain and needs to be looked after which means half part of my body needs care and that's why it's my duty as a husband to care for her (Dev, Hindu).

In addition to a discourse of duty, a narrative about the life after death was present in some of the Hindu responses:

I feel really honoured that I am doing a tiny bit of what my religion teaches me. I always make sure that he doesn't feel that we are doing a favour on him by doing all this. ... We are doing it because we want to earn some good marks from our God. Because whatever you do during your life ... good or bad deeds stay with you forever and when I die whether I will get place in heaven or hell ... it will be decided upon my deeds. So he is helping me and all of us to earn some good deeds (Bhav, Hindu).

It is also important to note that within the Indian language of Gujarati, there exists a specific word for caring:

Caring is the same word as 'sewa' which means doing something for somebody without anything in return. ... But honestly I do get tired and I do think it is a duty which I wished I did not have ... it is hard work. But it is my Karma (written) ... (Jia, Hindu).

Care means a kind of Sewa we say in Gujarati. Serving somebody because they are unable to do things on their own. ... Feeding somebody or doing a little chore for somebody is a care according to me ... (Oorja, Hindu).

Based on their narratives, the participants' religion was a dominating factor in why they were providing care. It informed how they understood the term 'informal care' which, in turn, is often not something they associated with the care they were providing to family members. They used their religious beliefs as Muslims and Hindus to provide what we would argue are narratives of care.

Conclusion

Gerontological research that has sought to understand the experience of ageing and later life among minority communities in Britain is developing as our migrant communities are on the verge of 'old age'. The emerging field of ethnogerontology has largely focused on a narrow range of topics such as health inequalities and access to health and social care services and has limited its endeavours to a single minority group. Attempts to examine the heterogeneity within and between minority groups as they age are much rarer. A key area of research is the provision of family-based care by minority communities, with a special focus on the Bangladeshi and Pakistani communities. The emphasis in these projects has been on the role of filial responsibilities for providing care to older people that are seen as central to the culture of these groups.

In our participant narratives we have identified a novel narrative, whereby caring is seen as a religious duty among Muslims and Hindus. Previous studies of caring in minority communities have not, to the best of our knowledge, identified religion as an impetus to care. This raises the question of why religion has emerged in our study but not in previous research on caring. There are several potential explanations. Methodologically speaking, the interviews we conducted were qualitative in nature and were undertaken by interviewers with appropriate language skills, who were predominantly market researchers rather than academic researchers. We may speculate that the nature of the interview encounter, because of the similarity between interviewer and interviewee in terms of status, enabled participants to talk about religion as a shared experience between them. The research encounter is always challenging, and explanations for why religion has not emerged as a narrative for caring may reflect other factors that contextualize this. Participants may provide answers that they think the interviewer wants to hear and may also self-censor their responses because of events within the wider sociopolitical context (the negative media image of Islam, for example). For example, perhaps participants in the early studies of caring and minority groups felt less confident in talking about their religious faith or felt that academic interviewers may not understand the nuances of their narratives.

Also, our interviews were focused on the definition of care and explored in depth *why* participants cared for their dependent relatives. This contrasts with other studies where the emphasis is on the details of caring – how much care is provided, to whom and for how long and with what consequences. Thus, our study enabled participants to talk in more detail about the specific circumstances around care provision. The interviews were based around the relationship to the dependent and the broader contextual drivers to care, thus facilitating the emergence of this religious narrative. This suggests that, potentially, previous studies have not investigated the deeper motives for caring because of a narrow policy focus. In addition, our study was based upon a nationally drawn sample and so did not confine the data collection to specific geographical communities – such as the Bangladeshi population in East London – where they may be specific cultural sub-norms.

Hence, it seems entirely plausible that there are a number of methodological characteristics of our study that enabled the importance of religion as a motivation to care emerge from our data for our Hindu and Muslim participants. However, this raises the question of why this did not emerge in the interviews with our Christian participants. We had study participants who were active Christians, yet none of those mentioned religion when talking about caring. Historically, Christianity has been an important driver for the establishment of hospitals and the provision of nursing and health care, but it did not seem important for our participants. Indeed, previous research looking at caring among the general population has not reported findings where religion has been offered as a reason to care. This may reflect the different nature of the faiths, the potential but unlikely notion that it is a 'taken for granted narrative for caring', or the possibility that no one has asked. Does our data then suggest that religion is now becoming more visible in ageing minority communities? We cannot answer this question on the basis of our small study. However, our findings do suggest that gerontologists may have underplayed the importance of religion in the experience of ageing and later life. There is clearly scope for further research to determine whether the findings of our study have a wider resonance.

Acknowledgements

This study was funded by the Leverhulme Trust and the National Institute for Social Care and Health Research (NISCHR). Professor Vanessa Burholt and Dr Wendy Martin were co-investigators.

15

Religion and transnational Roma mobilization: From local religious participation to transnational social activism in the case of the Finnish Roma

Raluca Bianca Roman

The Roma population of Europe is perhaps one of the most controversial groups in contemporary European societies. News stories, popular books, academic studies and official reports have been written on the apparently 'exotic' character and lifestyle of the Roma, as well as on the issue of cross-country marginalization of Roma communities (Abu Ghosh 2008; Barany 2002; Crowe 2007; Fraser 1995; Gheorghe and Acton 2001; Grill 2011; O'Nions 2007; Sigona and Trehan 2010; van Baar 2011). Presently, some 10 million Roma are thought to be living in the European Union alone, the majority in Eastern European countries.

The more recent presence of East European Roma migrants in Western (and, more recently, Nordic) European cities (such as London, Rome, Paris, Glasgow, Graz, Oslo, Stockholm and Helsinki) has brought a transnational dimension to the issues of both Roma marginalization and Roma mobilization (Benedik 2011; Engebrigtsen 2011; Grill 2011, 2012a, 2012b). What seemed to be an Eastern European 'problem' (i.e. Roma poverty, marginalization and social segregation) has now become a major element of debate not only among academics but also among European politicians and within Europe-wide institutions (O'Nions 2007; Sigona and Trehan 2010; van Baar 2011).

In this context, the rise of Roma mobilization and the possibility of a 'Roma movement' was premised on the undoubtedly marginal position held by Roma communities across Europe. The early Roma activism of the 1970s, a time when the International Romani Union was first established (Acton and Klimova 2001; Klimova-Alexander 2005), highlighted the need for unifying elements of belonging among very diverse Roma groups (Acton and Klimova 2001; Klimova-Alexander 2005; McGarry 2010; Vermeersch 2006) and contributed to a form of cross-country mobilization. Symbols of Roma identity started to be used in the political discourse of the time – symbols often resembling those of a modern nation state: a Roma flag (a carriage wheel on a green and red background), a (controversial) standardization of the Romani language, and a Roma hymn (Barany 2002; Gheorghe and Acton 2001; Klimova-Alexander 2005). The 'kinship' metaphor was used by those stressing cultural similarities, while the 'underclass' metaphor was used by those stressing socio-economic similarities among Roma groups across countries (Barany 2002; Ladányi and Szelényi 2006; Vermeersch, 2006).

The Roma mobilization of recent decades has, however, been a markedly elite affair. Members of grassroots Roma communities often know little about the movement happening at a higher level (Barany 2002; Stewart 1997, 1998), and the voices of the Roma partaking in transnational mobilization have been those of individuals in high-level positions, with access to financial, social and political resources (Barany 2002; McGarry 2010; Vermeersch 2006).

This chapter is therefore concerned with forms and processes of mobilization that reach beyond the elite strata of Roma communities. In recent years, one of the most significant – perhaps *the* most significant – sources of grassroots mobilization among diverse European Roma groups has been involvement in Pentecostal (and Evangelical) Christianity. I look at the ways in which a Pentecostal discourse of conversion and missionary work among the Roma in Finland plays a role in emphasizing the need for a social (and moral) engagement both within and outside the country. In other words, I focus on questions that emerge with the spread of Pentecostal movements among Roma groups: *Does belonging to a Pentecostal Church influence Roma mobilization, across different country contexts and how? What role does Pentecostal religious belonging have in enhancing ethnic solidarity among the Roma, across groups and national contexts? How does the 'kinship' metaphor*

used in the ethnic group discourse apply to the new layer of identity – a
religious identity – for the converted Roma?

The chapter is based on thirteen-month ethnographic research among the
Finnish Kaale (Finnish Roma) and was written while in the field. I lived with
Pentecostal Kaale families in the capital city of Helsinki and in south-eastern
Finland and participated in many family, religious and community events in
the areas where they live. Additionally, during spring 2014, I participated in
one of the regular transnational missionary 'movements' of Kaale believers to
Eastern European countries, by acting as a translator and interpreter during
a missionary trip organized by Finnish Roma Pentecostal believers to poor
Roma villages in Romania. My overview and arguments here are based on
in-depth participant observation, in addition to the collection of life stories,
conversion narratives and interviews with Kaale believers, Kaale pastors, non-
Kaale pastors and Kaale elders in the community. The aim of this chapter at
this stage is to provide an exploratory ethnographic 'picture' of the meaning
of Pentecostal belonging in social mobilization and to raise further theoretical
questions regarding the role of religion in shaping transnational identities for
individuals involved in cross-country missionary movements.

The theoretical conundrum: Personhood among the Roma and the meaning of the Christian self

Religious conversion and Pentecostal belonging for Roma across diverse
national contexts seems to present an apparent paradox for theorizing
Roma 'worldviews'. According to anthropological studies on Roma/Gypsies,
personhood (i.e. the understanding of what it means to be a person) within the
Roma worldview (also known as the *Romanes* or the *Romanipen* in the Romani
language) is inseparable from 'Gypsy-hood' (Gay y Blasco 1999; Okely 1983;
Stewart 1997; Sutherland 1975; Williams 2003). This broadly means that, for
the Roma, being a person is synonymous with being a 'Roma person'. Hence,
those not belonging to the (perceived or constructed) category of Roma would
be regarded as distinct category of beings (Gay y Blasco 1999: 14; Okely 1983:
82), with all the consequences that such a position entails: a Roma/non-Roma
dichotomy, taboos regarding interactions with the *Gadje* (the non-Roma),
rules regarding endogamy and different degrees of social closure and group
exclusivity (Gay y Blasco 1999; Miller 1998; Okely 1983, 1996; Stewart 1997;
Sutherland 1975).

Solidarity in Pentecostal Christianity, on the other hand, is argued to be
based on a common, non-mediated orientation to the divine (Cucchiari 1990;

Engelke 2004; Gifford 2004; Gill 1990; Meyer 1998; Scott 1994) rather than on any forms of ethnic, kin or friendship affiliations. Commitment is to be reinforced through ritualized practices in the religious community, such as memorization of biblical texts (Coleman 2009, 2011; Csordas 2001, 2009), active and bodily engagement within religious services, ritual healing and community prayers (Coleman 2000; Csordas 1990; Harding 1991). Conversion, therefore, arguably represents a major change or discontinuity in the Roma understanding of the 'person' and in the relations believers have with the Roma community (Canton Delgado 2010; Fosztó 2006; Rose Lange 2002; Slavkova 2007; Williams 1987). This, in turn, would arguably have implications for the so far underemphasized (but see Gay y Blasco 2002) perspective that looks at the impact of conversion and belonging on social engagement and at a type of Roma activism that reaches beyond the clearly political (or politicized) avenues of mobilization.

The Finnish Kaale

The Finnish Kaale are a Roma population living in Finland, officially recognized as a traditional minority in the country. The presence of the Kaale community in Finland dates back to the beginning of the sixteenth century, when Finland was still part of Sweden. As the argument goes, the Kaale travelled to present-day Finnish territories from other parts of the Swedish kingdom and settled there (Hernesniemi and Hannikainen 2000; Pulma 2006). Presently, there are approximately 10,000 Kaale living in Finland, with 3,000 more Finnish Kaale living in Sweden.

The Finnish Kaale are nowadays a sedentary population, living mainly in cities in southern Finland (e.g. the Helsinki metropolitan area, Imatra, Tampere), and, unlike many of the Roma communities in Eastern Europe, who speak a variant of Romani language, most Finnish Kaale speak Finnish as their mother tongue. The use of the Romani language among the Kaale has deteriorated greatly over centuries of assimilation attempts by the Finnish state (Granqvist 2006; Hedman 2009). According to scholars in the field, the industrialization and rural–urban migration occurring in Finland since the 1940s led the Kaale to abandon their itinerant lifestyles (Pulma 2006; Thurfjell 2013: 22). Of particular importance was a law, drafted in 1975, concerning the improvement of housing conditions for the Finnish Kaale. The law enabled access to cheap housing, making it possible for the community to buy or rent flats (Grönfors 1997: 308).

These housing policies also meant that only small families could live together in the same area. The consequences of this change are still emphasized by the elder Kaale, who often argue that the close ties of pre-settlement have been lost among the younger generations (Markkanen 2003). The Finnish Kaale continue to practice what are perceived (by the Kaale community and the majority) as age-old customs, purity rituals and community norms that differ from those of contemporary Finnish society: specific dress codes, maintenance of age and gender hierarchies and specific sexual taboos. All these elements have been argued to constitute reasons for distinction and marginalization from mainstream Finnish society (Markkanen 2003; Nordberg 2005).

The Pentecostal movement in Finland

The Pentecostal movement in Finland is closely tied with the global Pentecostal revival (Hokkanen 2007; see Martin 2002) and arrived in Finland in 1908 (Ruohomäki 2014), followed by waves of evangelization and revivalism that succeeded one another up to the present day (Hokkanen 2007). Until the early 2000s, the movement operated as independent congregations registered in the Register of Associations. However, in 2003, the Pentecostal Church of Finland was granted the status of official religious community, sparking some debate among believers about the institutionalization of their faith and making a distinction between the Pentecostal Church and independent Pentecostal congregations who did not want to become affiliated with the now 'official church'. Pentecostalism in Finland remains, however, to the largest extent, a loose, decentralized movement, and only one-fifth of all Pentecostal congregations are members of the Pentecostal Church of Finland (Hokkanen 2007; Kääriäinen et al. 2009: 16). Congregations differ especially in terms of the nature of their services, from the more conservative ones to the more charismatic, with Kaale believers belonging largely to the latter.

Many of the Pentecostal congregations have paid special attention to developing ministry and missionary work among the Roma. The Kaale are actively involved in local Pentecostal congregations, often preaching, singing or organizing events in the churches they belong to. In addition, two of the largest Roma organizations in the country, Romano Missio and Life and Light (*Elämä ja Valo*), are closely connected to the Pentecostal movement, with most of its members being devoted members of Pentecostal congregations. The churches my informants belong to are multiethnic Pentecostal congregations, often catering for a variety of groups, including new immigrant groups, such as members from the Philippines, Pakistan, Kenya, Sudan and Spain.

The ethnographic context: Belonging and identity among Pentecostal Kaale

One of the most striking elements in my fieldwork has been the major importance placed by my traditional Finnish Kaale host and her family (as well as many of my other Finnish Kaale acquaintances) on behaving with shame (*häpeä*) and respect (*kunnioitus*) in all circumstances. Shame and respect, I was told, are central in the culture of the Kaale and in the making of Kaale personhood. Shame, in particular, is not only a feeling expressed by Finnish Kaale but a practice, to a large extent. For the Kaale, showing shame (*hävetä*), in different ways and contexts, is a form of respecting (*kunnioittaa*) the community elders and, by it, the community traditions. Younger women must, therefore, be ashamed (*täytyy hävetä*) in front of elder women and reveal little (or nothing) about their personal or intimate lives, not even to their mothers. For women, especially, shame is central in showing their adherence to community customs. The entire period of pregnancy, for instance, is often conveyed under secrecy, and marriage (or 'getting a man') is a period during which the newlywed women must show this 'shame' in front of elder Kaale women. 'Being ashamed' (*hävetä*) is often a practice done by avoiding the gaze of one's elders and retreating to a separate room in larger gatherings. Shame, and avoiding those in front of whom one must show shame, often go hand in hand. The younger and the elder Kaale are thus separated by rules and customs throughout different life events (marriage and birth being the two central ones).

Conversion complements and enhances the need to be a virtuous human being for the Kaale, one who behaves with honour, respect and the very 'shame' that is required within the community itself. Such customs are by no means contradicted by either the religious worldview of Pentecostalism or by the pastors of Pentecostal congregations, who often argue that the moral bases of some Kaale customs are to be respected (!) in their entirety. Moreover, although conversions occur 'individually' – it is a personal path that each individual needs to choose in his or her own terms – there is no doubt that conversion is believed to be of significant importance for the Kaale society as a whole. This is an opinion often expressed not only by individual Kaale believers discussing their own conversions but also by non-Kaale pastors and members of the religious communities the Kaale belong to. More often than not, my informants would emphasize the ways in which being 'in faith' (*uskossa*) changes one's life in its entirety and becomes a bridge between the Kaale and the non-Kaale (i.e. the mainstream population), be it in the church context or outside it:

You become a different person. Your old life is forgotten. When the Holy Spirit talks to you, and when you listen to it, really listen, it all becomes clear. It all becomes easy. Giving up drugs, anger, alcohol, all those things that seemed impossible become possible. God makes that possible. The Holy Spirit gives you strength, speaks to you, speaks through you and makes you see the right path. It is what happens to most Kaale who come into faith. Everyone sees it. The hatred they have for the Kaaje (the non-Roma), the anger, the confusion, they all go away. It is not difficult, as long as you accept what God has in store for you (K, male Kaale believer, Helsinki).

At the same time, tradition still holds a central role among the Finnish Kaale. Tradition shows and highlights an individual's commitment and identity as Kaale. Belonging to Pentecostal movements does not necessarily change the shape of this 'tradition'. Some elements are selectively maintained, while others are abandoned. Traditional notions of virtuosity are nevertheless retained: a respectable Kaale is one who is devoted to self-control in the diverse manifestations of respect to members of the community. One's dress style, one's honouring of the elders, one's control of the body through notions of purity, avoidance of pollution and enhancement of tradition all reflect this image of virtue (cf. Throop 2009).

Pentecostal congregations and Kaale believers

The commitment, interest and work of Pentecostal pastors, missionaries and preachers among the Kaale have become elements in developing the attachment of the Roma community to Pentecostal congregations within the country. Although the work has a historical legacy to it (see Ruohomäki 2014; Tervonen 2010; Thurfjell 2013), nowadays Pentecostal congregations function in their role among Kaale by means of organizing regular 'Romani Days' across Finland. The aim of these large-scale events is to attract non-believer Kaale, often being initiated by local non-Kaale pastors or missionaries within the congregations themselves. Although song worship, believers' testimonies and preaching play a central role in these events, an unwritten rule is also to provide food and organize a feast where believers and their kin can get together between services. Breaking bread, talking about the news in their communities and discussing upcoming events in the churches all play a part in making the 'Romani Days' not only a religious gathering, but a social happening as well. It becomes a site where Kaale (closer or more distant) kin can meet, greet and worship at the same time.

A type of activity organized at the initiation of Kaale believers, and one that reaches out to non-believing Kaale kin, is the family Bible study camp. The camps are usually set up in large summer cottage areas around the Finnish countryside. Here, Kaale parents and Kaale children alike study the Bible under the guidance of Kaale evangelizers and discuss issues regarding the Kaale community from a biblical perspective. Emphasizing the need for education as a means to a better understanding of the Bible, and a closer connection to the written word, has become one of the central works of Christian Kaale organizations, such as Life and Light (*Elämä ja Valo*), who apply this approach in missionary countries as well. Moreover, in congregations with a significant Kaale membership, discussion about the role of the church in promoting the social inclusion of Kaale members by means of education is often one of the key concerns.

'Balkan' work: Kaale missionary work and transnational Roma mobilization

During my fieldwork, I was once again reminded of the fact that although conversion is a significant event in a person's life trajectory and identity construction, the effects of such a conversion almost always 'spill over' to the broader community (both Kaale and non-Kaale), particularly in the form of missionary work both within and outside Finland. The Kaale are often the most active participants in Pentecostal Sunday services, and 'speaking in tongues' is central in their external manifestation of Pentecostal belonging: speaking in tongues occurs not only within a church or religious context but in the most mundane of activities (while cleaning the house, driving the car, cooking or doing the laundry). It is a way of being in a constant communion with the Holy Spirit, and a way of feeling His presence in their everyday life. It is a language unknown even to those who speak it, the language of the Holy Spirit.

Speaking in tongues and participation in religious ceremonies are rarely, however, the sole markers of belonging. Through the activities organized within their local churches, and often after embracing the messages received from the Holy Spirit (in the form of dreams or prophecy), many Kaale believers become involved in local missionary work among other non-believer Kaale within and outside the country. My informants repeatedly argued that the process of conversion brings about not only a certainty of their individual salvation (acquired through the love of Jesus Christ) but also a sense of responsibility and duty to promote the word of God to non-believers. Missionary work (*lähetystyö*) becomes an important and essential external expression of God's presence in their lives. Moreover, while most of my informants considered missionary work (especially among Kaale non-believers) as the central aspect of reaching out to the world, they also saw social action as a necessary corollary to it.

Pentecostal belonging among disenfranchized communities has been argued to foster social mobility in diverse ways. This has particularly been the case of African Pentecostalism (Gifford 2004; Llera Blanes 2007; Meyer 1995, 1998), but similar cases among Roma communities in Europe have been noted (Canton Delgado 2010; Fosztó 2009; Ries 2011; Rose Lange 2002). Similarly, Pentecostal religious belonging among the Kaale appears to foster a sense of social engagement. Part of this takes form as social work within the Kaale community, part as engagement with social problems in the broader Finnish society and part – a growing trend – as missionary and social work abroad, among Roma communities in Eastern and south-eastern Europe.

In practice, transnational engagement takes many forms: it is organized by Pentecostal congregations, by Finnish Kaale organizations and by individual believers. The 'target' countries are selected based on contacts with local believers or pastors and according to perceived needs – material and spiritual alike – in the area. Missionaries work in small Roma villages or segregated Roma neighbourhoods. In the initial phase, the missionary trips last for a couple of weeks, in forms of outreach projects. At this point the main task of the missionary workers is to distribute clothing and resources. Later, regular religious services are organized in the local communities, and the trip is infused with religious meaning: evening prayers, special events and Bible schools are established with the support of local members. In some cases, the initial trips have led to the establishment of permanent links between the 'target' communities and the churches to which individual missionary workers belong. Provision of religious and social services is supervised by the appointment of 'local mediators', people with knowledge of the country context and who are perceived as leaders of local Roma communities.

As mentioned above, 'ethnic kinship' plays a role in the articulated motivations for missionary work. At the same time, encounters with Roma outside the national community may, at times, challenge ideas about ethnicity as the sole and central element of unity and similarity among missionaries and missionized. Massive disparity in living conditions and the social position of Roma in different national contexts is the obvious measure of difference, but perceptions of differences in tradition arise as well.

> You see them running around, showing their chest. That surprised me so much. This is not done among the Kaale. It would be completely inappropriate. But they (Romanian Roma) are so poor that they do not understand. It is like running on what you have and making use of what they have, their body. Their poverty goes deep and they do not know the full extent of their actions. But we can only pray that God will show them

the way. We are different, but we are brothers and sisters, in Christ first of all. And we are all Roma brothers and sisters second of all. We feel it every time we meet, when we get together, when we sing together. You feel it in your heart. A Roma is a Roma, no matter what kind of different social condition we have (H, Kaale man, Nokia).

During missionary trips, a marked element of distinction between communities is also the obligation of Kaale missionaries to abide by Kaale rules of cleanliness and purity in contexts in which these may differ to those of 'indigenous' Roma communities. As the rules of Kaale society go, elder Kaale cannot sleep in the same room with younger Kaale. Under conditions in which sleeping arrangements in the 'missionizing' countries make it harder to abide by such distinctions, local social conditions make it difficult for the maintenance of learnt traditional norms. Moreover, the poverty of the segregated Roma neighbourhoods in Eastern Europe and the behaviour of some Eastern European Roma women, in particular, who often breastfed their children and showed their chests in public, surprised Kaale believers. Showing any part of one's skin (in public or among elders) is considered a sign of disrespect and negligence of community rules, as pointed out by one missionary in the quote above. Local Roma behaviour was argued to be a consequence of the misery and poverty in which they live and from which only faith and God can help them emerge.

Despite observed differences, however, the unity between Kaale missionaries and Roma missionized were sought and emphasized during religious sermons and church events, recurrently referring to each other as 'God's Romani people' and 'brothers and sisters in Christ'. Finding and arguing for a sense of a doubly common 'belonging' (both Christian and Roma) was key in establishing rapport and relations between Kaale missionaries and local Roma communities in Eastern Europe and also key in strengthening the argument of Christian love and Christian Evangelism among brothers (and sisters) living outside Finland.

We (Kaale) all have a place to sleep, food to eat. Many of us have jobs. There it is devastating. They cannot even clean themselves, they cannot read, they have no roof over their heads, no electricity. I only heard these kinds of stories in Finland from my grandparents. But I never saw anything like that myself, not until I went to Ukraine. You learn how small things like that matter, and how lucky we are for having what we have here. So we must help, because we are in the position to help. And because, after all is said, we are Roma, they are our brothers and sisters and they need our help. I become more aware of this every time I go to a different country with my work (E, Kaale missionary worker, Helsinki).

In many ways, transnational social action has an impact not only on the receiving communities (for the Roma being helped/'missionized'), but also on the communities sending missionaries abroad (the Kaale), through the re-evaluation of one's belonging to a common society, based both on Christian identity and 'Roma kinship'. It could, in this sense, provide an alternative means for a form of transnational Roma mobilization, where the elements of common belonging are created not only via an exclusively 'ethnic discourse' but also through a religious discourse of missionary work incorporated in the everyday life of the Kaale believers.

God's work: From the local to the transnational

The meaning of religious missionizing among the Kaale appears to be not only individually but also community oriented: it is an individual drive to participate, but the missionary work is almost always conducted in Roma communities abroad, rather than poor communities more broadly. What the Pentecostal movement in Finland provides for the Kaale is the possibility for action, both spiritually and emotionally, giving them an 'alternative' voice and an alternative means of social engagement: a religiously based platform, fostering and grounded in social action.

The engagement is both national (among the Kaale non-believers) and transnational (through work among Roma communities outside of Finland), in both scale and action. Moreover, it is historically grounded in the religious revivalism among Kaale and non-Kaale in Finland, currently involving the collaboration of local churches, Pentecostal organizations, Kaale organizations and individual believers in a network of relations that seem to bridge not only the majority population (the Finnish members of the churches with whom Kaale engage) but also members of the Finnish Roma (Kaale) community to members of Roma communities outside of Finland.

Missionary work abroad, conducted by Roma for the Roma (rather than by non-Roma missionaries among impoverished Roma communities) thus brings about and highlights different types of understanding of the meaning of social integration, social activism and religious engagement among what are considered 'marginal' communities in Europe. Being an 'elective' activity, religious missionary work provides a space for Kaale believers to feel engaged in social work, in community involvement and in the establishment of relations with Roma communities abroad. In the long term, it might mean changing the very meaning of Roma/Kaale identity, through interaction with individuals and communities in a transnational context.

Acknowledgements

This chapter would not have been written without the moral support of Alex Archer, Paloma Gay y Blasco, Kimmo Granqvist, Titus Hjelm, Airi Markkanen, Aino Saarinen as well as the institutional support of Aleksanteri Insitute. My gratitude, love and friendship go to the Kaale families that have taken me in, taught me about life, and accepted me with all my faults.

16

Finding God in the process: Recovery from addiction in Sarajevo

Eleanor Ryan-Saha

Tito's Sarajevo is variously remembered as a 'European Jerusalem' and the apotheosis of the atheist, socialist dream that was Yugoslavia. Many people in Sarajevo, without fuss or ontological bother, manage to embrace both visions of their recent past as equally true. In so doing, they demonstrate a modus operandi that in this chapter will be referred to and examined as *capricious simultaneity*.

The shifting frontiers between public and private religious life in the former Yugoslav region during the late twentieth century were contemporaneous with and, indeed, implicated in a global intellectual re-assessment of the role of religion in the public world (Perica 2002: VII). The rise of ethno-religious nationalism that preceded and precipitated Yugoslavia's dismantlement served as an example with which many commentators furnished their points about the resurgence of religion in previously secular spaces. Numbering among such commentators, José Casanova drew two lessons from the changing position and role of religion from the 1980s onwards. The first, that in spite of Enlightenment predictions, religion was in no danger of disappearing. The second, that religion's public role would likely continue to be vital to 'the ongoing construction of the modern world' (Casanova 1994: 6).

Posing a critical complication to secularization and desecularization theories, this chapter will reconsider the ways in which public life in Sarajevo is inconsistently and unpredictably constructed as secular and religious. The new visibility of religion in contemporary Sarajevo will be explored through ethnographic data amassed during long-term fieldwork with people involved in addiction treatment. Taking Sarajevo's public addiction treatment milieu as an optic, this chapter will unpick the co-constituting and competing manifestations of religion and the secular in post-addiction recovery processes. It is an attempt to explain, without explaining away, the religious and secular aspects of these processes in terms of capricious simultaneity and, in so doing, to attain insight into post-siege public life in Sarajevo.

Secular, but to what extent?

Gaining a handle on the strength and success of secularization projects in pre-war Sarajevo is no small task, in part due to the very capricious simultaneity under discussion. In recollection, where one informant would reminisce about the religious pervasiveness and multifaith permissiveness of the socialist era with an anecdote about a Serb friend preparing them an Iftar meal, the other would stress the atheist aspects of their 'typical' family and 'normal' childhood. Outside of my informants' impressions, the extent to which the Yugoslav leadership pursued the secularization of public life – often an aim taken as given in state socialism – is hard to pin down. As Talal Asad has emphatically demonstrated, 'the secular', 'secularism' and 'secularization' as constructs must be genealogically situated within the history of West European thought. Taking, as Asad does, the secular to be 'neither singular in origin nor stable in its historical identity' (Asad 2003: 24), the secularization of public life will nonetheless, for the purposes of this discussion, be defined according to the typological instincts of another great theorist of the secular, Charles Taylor. It is 'a move from a society where belief in God is unchallenged and indeed, unproblematic, to one in which it is understood to be one option among others, and frequently not the easiest to embrace' (Taylor 2007: 3).

Much has been made of the principle of 'brotherhood and unity' in scholarship concerned with the dissolution of Yugoslavia, the rise of ethno-religious nationalism in the region and the wars of the 1990s. Ideologically, 'brotherhood and unity' was the lynch-pin of the secular Yugoslav nationalism championed by the party leadership as a salve for, or indeed silencer of, the traumas of the Second World War. One particularly problematic manifestation of this war in the Yugoslav region had been the series of interethnic atrocities perpetrated and suffered by communities who were subsequently expected to embrace each other within one state (Perica 2002: 100). Perica convincingly argues that 'brotherhood and unity' should be considered a civil religion in Bellah's sense of the term. As such, 'brotherhood and unity' was the multi-faceted 'keystone of the new Yugoslav nationalism' (Perica 2002: 94–5) and consisted of tales of Partisan victories and the nation's origin in the Second World War; the rebirth of the nation after Tito's 1948 split from Stalin; the unity of all ethnic groups within Yugoslavia; the cult of Tito; the Yugoslav model of self-managed socialism and the foreign policy of non-alignment; and patriotic support for the Yugoslav national teams (Perica 2002: 95).

If 'brotherhood and unity', with its simultaneously secular, mythical and ritual aspects, may be considered a civil religion, the question remaining is whether this civil religion was 'easiest to embrace' (Taylor 2007: 3); that is, whether and to what extent religious observance was discouraged or supressed under Yugoslav socialism. This may be fruitfully explored through the revelatory and well-documented case of the Muslims of Bosnia-Herzegovina. Islam, it seems, was regarded as a divisive threat insofar as Bosnian Muslims experienced themselves as 'different' from their Serb and Croat compatriots (Bringa 1995: 197). Strict adherence, therefore, was simply incompatible with personal advancement, since party membership, a prerequisite for such advancement, was denied to practicing Muslims (Bringa 1995: 204–5). The regulation of Islam in the Yugoslav socialist period was achieved through the state control of the *Islamska zajednica*[1] (Islamic community). In her seminal ethnography, Bringa explained the restraint and accommodating outlook she encountered among *Islamska zajednica* sponsored *hodžas* (imams) as inevitable given that 'they owed their positions to their cautious attitude and/or communist sympathies in the restrictive postwar years' (Bringa 1995: 199).

Islam was tolerated only under the state's aegis and, further, was regularly manipulated in order to serve state purposes. While Banac explains the revival of Islam in late Communism as the winning-out of 'the deep religiousness of a great majority of Muslims' (Banac 1994: 328), I suggest instead it was with foreign policy in mind that from the 1970s Yugoslav Muslims were favoured materially, given certain freedoms and conferred with a certain prestige. As Freidman has explained, 'Because Tito needed to form friendships in the Middle East and other Muslim-dominated areas to succeed in his policy of non-alignment, Bosnian Muslims were courted by Tito and his colleagues' (Freidman 1996: 167). In domestic policy, by granting the distinct nationhood of Muslims through the category of 'Muslim, in the sense of a nation', as introduced in the 1971 census (Malcolm 1994: 198), the state made a bid to undermine the religious component of this identity, and thus to co-opt the contemporaneous pan-Islamic sentiment and activism, and to further secularize Yugoslav society.

Ultimately, it is the lived reality of secularism that is of concern here. Various surveys shed light on this topic, foremost among these being the work of sociologist of religion Srđan Vrcan. Although only comprising a small minority of the population in census terms,[2] those identifying as 'Yugoslav' by nationality were the subject of one of Vrcan's investigations. Vrcan's data show that the overwhelming majority of these Yugoslavs declared themselves to be without religious affiliation (Vrcan 1986). For those who embraced the Yugoslav political system to the fullest by aligning their nationality with it, it seems that secularism, not religion, was the 'easiest to embrace.'

A revival era?

Vrcan's sociological work stretches into the post-Tito period of dismantlement and beyond. As such, he was able to carefully chart the rise of ethno-religious nationalism as a political force and to note the concurrent desecularization of the public sphere and the revitalization of religion as a political force in the region (Vrcan 2006). His observations speak volumes to the vastly increased prominence of religion in Sarajevo's public sphere in the post-Tito period. Yet, this increased prominence is certainly not a religious revival. In his vital discussion of religion in post-Soviet space, Pelkmans challenges 'the problematic notion that religious life after socialism can be characterized as a *revival* of repressed religious traditions' (Pelkmans 2009: 2). Ethnographic accounts of pre-war and wartime religiosity in Sarajevo serve accordingly to challenge this problematic revival narrative. Sorabji's description of the *mevlud*[3] landscape of the early 1990s illuminates exactly the processes underway following Tito's death when she notes that in 1990, two types of new women entered the scene (Sorabji 1994: 116):

> Firstly, there were women with less religious knowledge or experience than the typical *mevlud*-goer, women whose enthusiasm was stimulated by a political context in which the disapproval of atheist authorities was no longer relevant, in which religious expression seemed to be an expression of the changing times and of the new freedoms which western-style democracy would bring, and in which the assertion of religious/national identity appeared more vital than before. Secondly, there were young women and young *bulas* (or *mu'alimas*, the Arabic term with which the Zajednica wanted to replace *bula* and which many of the young preferred) with a less traditional and more radical vision of Islam than their elders.

Sorabji's account may be fruitfully read against Maček's ethnography of life under siege in Sarajevo. Maček spent time with doctors and other elite members of society and concluded that the source of their discomfort in terms of religion's re-entry into the public sphere was overwhelmingly the disjuncture between the private religiosity that was familiar to them and the concurrent politicization of religiosity as it entered and began to dominate the public realm. Maček writes that it was the 'April Muslims' – 'those who had become vocal and dedicated Muslims only after the beginning of the war in April 1992' (Maček 2007: 46) – who were regarded critically by her more secularized friends and informants. Religion was not 'new'; indeed, far from it. Rather, Maček observes that 'people were used to Islam's presence in their surroundings and had always respected religious Muslims, their beliefs and customs, as any other religious people. What caused the uncertainty was the growing importance (and power) of Islam in public space, which had been completely secularized before the war' (Maček 2007: 45).

Maček focuses upon the army, education and the media as principal sectors of public life that were secular before the war and were transformed by religion during it. Accounts abound of novel public displays of religiosity in Sarajevo during the war, with the dominance of Islam in these public displays mirroring the changing ethno-religious make-up of the city, from diversity and even ethnic ambivalence to an emphatically Muslim majority (Bougarel et al. 2007).[4] From changing street names and public greetings, to army uniforms and religiously motivated modes of dress, the politically charged public visibility of religion in Sarajevo, and especially Islam, increased throughout the siege and into the post-siege period (Bougarel 2007). Bougarel presents an emphatic example of this trend in his discussion of the new cult of šehidi (war martyrs). Unpicking the case of a father who wrote to the president in protest against his atheist son's posthumous valorization by the state as šehid, Bougarel takes the cult of šehidi as indicative of the top-down authoritarian methods through which religious and political leaders 'strove to impose their own conception of Islam and definition of Muslim national identity upon a largely secular population' (Bougarel 2007: 170).

The furore over Dani's[5] 'East and West Kiss' advertising campaign further underscores this point (Helms 2008). The ad pictured a scantily clad woman with a Santa hat kissing a woman in hijab and, as Helms describes, 'was created by this anti-nationalist, secular magazine in response to calls by Muslim religious nationalists to suppress the widely popular New Year celebration and its well-known symbol, Deda Mraz (Grandfather Frost) as un-Islamic' (Helms 2008: 88). The split in attendant public debate between secular-oriented Bosnians who enjoyed the ad for its humour, and the powerful religious elements of Bosnian political life as represented by the Bošnjak political party Stranka demokratske akcije, or SDA, whose leaders 'pressured the advertising company that had hung the posters to cancel Dani's contract, effectively removing their ads from public space' (Helms

2008: 97) speaks volumes to the dominant, if contested, position of religion in Sarajevo's contemporary public sphere. As such, it becomes clear that the new role and relevance of Islam and, indeed, other religions in Sarajevo's public sphere is more than simply a matter of 'revival'. Rather, it is more apt to speak in terms of a new departure typified by the appropriation of religion to serve personal and political ends, and the concurrent, contested and politicized desecularization of the public sphere.

Addiction and religion go public, together

From *Dani*'s 'East and West Kiss' in 1999 to 2012, and a small billboard on the side of a busy road, the main clogged artery into the heart of Sarajevo; as a favour, the owner of this advertising space has lent it out free of charge to a local non-governmental organization (NGO). Using money donated by an Evangelical pastor in the United States, this NGO has printed and is displaying a poster that urges its reader to 'Defeat Addiction' (*Pobjedite ovisnost*). 'Recovery is a Reality' (*Oporavak je realnost*), the billboard announces to motorists and tram passengers alike as they rumble along the road. Call our number and find out for yourself, it invites.

The scale, or even existence, of drug addiction in Sarajevo before the siege is hard to definitively pin down. Alone, Savelli's (2012) careful scholarship on the alcoholism 'epidemic' of the Communist era stands out, insofar as it renders a clear picture of one important facet of drug dependence that had a lasting effect on the development of psychiatric disciplines in the region (Savelli 2012). Savelli credits alcoholism, and the epidemiological study thereof, with shaping Yugoslav psychiatry along a social psychiatry model (Savelli 2012: 10). Referencing the rampant proliferation of journal articles on the topic of alcoholism, particularly from the 1960s through to the 1980s, Savelli notes that 'the threat that alcoholism posed to two of the country's ideological planks – namely citizens' right to health and the centrality of work to man's psychological development – ensured political support for tackling the disease' (Savelli 2012: 2).

Prominent contemporary Bosnian psychiatrists paint a grim and more often than not implicitly, and at times explicitly, moralizing picture of the causes of escalating drug addiction in Sarajevo and throughout the region. Their arguments may be distilled into two interrelated factors, namely war trauma and Western influence. In a highly revealing post-siege edited volume on the topic entitled *Drug Addiction* (*Ovisnost o drogama*), Hasanović cites the social and attendant psychological upheavals and traumas of the war in Bosnia as an explanatory factor for an attendant escalation of problem drug use (Hasanović

2001: 168). Hasanović further credits the coming of an 'explosion in the proliferation of various forms of psychoactive substance abuse'[6] during the aggression as being 'a direct consequence of open communication with "the West"'.[7] He goes on to accuse United Nations Protection Force employees and, indeed, employees of other international organizations of having 'literally infected'[8] the people of Bosnia with drug use (Hasanović 2001: 169).

Bosnia and, indeed, the Balkans have long been rhetorically portrayed by foreign and domestic commentators as a 'bridge' between East and West (Todorova 1997). To a certain extent, preoccupation with 'Western' influence and its role in shaping Bosnian society, such as Hasanović displays, is therefore a typical preoccupation, if not a defining feature of social analysis and criticism in Tito's Sarajevo and beyond into the contemporary moment (Hasanović 2001; Helms 2008). In rather more morally neutral terms, Vučetić expresses the 'Coca-Cola socialism' of Yugoslavia through the two-faced Roman mythological figure of Janus (Vučetić 2012: 401). As such, she describes Yugoslavia as having 'one face looking to the East, the other to the West; one face to foreign politics, the other to domestic politics; one face to Hollywood, the other to Black Wave cinema'[9] (Vučetić 2012: 401–2). However, whereas once it was the strength of the socialist man and Communist republic that was at stake in matters of drugs and Western influence (Vučetić 2012; Savelli 2012), Sarajevo's newly desecularized public sphere allows commentators to reframe theories about addiction in religious terms. Thus, it is incredibly telling that *Drug Addiction*, edited by distinguished Tuzla University psychiatrist Osman Sinanović, comprises seventeen chapters, seven of which touch directly on the topic of religion – specifically Islam – and addiction, with opening words provided by none other than Bosnia's *Reis-ul-Ulema* (Grand Mufti) Dr Mustafa Cerić.

Religion certainly plays an important role in framing the moralizing discursive public understanding of addiction. Yet beyond its public reception, what features have come to define the post-siege addiction crisis? During the course of my fieldwork, I spent one fascinating evening at my friend's kitchen table, pen in hand, transforming his recollections of pre-war life in Sarajevo into an ever more complex and entangled web of connections between different intoxicating substances, different genres of music, different dress styles and different youth subcultural groups. Did the punks do acid? No, that was the goths. Or was it the technos? Either way, there were plenty of drugs in Yugoslavia. By contrast, the vast majority of people involved personally and professionally in Sarajevo's drug treatment milieu understood and communicated the historical development of drug addiction in terms that tightly mirrored Hasanović's 'war trauma and Western influence' schematic. Addiction for them is a 'new' problem and represents, or embodies, a violent rupture with pre-war social life as far as the bulk of my informants are concerned: 'There were no drugs in Sarajevo before the war, it is something entirely new for us', or 'There were addicts before the war but they were a minority in prison. After the war heroin entered Sarajevo, and we lost our youth to it'.

Furthermore, addiction was overwhelmingly presented as a moral problem, rather than an amoral disease, by many of my friends and informants. Interestingly, these comments were framed through a language of morality that manifests in multiple aspects of daily life in Sarajevo as concern about 'values' (vrijednosti). Sitting with a group of female social workers one day, our talk turned to the videoed and highly publicized recent fight between two high school-age girls in Tuzla. 'Since the war no one is vrijedan', one woman lamented. Another friend and former addict explained it this way, 'In Sarajevo the whole nation has lost its sense of identity, in Sarajevo it is not one person that is the problem, the problem is the nation. We were brought up in the spirit of Communism, brought up to know that we are all one people, brought up according to brotherhood and unity.' The subject position of being a person of value or a worthy person (vrijedan čovjek) and concern about the lack of such people, along with the death of community spirit, is a well-worn trope in Sarajevo. Moral panic over a new valueless generation ties in with a great range of dissatisfactions that people in Sarajevo link to the post-siege changes in their city – from rampant corruption in politics and the incorporation of displaced and refugee 'uncultured villagers' (nekulturni seljaci/papci) who despoil the urban space, to the disintegration of 'traditional' family and neighbourhood structures and the new generation's spurning of customs and culture (Stefansson 2007). In addiction terms, young people, especially, are understood to be lacking in sources of values and examples of people of value as a result of war trauma, Western influence and – or, to say the same thing – Sarajevo's changing sociopolitical landscape. Substance misuse is overwhelmingly encountered by my informants as a direct and logical consequence of this valueless era.

Finally, posing a sharp departure from the specialized and professionalized field of alcoholism treatment and study in Tito's Yugoslavia (Savelli 2012), addiction has become a public problem. Since the early 2000s, when the first wave of post-treatment former addicts and state-sponsored care workers began to make moves towards developing specialized treatment provisions in Sarajevo, the visibility of addiction – in both the 'on the street' and public media discursive sense – has rapidly escalated. That is not to say that addicts and their families are publicly open about their predicament. Stigma, drugs and concern about malicious gossip and keeping up appearances within the mahala (neighbourhood) were frequently communicated to me through the almost-parable of a Bosnian woman who watched her son sell everything in the house for drug money, while still publicly maintaining the pretence of a happy home. Rather, as a phenomenon that is increasingly divorced from the particular and elevated to the politicized realm of the general, addiction has both a public life and a place in public debate. In this respect, religion and addiction are one and, indeed, share key similarities in their features as they manifest in Sarajevo's post-siege public sphere – they are 'new,' they carry moral baggage and they are public issues. We must therefore speak not of a revival of addiction or of religion, nor necessarily in terms of intensification of the drugs problem or of religious conviction, but of a transformation of both, in and through their new public omnipresence.

Finding God in the process

'Do you believe in God?' Anita, behind her computer, has her smile and attention trained on me at mine. It is my second week as an administrative assistant at this recovery NGO, and, as is often the case, Anita and I are alone in the office with our chat and our work and a suspect-smelling gas heater. Oporavak is an NGO that focuses on what it terms the 're-socialization' (*resocijalizacija*) aspect of the recovery process, and Anita is a key figure within this organization. Oporavak's bread-and-butter work is its weekly evening meetings, in which people who have, by and large, spent a considerable amount of time in rehab centres and who self-designate as 'recovered' meet to discuss their feelings and opinions in a loosely structured way. Further to this, the NGO tries to encourage people struggling with addiction to enter rehab programmes and pursues a variety of other related projects as and when funding permits. Crucially, Oporavak is Evangelical Christian in its fundamental aspects: its membership, its funding and its affiliations.

'Do you believe in God?' asks Elvir. We have just driven together up the winding road into the mountains – breath-taking in their autumnal blaze of colour – to the rehab centre where he is a middle manager and where I teach English. Zajednica is a state rehabilitation facility that comprises a population that, during my fieldwork, fluctuated between fifteen and twenty male 'clients' (*klijenti*) and about seventy members of staff. Zajednica is a 'typical' rehab centre in many senses: the treatment on offer is long term and residential, the staff includes social workers and psychiatrists and the centre has an established ethos and programme. Importantly, as a state facility it does not officially espouse one religion or favour one ethno-religious group over another in its treatment philosophy or in its practice. However, neatly reflecting the Sarajevo cantonal ethno-religious make-up, the clients and staff at Zajednica overwhelmingly identify as Bošnjak, or Muslim, or both.

In the first few months of my fieldwork, two 'discoveries' stood out. The first, that God and religion would present themselves as topics of conversation almost every day. The second, that unlike the disease model of addiction, which was more than familiar to me – a model that renders addiction as a chronic, relapsing condition – in Sarajevo, total recovery was a widely accepted reality. Anita, speaking both as a recovered addict and as a professional, would emphasize time and again that 'recovery is possible'. 'Recovery sets you free from addiction', she explained, 'so that you are no longer a slave'. In the same breath she would explain her recovery in religious terms: 'God saved me', she would say, or 'I found God and I converted'.

Perhaps unsurprisingly, it soon became clear that these 'discoveries' were interlinked. Full recovery as a rhetorical concept and ontological state is not exclusive to drug addiction in this context, as for instance Shohet demonstrates when she distinguishes between 'full recovery' and 'struggling to recover' narratives in anorexia (Shohet 2007). Crucially, Shohet locates recovery at the nexus between the individual and the social and defines it as 'neither fully determined by and situated in the personal psychology of any particular sufferer nor transcendent of that sufferer and her particular conceptions and relations' (Shohet 2007: 346). It is this tension between the individual addict's inner state and his or her outer social embeddedness that Ringwald touches upon when he notes that in addiction treatment 'society intervenes to change the person in a way much like the way medieval European society dealt with sinners. Only repentance and redemption will do. He or she must act differently as an outward sign of inner change' (Ringwald 2002: 24).

Newfound religiosity or conversion is just such an outward sign of inner change. As Ringwald explains, God, mind and chemistry are most often credited with the power to treat addiction (Ringwald 2002: 135). In this sense it is certainly not unusual for recovery and religion to be equated. Ringwald underscores this point when he notes that, in the American context, 'without a personal transformation, usually spiritual in nature, little happens over the long term. So in an odd way, we have this huge public policy apparatus aimed at effecting an internal change in the alcoholic' (Ringwald 2002: 24). As such, when conversion or newfound religiosity was cited by my informants in their accounts of their own recovery – as was often the case – religion in post-siege Sarajevo was in evidence once again, not as a revival movement but as a new departure: as Pelkmans notes of conversion after socialism, '[R]eligion served new needs and was linked to new imaginaries' (Pelkmans 2009: 2). Conversion in Sarajevo speaks to the debate on secularity and modernity insofar as it lends strength to the insights of Austin-Broos, who argues 'the view that the rise of the modern state with its bureaucratic modes would supersede religion has proven mistaken. New departures and confrontations involving the world's religions mean that the dynamics that draw people to one religion or away from another intrigue us as never before' (Austin-Broos 2003: 1).

In the Evangelical Christian case this is particularly clear, since in Sarajevo this is a markedly novel religious presence linked to new social and religious imaginaries.[10] Further, Evangelical Christianity has long been associated with addiction treatment through the promise of rebirth and a subsequent rupture from the damning chronicity of addiction (Garcia 2010) and, as such, serves the relatively new or at least arguably intensified desire of Sarajevo's addicted population to become recovered. Importantly, the same explosion of international presence in Sarajevo during and subsequent to the siege is rhetorically associated with the spread of addiction (Hasanović 2001) and with the rise of Evangelical Christianity in the city. At the heart of both phenomena is the thorny issue of globalization, which has been credited as both the conduit for Evangelical Christianity's dissemination outside the United States and, simultaneously, a major source of contemporary existential insecurity that leads people towards Evangelical faith (Micklethwait and Wooldridge 2009: 242; Pelkmans 2009: 2).

Pelkmans observes that in the post-Soviet context 'the "new" religious movements balance and prosper on the junction between forces of globalization and localization. They are embedded in wider transnational networks yet vigorously adjust religious messages to local concerns and translate them into a locally contextualized vocabulary' (Pelkmans 2009: 9–10). His insights clearly apply to evangelicalism. However, if we consider Islam's public presence in Sarajevo as a new departure rather than a revival, it becomes clear that Islam – though not strictly 'new' – prospers on this same junction in the post-siege era. Substituting the contentious term 'globalization' for 'internationalization', it can be said that while practicing Muslims in Bosnia had previously been internationalized through their connections with the global ummah, the ummah presented itself on their doorsteps during and after the war, transforming in many respects the nature of Islam in Sarajevo (Maček 2007). In the post-siege rebuilding of mosques, for example, we see rich Islamic countries placating 'local concerns' and using a 'locally contextualized vocabulary' (Pelkmans 2009: 9–10) by pandering to public dismay surrounding the destruction of cultural and religious buildings during the siege, while simultaneously spending vast amounts of money in the hopes of advancing their own 'brand' of Islam.

Though religion greeted me at every turn in my fieldwork contexts, a revealing aspect of Sarajevo's treatment milieu was the conspicuous absence of Higher Power (*viša sila*). Higher Power, a concept coined and popularized by Alcoholics Anonymous co-founders Bill Wilson and Bob Smith, is a 'partially secularized and highly subjectivist image of the supernatural' (Hood 2012: 90). Its absence in Sarajevo was explained by a former addict and NGO manager in his recollections of the development of Sarajevo's addiction treatment milieu:

> I tried to organize NA [Narcotics Anonymous] groups here and it, and it you know happens for a couple of years we meet but not really as a genuine NA twelve step group ... two issues were very hot about twelve step

in the Bosnian context. The first one is spirituality: Which Higher Power? [*laughs*] So which Serenity, how will you make the Serenity declaration in the beginning? God?! Should we say Bože or Allah or?! You know it was tricky, you know in the Bosnian context it was very tricky.

Here, an important facet of religion and addiction treatment in Sarajevo is underscored. When religion was cited by my informants as the key to their recovery, they were undoubtedly speaking of faith and inner change – of finding God personally – but, in an important sense, they were also referencing the social, public-oriented aspects of religion. Addiction, religion and recovery are thus individual and public in a mutually reinforcing sense, and therefore Higher Power simply does not cut it in Sarajevo. While Heelas has contended that religion in late modernity has capitulated not to secularism, as predicted, but to spirituality (Heelas 2009: 413), in Sarajevo this simply is not the case. Spirituality (*duhovnost*) is not common parlance or widely intelligible in this context; instead, a team must be picked. One must not only privately submit to Bože or Allah in recovery but, more often than not, must also publicly declare and explicitly cite affiliation when publicly projecting one's recovered self.

Capricious simultaneity

Ringwald writes of religious and secular addiction recovery programmes that 'different roads to recovery cover much of the same terrain' (Ringwald 2002: 158). In his comparative ethnography of Recovery House and Redemption House, Hood takes this point further. Of the programmes at both centres, he writes that 'these rituals, mechanisms, and strategies are mobilized in both Houses in order to re-socialize the clientele into quite similar alternative moral logics, namely Right living at Recovery House and Christian living at Redemption House' (Hood 2011: 198). He further asserts that 'therapeutic community treatment seems in large part a secularized form of evangelical religious conversion used to correct, control, and conventionalize people whose drug use has been labelled deviant' (Hood 2011: 198).

In my fieldwork contexts different roads were taken, but it is not the religious aspects of recovery that constitute the same terrain. That is, the ethos and programme at Zajednica is not simply a 'secularized form' (Hood 2011: 198) of religious practices and imperatives. Nor were the principles and practices of Oporavak necessarily religious versions of secular treatment orthodoxies, or indeed strictly religious at all. Rather, the similarities or shared terrain between Oporavak and Zajednica manifested in their common pragmatic and situational shifting between religious and secular models of thought and modes of action, a phenomenon that I describe as the capricious simultaneity of religion and the secular.

Ethnographic examples of these processes abound in my field notes. In Zajednica, it became a running joke among the clients and many members of staff that Sead, a client, had taught me to furnish the friendly enquiry 'How are things at home?' with the Arabic adopted Bosnian Muslim response '*Elhamdulillah*' (literally Hallelujah, but meaning 'All is well praise God'). Yet, one day while outside with a social worker on her cigarette break, I watched Sead receive a barrage of shouted reprimands from one of the managers as he crossed the lawn. Heading inside after a period of gardening work – part of daily work therapy at the centre – Sead had shouted out in greeting to this manager '*Selam alejkum*!' A self-designated devout Muslim, this manager would join his male colleagues every Friday during the working day to go to the nearest mosque for prayer, yet would not accept this show of public religious preference in the rehab centre: 'Where do you think you are, Pakistan?! he bellowed. This tension between the religious and secular was particularly clear during *Ramazan* (Ramadan), where the usual focus on abstinence from drugs – a focus that was officially expressed in secular, scientific terms – came into tension with the religious imperative to fast and abstain from vices in general. On the one hand, for example, many colleagues suggested that clients should focus on the physically and psychologically challenging task of staying clean and that fasting in their case was absurdly, even ludicrously, premature. Yet, on the other, the question 'Are you fasting?' rang out every day throughout the centre, with an unmistakable attendant 'sizing up' of the values and commitment of the person – client or staff – who answered in the affirmative or negative.

At Oporavak, the religious and the secular happily mixed, with the former trumping the latter so frequently as to seem almost strange, given the Evangelical Christian underpinnings of the organization. In one women's support session, for example, we spent almost the entire time as a group discussing the differences between men and women in Bosnia, with ribald humour and a more than a little righteous indignation. The list we drew up was as follows: Women are expected to get married, to stay in the kitchen, to be good housewives, not to fight or cheat, to dress appropriately, not to go out, to do all the work. Alternatively, men can make money, have better jobs, go out more, have more money, cheat on their wives, have many girlfriends, and fight. Shifting hurriedly to the religious frame of reference, it was only right at the end that the group's leaders brought in the biblical underpinnings of the session by inviting us all to consider Genesis 1:27 – 'So God created man in his own image, in the image of God he created him; male and female he created them'. Anita herself demonstrated a capricious attitude towards religion in the public sphere. At a youth conference that we attended together, she was vociferously appalled that a football coach had stood up during the question and comments session, expressing himself and his ideas through language peppered with Bošnjak or Muslim phraseology. It was her decided opinion, that day, that religion had no place in Sarajevo's public discourse. And yet, she would be the last person to shy away from publicly testifying to the miracles God has wrought in her life, which she did regularly and with entirely understandable gusto.

Why, then, is this ethnographically evident capricious simultaneity important? I suggest that it speaks to a wider, ongoing process in Sarajevo, whereby the public sphere is being reshaped, but in an awkward, contradictory and unpredictable manner. Watching the post-match, on-pitch, televised interviews of Bosnian football players on the evening they secured a place in the 2014 World Cup, I saw capricious simultaneity in action. The Bosnian national team and their path to Brazil 2014 was tightly enmeshed in hopes that affiliation to Bosnia as a nation could trump divisive ethno-religious nationalist loyalty. One commentator on the pitch that evening had garnered a huge national fan base both for his energetic style and for the passionate – and, as a Bosnian Serb, potentially more striking – tenor of his support for the national team and, by extension, for Bosnia. Yet, for a few awkward moments, his fellow commentator threatened the congenial and decidedly secular celebratory mood when he decided to comment on how wonderful it was that this win coincided with *Kurban Bajram* (a Muslim holiday) and to extend a traditional *Bajram* greeting to the viewers.

In this sense and many others, recovery from addiction in Sarajevo holds a mirror up to society in general. In this mirror, we see capricious simultaneity reflected in the way in which my informants hark back to a bygone Sarajevo of secular state socialism and, at the same time, multifaith permissiveness. It is apparent in the ways and means by which addiction and religion have entered the post-siege public sphere, together. Above all, we may see capricious simultaneity reflected with startling clarity in the way that my informants talk about and try to achieve recovery in a public and private sense, and in the intrigues of their daily lives as members of Sarajevo's drug treatment milieu.

Notes

Chapter One

1 Interestingly, the original subtitle of Micklethwait and Wooldridge's book is *How the Global Rise of Faith is Changing the World*. In a later edition, there is a subtle but significant change to *How the Global Revival of Faith is Changing the World* – a movement from something unprecedented to something how things used to be.

2 The basis of these assertions is unclear: The National Health Service, the secular utopian project, enjoys historically high levels of satisfaction among the British public (e.g. http://www.kingsfund.org.uk/projects/bsa-survey-2012/satisfaction-nhs-overall [accessed 25 September 2014]). Similarly, it is very likely safe to say that the vast majority of Britons still prefer to have their cancer treated by a GP rather than a faith healer.

3 As an aside, despite disagreeing with the argument, I welcome the openly political position that Woodhead takes in her chapter (Woodhead 2012). Sociology of religion – with the exception of feminist work – has traditionally shied away from openly political commitments, in my opinion to the detriment of the sub-discipline. However, even if I laud the commitment, I do not share the politics and find it hard to avoid a comparison with famous left-wing historian Eric Hobsbawm's assessment of a nineteenth-century conservative: 'The British jurist, A.V. Dicey (1835–1922) saw the steamroller of collectivism, which had been in motion since 1870, flattening the landscape of individual liberty into the centralized and levelling tyranny of school meals, health insurance and old age pensions' (Hobsbawm 1987: 103).

Chapter Two

1 Liberal morning paper *Dagens nyheter*, Conservative morning paper *Svenska dagbladet* and Liberal popular paper *Expressen*. In a parallell study, master student Maximilian Broberg (2013) studied Social Democratic popular paper *Aftonbladet*, with similar results (Broberg 2013).

Chapter Three

1 This study is undertaken within the project 'The Resurgence of Religion?! A study of religion and modernity in Sweden with the daily press as case', which was funded by the National Research Council of Sweden 2010–14.

2 The study consists of nearly 5,000 articles published in fourteen newspapers in Finland, Sweden, Norway, Denmark and Iceland, from four two-week periods in 1988, 1998 and 2008.

3 *Aftonbladet, Arbetet, Expressen, Dagens Nyheter, Dagens Industri, Göteborgs-Posten, Göteborgs-Tidningen, Kvällsposten, Svenska Dagbladet, Sydsvenska Dagbladet, Helsingborgs Dagblad.*

4 Search word categories (translated from Swedish): Religion, Islam, Christianity, Judaism, world-religion (includes Hinduism and Buddhism), new forms of spirituality, religious metaphor.

5 Search words and indicators were chosen from a previous research project charting indicators of cultural change in editorials: 'Kulturindikatorer: svensk symbolmiljö 1945–1975' (Block 1984). The main categories used are freedom, democracy, equality, Socialism, security, economic growth, environment, regulation.

6 In four of the editorials the coding is unclear, and these have been left out of the qualitative analysis.

7 A few cases (six) overlap between categories as articles that mainly use religion as a description but also comment on its role in political conflicts.

8 The authors made translations of the Swedish texts into English.

Chapter Four

1 The White Paper on European Governance stated in 2001: 'The organisations which made up civil society mobilise people and support, for instance, those suffering from exclusion or discrimination' (European Commission: Com [2001], 428 final p. 14).

2 Lipset and Rokkan (1967: 47) suggest that cleavages mark social positions that translate into support or opposition to certain political issues. In other words, 'cleavages' denote already perceived (and thereby not unnoticed) differences that have the potential to transform (under certain circumstances) into political positions and into conflicts.

3 The article does not, however, contribute to minority studies, and aspects of the exclusive powers of religion are touched only indirectly.

4 It is important to distinguish between national identity referring to affiliations, feelings of commitment and loyalty on the one hand and the mere administrative act of granting (or neglecting) citizenship with access to social policy systems on the other.

5 In contrast to other concepts of social cohesion (e.g. 'generalized trust'), it provides an objectivation for individual identification. Generalized trust

became the key component of social capital. Most survey-related research refers to the question, 'Generally speaking, would you say that most people can be trusted or that you need to be very careful in dealing with people?' generated by Noelle-Neumann in 1948. This operationalization, however, makes it problematic to compare the radius of trust between individuals and between countries (e.g. Welch et al. 2007; Delhey et al. 2011). Therefore we decided to use the concept of national identity instead.

6 There are two well-established versions of national identity (Smith 1991; Jones and Smith 2001): the ethnic version is characterized by ascribed/objective features, such as country of birth or common ancestry. The civic/voluntaristic aspect includes a community of laws and institutions, a single political will, equal rights for members of the nation and a minimum of common values, traditions or a sentiment. As research has repeatedly shown, these two aspects of collective national identity are often seen as a country's master-narrative (e.g. Meuschel 1988). But empirically, they refer to two different dimensions of attachment that are realized at the same time rather than two mutually exclusive categories. Consequently, the population of countries can exhibit different strengths of national identity and the two dimensions can be mixed in different ways (e.g. Lilli and Diehl 1999; Hjerm 1998, 2007). Crucially, it is expected that different types of national identity are more prevalent in certain countries than in others.

7 For a mere statistical reason, we restricted the analysis to those countries for which EUROSTAT-Data are available.

8 Data are not reported here but can be requested from the author.

9 Using the regression method, the factor scores are standardized between 0 and 10. Data are not reported here but can be requested from the author.

10 National identity in this sense of ethnic national identity should be higher in countries where the state and the nation coincide. The two dimensions of ethnic and civic national identity have proven to be sufficient independent of each other so that an analysis only of the former is justified (Lilli and Diehl 1999 or Hjerm 1998).

11 We are aware that the Herfindahl-Index is not uncontested (e.g. Voas et al. 2002). It seems to be sensitive to group size. It is however, a sufficiently good measurement if one is only interested in effects of majority relations – regardless of the particular groups involved. We calculated the measurement from the percentages of Catholic, Protestant, Orthodox, other religions and a-religious persons. The higher the index is, the more homogeneous is the society.

12 For the following analysis, we are not interested in the particular content or dogma of the different denominations. We are interested in the individual attitudes.

13 We tested both aspects of individual religiosity separately. They pointed in the same direction in all models. Therefore, it seemed sensible to reduce variables by collapsing them.

14 Institutional feedback effects are extensively discussed by Pierson (2000), Mau (2002) and Svallfors (2012).

15 Diez-Roux developed this argument on the basis of the following example: income and coronary heart disease mortality are correlated inversely on the individual level; per capita income and coronary heart disease mortality are correlated positively on the country level when non-European countries are considered (Diez-Roux 1998).

16 We are not particularly interested in country-specific differences in national identities beyond their interaction with religion. Therefore we keep the description of the European national landscape brief and do not discuss further implications.

17 In this case, Orthodoxy and Russian national identity are so closely linked that religion became part of the ethnic identity frame of the Russians, making it even harder to integrate into the host societies.

18 Data are not reported here but can be requested from the author. The weak impact of Orthodoxy in countries with an Orthodox majority is statistically due to both high levels of individual religiousness and national identity without much variance in both variables.

19 Results are not reported here but can be displayed on request.

20 For the latter, see for example Hjerm (2007); similarly King and Wheelock (2007) or Banting and Kymlicka (2006).

21 See for example Brubaker and Laitin (1998), Appleby (1999) or Yuval-Davis (2010).

22 For a critical view on the widespread methodological nationalism that treats the nation state as an undifferentiated independent variable, see Glick Schiller et al. (1995).

23 The EU's attempts to harmonize European societies show in their different initiatives concerning religion: anti-discrimination regulation concerning the freedom of religion, the attempt to create a constitution including a reference to Christianity and the increased dialogue between the EU Commission and the churches in order to give 'a soul to Europe' (Grötsch and Schnabel 2012).

Chapter Six

1 See http://www.independent.co.uk/news/uk/home-news/war-on-wonga-were-putting-you-out-of-business-archbishop-of-canterbury-justin-welby-tells-payday-loans-company-8730839.html [accessed 5 June 2014].

2 Space here precludes examination of the historic engagements of evangelicals in modes of religious publicity, or of non-conformist traditions in shaping the public sphere. For more on this, see Engelke (2013) and Van Horn Melton (2001).

3 I conducted fieldwork at St John's – a large conservative evangelical Anglican church – from February 2010 to August 2011, attending two of the three weekly Sunday services during this period. I also participated in weekly Bible study groups, attended other church and social events and conducted interviews with members of the church. I have been carrying out fieldwork at Riverside – an influential 'open' evangelical church – since February 2013. This has involved attending Sunday services, midweek groups and other activities and events organized by the church.

4 Timothy Larsen offers a helpful discussion of the problems of defining and locating evangelicals (Larsen 2007: 1–14).

5 Rob Warner examines tensions between charismatics and conservatives within post-war British evangelicalism: charismatics tend to be defined more by an orientation towards conversionism and activism, while conservatives tend to be shaped by Biblicism and crucicentrism (Warner 2007: 240).

6 For example in the Civil Partnership Act of 2004, Equality Acts of 2006 and 2010 and Marriage (Same Sex Couple) Act 2013.

7 The Christians in Parliament (2012) report 'Clearing the Ground' found in contrast that Christians are not persecuted or marginalized in public life. http://www.eauk.org/current-affairs/publications/clearing-the-ground.cfm. See also Trigg's *Equality, Freedom and Religion* for further discussion about religion and hierarchies of rights (Trigg 2012: 27–40).

8 http://www.wilberforceacademy.org.uk/#2 [accessed 22 March 2013].

9 With male headship in marriage and male leadership in the church.

10 Sex is seen as acceptable only in the context of heterosexual marriage.

11 See Strhan 2012 and 2013 for further discussion.

12 The two are not necessarily mutually exclusive, and there is some fluidity here, but open evangelicals tend to place less emphasis on the role of the Holy Spirit and spiritual gifts in their theology and ministry and are critical of some standard charismatic positions on moral issues, for example, open evangelicals accept same-sex marriage where most charismatics would oppose this.

13 It is worth noting that some open and charismatic evangelicals have also spoken publicly about issues related to sexuality, for example, the open evangelical Steve Chalke's statements in favour of gay marriage, which led to Oasis being expelled from the Evangelical Alliance (UK), who disagreed with his stance on this.

14 http://www.church-poverty.org.uk/news/britainisnteating [accessed 13 February 2014].

Chapter Seven

1 There have been attempts to put local and global figures on numbers of Pagans. After a rapid expansion from the last two decades of the twentieth century through until the first decade of the twenty-first century, growth slowed by the end of that decade, in part due to the end of the 'Teen Witch' fad (Lewis 2012: 128). According to the American Religious Identification Survey, carried out in 2008 by the Graduate Center of the City University of New York, American Pagans numbered 711,000 (to the nearest thousand), a statistical extrapolation based on a survey of 50,000 people in the United

States (Lewis 2012: 133). The 2011 Canadian census recorded 26,495 Pagans (e-mail from Shai Feraro to New Religious Movements Scholars group, 28 September 2013). In the 2006 New Zealand census Pagans numbered 7,122, and in the 2011 Australian census the figure was 32,083 (Lewis 2012: 134–5).

2 Wicca is the best-known modern Pagan tradition. It is a primarily duotheistic religion that developed in Britain in the first half of the twentieth century and was popularized by Gerald Gardner in the 1950s and early 1960s (Hutton 1999). Wiccan rituals incorporate magical practice and celebration of the lunar and solar cycles. Eight seasonal festivals make up the 'Wheel of the Year'. Wicca further subdivides into a number of traditions, including the initiatory Gardnerian and Alexandrian traditions, Celtic Wicca and Dianic Wicca (whose members venerate only a goddess, rather than a goddess and god).

3 The 2011 census figure for Pagans in England and Wales was 78,566 (Lewis 2012: 132).

4 A documentary film titled *Fire on the Mountain: A Gathering of Shamans* was made about this event by Canadian director David Cherniack. http://www.youtube.com/watch?v=SsR8H0ZLncE&feature=youtu.be [accessed 18 February 2014].

5 I have been unable to locate academic studies of modern Greek Pagans, although their activities are quite well covered in the media (especially in regard to their attempts to hold rituals at Greek temple sites) and in several books by members of modern Pagan groups. I have been advised by Alexandros Sakellariou, Panteion University of Social and Political Sciences of Athens, that this field is under-studied because of the powerful Greek Orthodox Church, which dominates the public sphere (personal communication, 12 October 2012). I am very grateful to him for passing on weblinks to me.

6 Similar Pagan faiths or ideologies were also created in several other European countries at the beginning of the twentieth century, for example, Poland and Latvia (Shnirelman 2002: 200). This is important to note because it shows that there was already Pagan activity in Central and Eastern Europe prior to the post-Socialist revival of religiosity.

Chapter Eight

1 Monsma appeals to a functional schema very similar to the Luhmannian one to pinpoint the field of action of the two principles (Monsma 2000: 33).

2 The product of this structural coupling is destined to play a global role. For the universal Catholic tradition, this became evident with the Vatican II declaration on religious liberty *Dignitatis humanae* (1965).

3 Not by chance, the crisis of secularism is due to the crisis of the state much more than the return of religion (Modood 2012a: 132). See also Diotallevi (2010) and Cassese (2013) on the post-state global polity.

4 From the perspective of multiple secularities, *laïcité* seems to be an increasingly marginal and fragile exception (Modood 2012a: 64; Calhoun et al. 2011: 8–12; Casanova 2011: 56). The original ambivalence of the *saeculum* has been analysed earlier by R. A. Markus, for example (Markus (1970, 2006). For some recent attempts in this vein, see Cacciari (2013) and Diotallevi (2013).

5 However, I am not arguing that the British model is exempt from tensions and transformations. On the contrary, such processes are clearly evident (e.g. Rivers 2012).

6 See Ferrari (1999). More recently, Ferrari has suggested a less homogenous picture of the presence and role played by religious actors within European public space (Ferrari 2012).

Chapter Nine

1 For a more detailed account see Bonney (2014).

Chapter Ten

1 The next largest religious group are Muslims, comprising 1.4 per cent of the population (Census 2011).

2 Interestingly, as I chatted to one of the local Yes Cardenden activists who had booked the hall, she told me how she had extended an invitation to the members of the local congregation and then made a point of telling me how the woman she had spoken to had 'firmly' advised that no one from their Church would attend such an event, meaning that as a matter of principle they would not attend a meeting to listen to Tommy Sheridan.

3 The two Catholic informants originally in favour of independence in 2013 were still intending to vote 'Yes' a year later, while the two Catholic men (Andy and Jim) who were against independence remained so when I interviewed them again in August 2014. Interestingly, with the help of a member of the Yes Cardenden group who is also a long-term member of the local Church of Scotland congregation, I learnt that none of my Church of Scotland informants had changed their views, so that there was no movement towards 'Yes' among my elderly Church of Scotland informants.

4 On the day of the referendum itself a Yes Cardenden activist (Dave Clark) manning the polling station at Denend School quickly sensed that old people were 'doing their bit' to stop Scottish independence and joked: 'Ah'm not ageist but Ah wish all these old age pensioner bastards had died in their sleep last night!' Dave's judgement regarding a generational split was borne out by a poll of 2,047 voters conducted on 18 and 19 September which found that, in every age cohort under fifty-five years old, most respondents had voted Yes, while among voters aged fifty-five to sixty-four and sixty-five+

only 43 per cent and 27 per cent, respectively, had voted for independence. See www.LordAshcroftPolls.com. On the existence of what I term the 1945 generation and an ethnographic description of its long-standing antipathy towards the return of Scottish sovereignty see Gilfillan (2014).

Chapter Eleven

1 The official English language name of the party is The Greens of Finland.

2 'LA' stands for *lakialoite* (Member's Initiative), and 157/2005 vp is the official diary number of the initiative.

3 The Orthodox Church in Finland enjoys some of the same privileges as the Lutheran Church (such as state collected church tax), although its status is not defined in the constitution. In the context of this chapter the Orthodox Church is pertinent in the case of the Education Acts and the provisions on public broadcasting, where it is separately mentioned. It is also mentioned in the actual debate, but always in conjunction with the Lutheran Church.

4 The diary number for the plenary debate is PTK 8/2006 vp. The transcript can be found online at http://www.eduskunta.fi/triphome/bin/akxhaku. sh?lyh=PTKSUP?lomake=akirjat/akx3100 → Asian tunnus: LA 157/2005 → Hae [accessed 14 July 2012].

5 For a full discussion on CDA, see Hjelm 2013; 2014d, Chapter 5.

6 These discourses emerge from various discussions of individual amendments in the initiative but mostly regardless of and/or in addition to the particular amendment suggestions. That is why it makes more sense to analyse the material in the framework of broader discourses than individual law amendments. The reason the comments from the floor don't necessarily even refer to the actual proposals has to do with the nature of the preliminary debate (where no decisions regarding amendments can be made), but also, in my opinion, because of MP Räsänen's strong contextualization of the initiative as an attack on the church in the beginning of the discussion.

7 The latter is the most controversial part of church funding as it means that a part of a, say, Muslim shopkeeper's tax payments will be used to support the Lutheran Church.

8 Despite the fact that the signatories left out perhaps the most significant issue, the church tax, because 'religious communities do important social work' (Krohn 2006).

9 For an outline of the legislative process see the Parliament home pages: http:// web.eduskunta.fi/Resource.phx/parliament/aboutparliament/legislativework. htx [accessed 14 July 2012].

10 All translations are the author's. I have retained grammatical errors but have not added the usual *sic*.

11 Krohn probably means 'position' here, but the Finnish word she uses is *tilanne* (situation).

12 Traditionally, the Greens and the Left Alliance especially, but also urban politicians (e.g. Helsinki's Krohn and Tampere's Meriläinen) in general have been more critical of the status quo, whereas stronger support for the current legislation comes from the Christian Democrats and rural MPs (especially in the Centre Party). Hence the references to the MPs home constituencies here.

13 It should be noted that 'civil religion' can be used for ideological purposes, of course (and, some would argue, has been so used). The distinction here is analytical, the actual uses murkier. 'Civil religion' was discussed mostly in the 1980s in Finland (Sundback 1984; Lampinen 1984) and, as the LA 157/2005 vp discussion attests, has not 'trickled down' to everyday use.

Chapter Fourteen

1 This is the definition we used for the purpose of our research.

Chapter Sixteen

1 All translations by the author.

2 In 1971, Yugoslavs comprised 1.3 per cent of the population, and in 1981 this figure had risen to 5.4 per cent of the population.

3 *Mawlid* in Arabic, the Prophets' (*pbuh*) birth and celebration thereof.

4 The 2013 Census results are projected to emphatically confirm this trend.

5 *Dani* is a popular Bosnian news magazine.

6 '*dolazi do eksplozije u širenju različitih oblika zloupotrebe psihoaktivnih supstancija*' (Hasanović 2001: 168).

7 '*što je direktna posljedica otvorenije komunikacije prema "Zapadu"'* (Hasanović 2001: 168).

8 '*čiji su uposlenici bukvalno zarazili*' (Hasanović 2001: 169).

9 '*Jednim licem Jugoslavija je gledala na Istok, drugim na Zapad; jednim licem na spoljnu politik, drugim na unutrašniju; jednim na Holivud, drugim na crni talas*' (Vučetić 2012: 401–2).

10 Black Wave cinema was a Yugoslav film movement of the 1960s and 1970s typified by dark, comic and critical treatment of modern themes, which garnered popularity in Yugoslavia and abroad.

11 Evangelical Christianity had been established in Yugoslavia in the 1980s and had more than forty ministers throughout the region before the war broke out in Bosnia (Perica 2002: 13), and previous to that a Protestant community existed in Sarajevo (Branković 2006). However, neither of these presences could be considered significant numerically.

Bibliography

Abu Ghosh, Y. (2008), *Escaping Gypsyness: Work, Power and Identity in the Marginalization of Roma*, Prague, Czech Republic: Charles University.

Acton, T. and Klimova, I. (2001), 'The International Romani Union: an East European answer to West European questions?', in W. Guy (ed.), *Between Past and Future: the Roma of Central and Eastern Europe*, Hatfield, UK: University of Hertfordshire Press, pp. 157–219.

Adamson, J. and Donovan, J. (2005), 'Normal disruption: South Asian and African/Caribbean relatives caring for an older family member in the UK', *Social Science and Medicine*, 60(1): 37–48.

Ahdar, R. and Leigh, I. (2005), *Religious Freedom in the Liberal State*, Oxford, UK: Oxford University Press.

Ahmed, N. and Jones, I. (2008), 'Habitus and bureaucratic routines', cultural and structural factors in the experiences of informal care', *Current Sociology*, 56: 57–78.

Aitamurto, K. and Simpson, S. (eds) (2013), *Modern Pagan and Native Faith Movements in Central and Eastern Europe*, Durham, UK: Acumen Publishing.

Ajrouch, K. J. and Fakhoury, N. (2013), 'Assessing needs of aging Muslims: A focus on metro-Detroit faith communities', *Contemporary Islam*, 1–20.

Alexander, J. C. (2006), *The Civil Sphere*, Oxford, UK: Oxford University Press.

Alexander, T. (2007), *A Beginner's Guide to Hellenismos*, self-published online: Lulu Press Inc.

Ališauskienė, M. and Schröder, I. (2012), 'Introduction', in M. Ališauskienė and I. Schröder (eds), *Religious Diversity in Post-Soviet Society: Ethnographies of Catholic Hegemony and the New Pluralism in Lithuania*, Farnham, UK: Ashgate, pp. 1–15.

Ammerman, N. (2007), *Everyday Religion: Observing Modern Religious Lives*, Oxford, UK: Oxford University Press.

Amster, M. (2015), 'It's not easy being apolitical: reconstruction and eclecticism in Danish Asatro', in K. Rountree (ed.), *Contemporary Pagan and Native Faith Movements in Europe: Colonialist and Nationalist Impulses*, New York, NY: Berghahn, pp. 43–63.

Anderson, B. (1983), *Imagined Communities: Reflections on the Origin and Spread of Nationalism*, London, UK: Verso.

Anderson, K. M. (2009), 'The church as nation? The role of religion in the development of the Swedish welfare state', in K. van Kersbergen and P. Manow (eds), *Religion, Class Coalitions, and Welfare States*, Cambridge, UK: Cambridge University Press, pp. 210–325.

Andersson, J., Vanderbeck, R. M. and Valentine, G. (2011), 'New York encounters: religion, sexuality, and the city', *Environment and Planning A*, 43: 618–33.

Appleby, S. R. (1999), *The Ambivalence of the Sacred: Religion, Violence, and Reconciliation*, Lanham, MD: Rowman & Littlefield Publishers.

Asad, T. (2003), *Formations of the secular: Christianity, Islam, Modernity*, Stanford, CA: Stanford University Press.

Aslan, R. (2011), '"Sharia" in the new Middle East', *The Washington Post*, 30 October [online], http://www.washingtonpost.com/blogs/guest-voices/post/sharia-in-the-new-middle-east/2011/10/30/gIQAW23PXM_blog.html [accessed 30 March].

Atkin, K. and Rollings, J. (1992), 'Informal care in Asian and Afro Caribbean Communities', *British Journal of Social Work*, 22(4): 405–18.

Austin-Broos, D. (2003), 'The anthropology of conversion: an introduction', in A. Buckser and S. D. Glazier (eds), *The Anthropology of Religious Conversion*, Lanham, MD and Oxford, UK: Rowman & Littlefield.

Axner, M. (2013), *Public Religions in Swedish Media: A Study of Religious Actors on Three Newspaper Debate Pages 2001-2011*, Uppsala, Sweden: Acta Universitatis Upsaliensis.

Bäckström, A. and Davie, G. (2010), 'A preliminary conclusion: gathering the threads and moving on', in A. Bäckström and G. Davie, with N. Edgardh and P. Petterson (eds), *Welfare and Religion in 21st Century Europe: Volume 1*, Farnham, UK: Ashgate, pp. 183–98.

Bäckström, A., Davie, G., Edgardh, N. and Pettersson, P. (2010), *Welfare and Religion in 21st Century Europe: Volume 1, Configuring the Connections*, Farnham, UK: Ashgate.

Bajekal, M., Blane, D., Grewal, I., Karlsen, S. and Nazroo, J. (2004), 'Ethnic differences in influences on quality of life at older ages', *Ageing and Society*, 24(5): 709–28.

Banac, I. (1994), 'Bosnian Muslims: from religious community to socialist nationhood and postcommunist statehood, 1918–1992', in M. Pinson (ed.), *The Muslims of Bosnia-Herzegovina: Their Historic Development from the Middle Ages to the Dissolution of Yugoslavia*, Cambridge, MA: Harvard University Press.

Banting, K. and Kymlicka, W. (2006), *Multiculturalism and the Welfare State*, Oxford, UK: Oxford University Press.

Barany, Z. (2002), *The East European Gypsies. Regime Change, Marginality and Ethnopolitics*, Cambridge, UK: Cambridge University Press.

Barbalet, J., Possamai, A. and Turner, B. (eds) (2011), *Religion and the State: A Comparative Sociology*, London, UK: Anthem Press.

Barrington, L. (1997), '"Nation" and "nationalism": the misuse of key concepts in political science', *Political Science and Politics*, 30(4): 712–18.

Bauman, Z. (1976), *Towards A Critical Sociology: An Essay on Commonsense and Emancipation*, London, UK: Routledge.

Bayat, A. (2006), 'The political economy of social policy in Egypt', in M. Karshenas and V. Moghadam (eds), *Social Policy in the Middle East*, UNRISD Social Policy in a Development Context Series, New York, NY: Palgrave Macmillan, pp. 135–55.

BBC (2012), 'Whatever happened to Methodist Central Halls?' http://www.bbc.co.uk/news/magazine-19341345 [accessed 30 August].

Beaman, L. (2013), 'The will to religion: obligatory religious citizenship', *Critical Research on Religion*, 1(2): 141–57.

Beaumont, P. (2011), 'Political Islam poised to dominate the new world bequeathed by Arab Spring', *The Guardian*, 3 December [online], http://www.theguardian.com/world/2011/dec/03/political-islam-poised-arab-spring [accessed 13 March].

Bebbington, D. (1989), *Evangelicalism in Modern Britain*, Abingdon, UK: Routledge.

Beblawi, H. (1990), 'The rentier state in the Arab world', in G. Luciani (ed.), *The Arab State*, London, UK: Routledge, pp. 85–98.

Beck, U. (2008), *Der eigene Gott*, Frankfurt and Leipzig, Germany: Verlag der Religionen.

Beckford, J. A. (1990), 'The sociology of religion and social problems', *Sociological Analysis*, 51(1): 1–14.

Beckford, J. A. (2004), '"Laïcité", "dystopia", and the reaction to new religious movements in France', in J. T. Richardson (ed.), *Regulating Religion*, New York, NY: Kluwer, pp. 27–40.

Beckford, J. A. (2010), 'The return of public religion? A critical assessment of a popular claim', *Nordic Journal of Religion and Society*, 23: 121–36.

Beckford, J. A. (2011), 'Religious diversity and social problems: the case of Britain', in T. Hjelm (ed.), *Religion and Social Problems*, New York and London: Routledge, pp. 53–66.

Beckford, J. A. (2012), 'SSSR Presidential Address: public religions and the postsecular: critical reflections', *Journal for the Scientific Study of Religion*, 51(1): 1–19.

Beckford, J. and Richardson, J. (2007), *The Sage Handbook of Sociology of Religion*, London, UK: Sage.

Bellah, R. N. (1967), 'Civil religion in America', *Daedalus*, 96(1): 1–21.

Benedik, S. (2011), 'Harming "cultural feelings": images and categorisation of temporary Romani migrants in Graz/Austria', in M. Stewart and M. Rövid (eds), *Multi-disciplinary Approaches to Romani Studies*, Budapest, Hungary: CEU Press, pp. 71–88.

Benthall, J. and Bellion-Jourdan, J. (2003), *The Charitable Crescent*, London, UK: IB Tauris.

Berger, P. L. (1967), *The Sacred Canopy: Elements of a Sociological Theory of Religion*, Garden City, NY: Anchor.

Berger, P. L. (1999a), 'The desecularization of the world: a global overview', in P. L. Berger (ed.), *The Desecularization of the World: Resurgent Religion and World Politics*, Grand Rapids, MI: Eerdmans, pp. 1–18.

Berger, P. L. (1999b), *The Desecularization of the World: Resurgent Religion and World Politics*, Grand Rapids, MI: Eerdmans.

Berger, P., Davie, G. and Fokas, E. (2008), *Religious America, Secular Europe? A Theme and Variations*, Aldershot, UK: Ashgate.

Berman, H. J. (1983), *Law and Revolution. The Formation of the Western Legal Tradition*, Cambridge, MA: Harvard University Press.

Beyer, P. (2012), 'Socially engaged religion in a post-Westphalian global context: remodeling the secular/religious distinction', *Sociology of Religion*, 2: 109–30.

Bhargava, R. (2011), 'Rehabilitating secularism', in C. Calhoun, M. Juergensmeyer and J. VanAntwerpen (eds), *Rethinking Secularism*, Oxford, UK: Oxford University Press.

Bhopal, R. (2004), 'Glossary of terms relating to ethnicity and race: for reflection and debate', *Journal of Epidemiology and Community Health*, 58: 441–5.

Bjarnason, T. (1998), 'Parents, religion and perceived social coherence: a Durkheimian framework of adolescent anomie', *Journal for the Scientific Study of Religion*, 37(4): 742–54.

Blair, T. (2008), 'Faith and globalisation', lecture at Westminster Cathedral, London, UK, 3 April.

Block, E. (1984), 'Freedom, equality, et cetera: values and valuations in Swedish domestic political debate, 1945–1975', in G. Melischek, K. E. Rosengren and J. Stappers (eds), *Cultural Indicators: An International Symposium Veröffentlichungen des Instituts für publikumsforschung o.* (8), Vienna, Austria: Verlag der Österreichischen Akademie der Wissenschaften.

Bohn, C. and Hahn, A. (2002), 'Patterns of inclusion and exclusion: property, nation and religion', *Soziale Systeme*, 8(1): 8–26.

Bonner, M. (2003), 'Poverty and charity in the rise of Islam', in M. Bonner, M. Ener and A. Singer (eds), *Poverty and Charity in Middle Eastern Contexts*, New York, NY: Suny Press, pp. 13–30.

Bonney, N. L. (2012), 'Some constitutional issues concerning the installation of the monarch', *British Politics*, 7: 163–82.

Bonney, N. L. (2013), *Monarchy, Religion and the State: Civil Religion in the UK, Canada, Australia and the Commonwealth*, Manchester, UK: Manchester University Press.

Bonney, N. L. (2014), 'The Cenotaph: a contested and consensual monument of remembrance', http://www.secularism.org.uk/uploads/cenotaph-a-consensual-and-contested-monument-of-remembrance.pdf.

Bougarel, X. (2007), 'Death and the nationalist: martyrdom, war memory and veteran identity among Bosnian Muslims', in X. Bougarel, G. Duijzings and E. Helms (eds), *The New Bosnian Mosaic: Identities, Memories and Moral Claims in a Post-War Society*, Aldershot and Hampshire, UK: Ashgate.

Bougarel, X., Duijzings, G. and Helms, E. (2007), 'Introduction', in X. Bougarel, G. Duijzings and E. Helms (eds), *The New Bosnian Mosaic: Identities, Memories and Moral Claims in a Post-War Society*, Aldershot and Hampshire, UK: Ashgate.

Bowen, J. R. (2007), *Why the French Don't Like Headscarves: Islam, the State, and Public Space*, Princeton, NJ: Princeton University Press.

Bowling, A. (2009), 'Perceptions of active ageing in Britain: divergences between minority ethnic and whole population samples', *Age and Ageing*, 38(6): 703–10.

Bradley, J. R. (2011a), 'The tyrant must go, but beware of what comes next', *The Daily Mail*, 31 January [online], http://www.dailymail.co.uk/debate/article-1352090/EGYPT-RIOTS-Hosni-Mubarak-beware-comes-next.html [accessed 13 March].

Bradley, J. R. (2011b), 'The terrifying truth behind the so-called Arab Spring', *The Daily Mail*, 20 December [online], http://www.dailymail.co.uk/news/article-2076355/Arab-Spring-The-terrifying-truth-revolution.html [accessed 13 March].

Bradley, J. R. (2011c), 'The domino effect: Tunisia engulfed. Egypt in flames. Jordan teetering. As the Arab world unravels, should the West be worried?', *The Daily Mail*, 3 February [online], http://www.dailymail.co.uk/news/article-1353088/Egypt-protests-Tunisia-Jordan-unravel-West-worried.html [accessed 13 March].

Bragg, M. (2011), *The Book of Books*, London, UK: Hodder and Stoughton.

Branković, T. (2006), *Protestantske zajednice u Jugoslaviji, 1945-1991: društveni i politički aspekti delovanja*, Niš, Serbia: Junir; Belgrade, Serbia: Signature.

BRIN (2014), 'Religion in the armed forces', British Religion in Numbers, http://www.brin.ac.uk/news/2010/religion-in-the-armed-forces/.

Bringa, T. (1995), *Being Muslim the Bosnian Way: Identity and Community in a Central Bosnian Village*, Princeton, NJ and Chichester, UK: Princeton University Press.

British Social Attitudes (2012), British Social Attitudes, 28th report.

Broberg, M. (2013), 'Religious actors on the debate page of *Aftonbladet*', master thesis, Uppsala, Sweden: Uppsala University, Department of Theology.

Brown, C. (2009), *The Death of Christian Britain*, London, UK: Routledge.

Brubaker, R. and Laitin, D. (1998), 'Ethnic and nationalist violence', *Annual Review of Sociology*, 24: 423–52.

Bruce, S. (2001), 'The curious case of the unnecessary recantation: Berger and secularization', in L. Woodhead with P. Heelas and D. Martin (eds), *Peter L. Berger and the Study of Religion*, London, UK: Routledge, pp. 87–100.

Bruce, S. (2002), *God is Dead: Secularization in the West*, Oxford, UK: Blackwell.

Bruce, S. (2011), *Secularization: In Defence of an Unfashionable Theory*, Oxford, UK: Oxford University Press.

Buckman, S. K. (2011), 'Performing Allah's work: experiences of Muslim family carers in Britain', unpublished PhD thesis, University of Nottingham, UK.

Bugra, A. (2007), 'Poverty and citizenship: an overview of the social policy environment in Republican Turkey', *International Journal of Middle Eastern Studies*, 39(1): 33–52.

Bugra, A. and Keyder, C. (2006), 'The Turkish welfare regime in transformation', *Journal of European Social Policy*, 16(3): 211–28.

Butler, J. (2009), *Frames of War*, London, UK: Verso.

Butler, J., Habermas, J., Taylor, C. and West, C. (2011), 'Concluding Discussion', in E. Mendieta, J. VanAntwerpen and C. J. Calhoun (eds), *The power of religion in the public sphere*, New York, NY: Columbia University Press.

Cacciari, M. (2013), *Il potere che frena*, Milan, Italy: Adelphi.

Calhoun, C. (1993), 'Nationalism and civil society: democracy, diversity and self-determination', *International Sociology*, 8(4): 387–411.

Calhoun, C., Juergensmeyer, M. and VanAntwerpen, J. (2011a), 'Introduction', in C. Calhoun, M. Juergensmeyer and J. VanAntwerpen (eds), *Rethinking Secularism*, Oxford: Oxford University Press, pp. 1–30.

Calhoun, C., Juergensmeyer, M. and VanAntwerpen, J. (2011b), *Rethinking Secularism*, New York, NY: Oxford University Press.

Callinicos, A. (2007), *Social Theory: A Historical Introduction*, Cambridge, UK: Polity Press.

Cameron, D. (2011), 'Prime minister's King James Bible speech', 16 December, http://www.number10.gov.uk/news/king-james-bible/.

Canton Delgado, M. (2010), 'Gypsy Pentecostalism, ethnopolitical uses and construction of belonging in the South of Spain', *Social Compass*, 57(2): 253–67.

Carman, C., Johns, R. and Mitchell. J. (2011), *Scottish Election Study 2011*, http://www.strath.ac.uk/humanities/research/cers/scottishelectionstudy2011.

Casanova, J. (1994), *Public Religions in the Modern World*, Berkeley, CA: University of California Press.

Casanova, J. (2000), *Oltre la secolarizzazione*, Bologna, Italy: Il Mulino.

Casanova, J. (2004), 'Religion, European secular identities and European integration', *Eurozine*, pp. 1–13, http://www.eurozine.com/pdf/2004-07-29-casanova-en.pdf, 2012-08-12.

Casanova, J. (2006a), 'Rethinking secularization: a global comparative perspective', After Secularization, *The Hedgehog Review*, 8(1/2).

Casanova, J. (2006b), 'Secularization revisited: a reply to Talal Asad', in D. Scott and C. Hirschkind (eds), *Powers of the Secular Modern: Talal Asad and His Interlocutors*, Stanford, CA: Stanford University Press, pp. 12–30.

Casanova, J. (2008), 'Public religion revisited', in H. de Vries (ed.), *Religion: Beyond a Concept. The Future of the Religious Past*, New York, NY: Fordham University Press.

Casanova, J. (2009), 'The secular and secularism', *Social Research*, 4: 1049–66.

Casanova, J. (2011), 'The secular, secularizations, secularisms', in C. Calhoun, M. Juergensmeyer and J. VanAntwerper (eds), *Rethinking Secularism*, Oxford, UK: Oxford University Press, pp. 54–74.

Cassese, S. (2013), *Chi governa il mondo?*, Bologna, Italy: Il Mulino.

Census (2011), http://www.scotlandscensus.gov.uk/en/news/articles/release2a.html [accessed 26 November 2013].

Chaves, M. and Cann, D. E. (1992), 'Regulation, pluralism, and religious market structure: explaining religion's vitality', *Rationality and Society*, 4(3): 272–90.

Chen, S. and Ravallion, M. (2008), 'The developing world is poorer than we thought, but no less successful in the fight against poverty', Policy Research Working Paper, no. 4703, Washington, DC: World Bank.

Christ, C. P. (1997), *Rebirth of the Goddess: Finding Meaning in Feminist Spirituality*, New York, NY: Routledge.

Christensen, E. (1995), 'Is the Lutheran Church still the state church? An analysis of church–state relations in Finland', *Brigham Young University Law Review*, 2: 585–601.

Christensen, H. R. (2012), 'Mediatization, deprivatization, and vicarious religion. Coverage of religion and homosexuality in the Scandinavian mainstream press', in S. Hjarvard and M. Lövheim (eds), *Mediatization and Religion: Nordic Perspectives*, Gothenburg, Sweden: Nordicom, pp. 63–78.

Christian Concern (not dated), 'Not ashamed: about', *Not Ashamed* [online], http://www.notashamed.org.uk/about.php [accessed 13 January 2012].

Christian Concern For Our Nation (2010), 'The "Big Society" and the Church', press release, 19 July.

Christian Concern For Our Nation (2011), 'Religious freedom', http://www.christianconcern.com/taxonomy/term/12/all.

Christian Institute (2009), 'Marginalising Christians: instances of Christians being sidelined in modern Britain', http://www.christian.org.uk/resource/marginalising-christians/.

Christians in Parliament (2012), 'Clearing the Ground inquiry, preliminary report into the freedom of Christians in the UK', February.

Church of England (2011), 'Challenges for the new quinquennium: a report from the House of Bishops and the Archbishops' Council', GS 185, Church House, Westminster, London, UK, January.

Church of England (2014a), 'The Church of England', http://www.churchofengland.org/about-us/structure/churchlawlegis/canons/section-a.aspx#Head1-7.

Church of England (2014b), 'Presentation on military chaplaincy', GS 1776 http://www.churchofengland.org/media/39111/gs1776.pdf.

Church of England, Mission and Public Affairs Council (2010), '"The Big Society" and the Church of England', GS1804.

Clark, J. A. (2004), *Islam, Charity and Activism: Middle Class Networks and Social Welfare in Egypt, Jordan and Yemen*, Bloomington/Indianapolis, IN: Indiana University Press.

Clark, L. S. (2003), *From Angels to Aliens: Teenagers, the Media, and the Supernatural*, Oxford, UK: Oxford University Press.

Clarke, G. and Jennings, M. (2008), 'Introduction', in G. Clarke and M. Jennings (eds), *Development, Civil Society and Faith-Based Organizations – Bridging the Sacred and the Secular*, Basingstoke, UK: Palgrave Macmillan.

Clarke, J. (2004), *Changing Welfare, Changing State – New Directions in Social Policy*, London, UK: Sage Publications.

Clements, B. and Spencer, N. (2014), *Voting and Values in Britain: Does Religion Count?*, London, UK: Theos.

Clifford, J. (1986), 'Introduction: partial truths', in J. Clifford and G. Marcus (eds), *Writing Culture*, Berkeley, CA: University of California Press.

CNN (2013), 'Muslim Vigilantes Bring Sharia Law to London', http://www.youtube.com/watch?v=b2liSHQntis [accessed 29 September 2014].

Cohen, A. P. (1996), 'Symbolising boundaries: identity and diversity in British cultures', in M. Anderson and E. Bort (eds), *The Frontiers of Europe*, London, UK: Wellington House, pp. 22–36.

Coleman, J. S. (1988), 'Social capital in the creation of human capital', Supplement: Organizations and Institutions, *American Journal of Sociology*, 94: S95–S120.

Coleman, J. S. (1994), *Foundations of Social Theory*, Cambridge, MA: Harvard University Press.

Coleman, J. S. (2000), *The Globalization of Charismatic Movements. Spreading the Gospel of Prosperity*, Cambridge, UK: Cambridge University Press.

Coleman, J. S. (2009), 'Transgressing the self: making Charismatic saints', *Critical Inquiry*, 35(3): 417–39.

Coleman, J. S. (2011), '"Right now!": Historiopraxy and the embodiment of charismatic temporalities', *Ethnos*, 76(4): 37–41.

Collins-Hill, P. (1986), 'Learning from the outsider within: The sociological significance of black feminist thought', *Social Problems*, 33(6): 14–32.

Connelly, A. (2014), 'Methodist central halls', http://www.religionandsociety.org.uk.

Conversi, D. (2007), 'Homogenisation, nationalism, and war: should we still read Ernest Gellner?', *Nations and Nationalism*, 13(3): 371–94.

Costa, P. (2003), 'Lo Stato di diritto: un'introduzione storica', in P. Costa and D. Zolo (eds), *Lo Stato di diritto. Storia, teoria e critica*, Milan, Italy: Feltrinelli, pp. 89–172.

Couldry, N. (2003), *Media Rituals: A Critical Approach*, London, UK: Routledge.

Couldry, N. (2008), 'Mediatization or mediation? Alternative understandings of the emergent space of digital storytelling', *New Media Society*, 10(3): 373–91.

Crenshaw, K. (1989), '*Demarginalising the intersection of race and sex: a black feminist critique of anti-discrimination doctrine feminist theory and anti-racist politics*', University of Chicago Legal Forum, pp. 139–67.

Crowe, D. (2007), *A History of Gypsies of Eastern Europe and Russia*, London, UK: Palgrave Macmillan.

Csordas, T. J. (1990), 'Embodiment as a paradigm for anthropology', *Ethos*, 18(1): 5–47.

Csordas, T. J. (2001), *Language, Charisma and Creativity. Ritual Life in the Catholic Charismatic Renewal*, New York, NY: Palgrave.

Csordas, T. J. (2009), 'Growing up Charismatic: morality and spirituality among children in a religious community', *Ethos*, 37(4): 414–40.

Cucchiari, S. (1990), 'Between shame and sanctification: patriarchy and its transformation in Sicilian Pentecostalism', *American Ethnologist*, 17(4): 687–707.

Cumper, P. and Lewis, T. (eds) (2012), *Religion, Rights and Secular Society. European Perspectives*, Cheltenham, UK: Edward Elgar.

Curran, J. and Liebes, T. (eds) (1998), *Media, Ritual and Identity*, London, UK: Routledge.

Davey-Smith, G., Chaturvedib, N., Harding, S., Nazroo, J. and Williams, R. (2000), 'Ethnic inequalities in health: a review of UK epidemiological evidence', *Critical Public Health*, 10(4): 375–408.

Davie, G. (1990), 'Believing without belonging. Is this the future of religion in Britain?', *Social Compass*, 37(4): 455–69.

Davie, G. (1994), *Religion in Britain since 1945*, Oxford: Blackwell.

Davie, G. (2001), 'Patterns of religion in Western Europe: an exceptional case', in R. Fenn (ed.), *The Blackwell Companion to Sociology of Religion*, Malden and Oxford, UK: Blackwell Publishing, pp. 264–78.

Davie, G. (2006), 'Is Europe an exceptional case?', *International Review of Mission*, 95: 247–58, 378–9.

Davie, G. (2007), 'Vicarious religion', in N. Ammerman (ed.), *Everyday Religion*, Oxford, UK: Oxford University Press, pp. 21–35.

Davis, D. H. (2000), *Religion and the Continental Congress 1774–1789: Contributions to Original Intent*, New York, NY: Oxford University Press.

Davis, D. H. (2011), 'George W. Bush and church–state partnerships to administer Social Service programs: cautions and concerns', in T. Hjelm (ed.), *Religion and Social Problems*, New York, NY and London, UK: Routledge, pp. 186–97.

Davy, B. (ed.) (2009), *Paganism: Critical Concepts in Religious Studies*, 3 vols, London, UK and New York, NY: Routledge.

Dayan, D. and Katz, E. (1992), *Media Events: The Live Broadcasting of History*, Cambridge, MA: Harvard University Press.

Deanoeux, G. (1993), *Urban Unrest in the Middle East – A Comparative Study of Informal Networks in Egypt, Iran and Lebanon*, Albany, NY: State University of New York Press.

Delhey, J., Newton, K. and Welzel, C. (2011), 'How general is trust in "most people"? Solving the radius of trust problem', *American Sociological Review*, 76(5): 786–807.

Deneulin, S. and Rakodi, C. (2012), 'Revisiting religion: development studies thirty years', *World Development*, 39(1): 45–54.

Dibdin, Sir L. (1932), *Establishment in England: Essays on Church and State*, London, UK: McMillan and Co.

Didion, J. (2003), *Fixed Ideas: America Since 9.11*, New York, NY: New York Review of Books.

Diez-Roux, A. V. (1998), 'Bringing context back into epidemiology: variables and fallacies in multilevel analysis', *American Journal of Public Health*, 88(2): 216–22.

Dillon, M. (2010), 'Can post-secular society tolerate religious differences?', *Sociology of Religion*, 71(2): 39–56.

Dinham, A. (2009), *Faiths, Public Policy and Civil Society: Problems, Policies, Controversies*, London: Palgrave Macmillan.

Dinham, A. and Jackson, R. (2010), 'Religion, welfare and education', in L. Woodhead and R. Catto (eds), *Religion and Change in Modern Britain*, London, UK: Routledge, pp. 271–94.

Diotallevi, L. (2007), 'Church–state relations in Catholic Europe and the crisis of the European social model', in G. Motzkin and Y. Fisher (eds), *Religion and Democracy in Contemporary Europe*, vol. 1, London, UK: The Van Leer Jerusalem Institute & NEF, pp. 125–40.

Diotallevi, L. (2010), *Una alternativa alla laicità*, Soveria Mannelli, Italy: Rubbettino.

Diotallevi, L. (2013), *La pretesa. Quale rapporto tra vangelo e ordine sociale*, Soveria Mannelli, Italy: Rubbettino.

Dobbelaere, K. (1981), *Secularization: A Multi-Dimensional Concept*, London, UK: Sage.

Doe, N. (2010), 'Towards a "common law" on religion in the European Union', in L. N. Leustean and J. T. S. Madeley (eds), *Religion, Politics and Law in the European Union*, London, UK: Routledge, pp. 141–60.

Doe, N. (2011), *Law and Religion in Europe: A Comparative Introduction*, Oxford, UK: Oxford University Press.

Durkheim, E. (2010[1912]), *Die elementaren Formen des religiösen Lebens*, Frankfurt and Leipzig, Germany: Verlag der Weltreligionen.

Dwyer, C. and Bressey, C. (2008), *New Geographies of Race and Racism*, London, UK: Ashgate.

Dwyer, P. (2004), *Understanding Social Citizenship*, Bristol, UK: The Policy Press.

Easterly, W., Ritzen J. and Woolcock, M. (2006), 'Social cohesion, institutions, and growth', *Economics & Politics*, 18(2): 103–20.

Ehrlich, M. C. (1996), 'Using "Ritual" to Study Journalism', *Journal of Communication Inquiry*, 20: 3–17.

El-Ghonemy, R. (1998), *Affluence and Poverty in the Middle East*, London, UK: Routledge.

Eller, C. (1993), *Living in the Lap of the Goddess: The Feminist Spirituality Movement in America*, Boston, MA: Beacon Press.

El-Menouar, Y. and Becker, M. (2011), 'Islam and integration in German media discourse', in T. Hjelm (ed.), *Religion and Social Problems*, New York and London: Routledge, pp. 229–44.

Engebrigtsen, A. I. (2011), 'Within or outside? Perceptions of self and other among Rom groups in Romania and Norway', *Romani Studies*, 21(2): 123–44.

Engelke, M. E. (2004), 'Discontinuity and the discourse of conversion', *Journal of Religion in Africa*, 34(1/2): 82–109.

Engelke, M. E. (2013), *God's Agents: Biblical Publicity in Contemporary England*, Berkeley, CA: University of California Press.

Enyedi, Z. (2003), 'Conclusion: emerging issues in the study of church–state relations', in J. T. S. Madeley (ed.), *Church and State in Contemporary Europe: The Chimera of Neutrality*, London, UK: Frank Cass, pp. 218–32.

Ettema, J. S. and Whitney, D. C. (1987), 'Professional mass communicators', in C. R. Berger and S. H. Berger (eds), *Handbook of Communication Science*, Newbury Park, CA: Sage, pp. 747–80.

Evangelical Alliance (2006), 'Faith and nation: report of a commission of inquiry to the UK Evangelical Alliance', http://www.eauk.org/current-affairs/publications/faith-and-nation.cfm.

Evangelical Alliance (2010), 'Churches should get stuck in to the Big Society', press release, 20 July.

Fairclough, N. (1992), *Discourse and Social Change*, Oxford, UK: Polity Press.

Farnsley, A. E. (2007), 'Faith-based initiatives', in J. A. Beckford and N. J. Demerath (eds), *The Sage Handbook of the Sociology of Religion*, London, UK: Sage, pp. 345–56.

Fedele, A. (2013), 'The metamorphoses of Neopaganism in traditionally Catholic countries in southern Europe', in R. Blanes and J. Mapril (eds), *Sites and Politics of Religious Diversity in Southern Europe: The Best of All Gods*, Leiden, Netherlands and Boston, MA: Brill, pp. 51–72.

Ferrari, S. (1999), 'The new wine and the old cast: tolerance, religion, and the law in contemporary Europe', in A. Sajò and S. Avineri (eds), *The Law of Religious Identity. Models for Post-Communism*, The Hague, Netherlands: Kluwer Law International, pp. 1–16.

Ferrari, S. (2012), 'Law and religion in a secular world: a European perspective', *Ecclesiastical Law Journal*, 14(3): 355–70.

Fonneland, T. (2015 in press), 'Approval of the Shamanistic Association: a local northern Norwegian construct with trans-local dynamics', in J. Lewis and I. T. Bårdsen (eds), *Nordic New Religions*, Leiden, Netherlands: Brill.

Förtroendebarometern (2014), http://medieakademien.se/wp-content/uploads/2014/03/2014_MedieAkedemins_Fortroendebarometer_140228.pdf [accessed 10 March].

Fosztó, L. (2006), 'Mono ethnic churches, the "undertaker parish", and rural civility in postsocialist Romania', in C. Hann (ed.), *The Postsocialist Religious Question: Chris Hann & the 'Civil Religion' Group*, Halle, Germany: LIT Verlag, pp. 269–92.

Fosztó, L. (2009), *Ritual Revitalisation after Socialism: Community, Personhood, and Conversion among Roma in a Transylvanian Village. Halle Studies in the Anthropology of Eurasia*, Halle, Germany: LIT Verlag.

Fox, J. (2004), The Religion and State Project, http://www.religionandstate.org/ 2010-03-30.

Fox, J. (2006), 'World separation of religion and state into the 21st century', *Comparative Political Studies*, 39(5): 537.

Fox, J. (2008), *A World Survey of Religion and the State*, Cambridge, UK: Cambridge University Press.

Fox, J. and Flores, D. (2009), 'Religions, constitutions and the state: a cross-national study', *The Journal of Politics*, 71(4): 1499–1513.

Fraser, A. (1995), *The Gypsies*, 2nd edn, Oxford, UK: Blackwell.

Freidman, F. (1996), *The Bosnian Muslims: Denial of a Nation*, Oxford, UK: Westview Press.

Fukuyama, F. (2001), 'Social capital, civil society and development', *Third World Quarterly*, 22(1): 7–20.

Furness, H. (2013), 'Grassroots Tories "betrayed" by David Cameron over same-sex marriage', *Telegraph*, 3 February.

Furness, S. and Gilligan, P. (2010), *Religion, Belief and Social Work*, Bristol, UK: The Policy Press.

Garcia, A. (2010), *The Pastoral Clinic: Addiction and Dispossession Along The Rio Grande*, Berkeley, CA and London, UK: University of California Press.

Gardell, M. (2003), *Gods of the Blood: The Pagan Revival and White Separatism*, Durham, NC: Duke University Press.

Gay y Blasco, P. (1999), *Gypsies in Madrid. Sex, Gender and the Performance of Identity*, Oxford, UK: Berg.

Gay y Blasco, P. (2002), 'Gypsy/Roma diasporas: introducing a comparative perspective', *Social Anthropology*, 10: 173–88.

Gellner, E. (1983), *Nations and Nationalism*, Oxford, UK: Blackwell.

General Household Survey, www.ons.org.uk.

Gerecht, R. M. (2011), 'How democracy became halal', *The New York Times*, 6 February [online], http://www.nytimes.com/2011/02/07/opinion/07gerecht.html?pagewanted=all&_r=0 [accessed 13 March].

Gerhards, J. (2004), 'Europäische Werte–Passt die Türkei kulturell zur EU', *Aus Politik und Zeitgeschichte*, 38: 14–20.

Gheorghe, N. and Acton, T. (2001), 'Citizens of the world and nowhere: minority, ethnic and human rights for Roma', *Between Past and Future: The Roma of Central and Eastern Europe*, Hatfield, UK: University of Hertfordshire Press, pp. 54–70.

Ghersetti, M. and Levin, A. (2002), 'Muslimer och islam i svenska nyhetsmedier Om rapporteringen av terrorattackerna i USA den 11 september 2001', Gothenburg, Sweden: Göteborgs universitet.

Gifford, P. (2004), *Ghana's New Christianity: Pentecostalism in a Globalizing African Economy*, Bloomington, IN: Indiana University Press.

Gilfillan, P. (2009), 'Fundamental ontology versus *esse est percipi*: theorizing (working class) being and liberation', *Space and Culture*, 12(2): 250–62.

Gilfillan, P. (2014), *A Sociological Phenomenology of Christian Redemption*, Guildford, UK: Grosvenor House Publishing.

Gilfillan, P., Phipps, A. and Aitken, E. (2013), 'A research report on the reception of the 2005 Religious Observance Guidelines in Scotland', *British Journal of Religious Education*, 35(1): 98–109.

Gill, L. (1990), '"Like a veil to cover them": women and the Pentecostal movement in La Paz', *American Ethnologist*, 17(4): 708–21.

Gilroy, P. (1993), *The Black Atlantic: Modernity and Double Consciousness*, Cambridge, MA: Harvard University Press.

Glasser, T. L. and Ettema, J. S. (1991), 'Investigative journalism and the moral order', in R. K. Avery and D. Eason (eds), *Critical Perspectives on Media and Society*, New York, NY: Guilford, pp. 203–25.

Glick Schiller, N., Basch, L. and Szanton Blanc, C. (1995), 'From immigrant to trans-migrant: theorizing transnational migration', *Anthropological Quarterly*, 68(1): 48–63.

Goffman, E. (1981), *Forms of Talk*, Oxford, UK: Basil Blackwell.

Göle, N. (2010), 'Manifestations of the religious-secular divide: self, state, and the public sphere', in L. E. Cady and E. S. Hurd (eds), *Comparative Secularisms in a Global Age*, Basingstoke, UK: Palgrave Macmillan, pp. 41–53.

Göle, N. (2011), 'The public visibility of Islam and European politics of resentment: the minarets–mosques debate', *Philosophy & Social Criticism*, 37(4): 383–92.

Gorski, P. S. (2000), 'Historicizing the secularization debate: church, state, and society in late medieval and early modern Europe, ca. 1300 to 1700', *American Sociological Review*, 65: 138–67.

Gorski, P. S., Kim, D. K., Torpey, J. and VanAntwerpen, J. (2012a), *The Post-secular in Question: Religion in Contemporary Society*, New York, NY: New York University Press.

Gorski, P. S., Kim, D. K., Torpey, J. and VanAntwerpen, J. (2012b), 'The post-secular in question', in P. S. Gorski, D. K. Kim, J. Torpey and J. VanAntwerpen (eds), *The Post-secular in Question: Religion in Contemporary Society*, New York, NY: New York University Press, pp. 1–22.

Goulbourne, H. and Solomos, J. (2003), 'Families, ethnicity and social capital', *Social Policy and Society*, 2(4): 329–38.

Gramsci, A. (1999), 'Selections from the prison notebooks', in A. Gramsci (ed.), *The Revolutionary Reader*, London, UK: Electric Book.

Granqvist, K. (2006), '(Un) wanted institutionalization: the case of Finnish Romani', *Romani Studies*, 16(1): 43–62.

Greeley, A. (1997), 'Coleman revisited: religious structures as a source of social capital', *American Behavioral Scientist*, 40(5): 587–94.

Greenwood, S. (2000), *Magic, Witchcraft and the Otherworld: An Anthropology*, Oxford, UK: Berg.

Gregorius, F. (2015), 'Modern Heathenism in Sweden: a case study in the creation of a traditional religion', in K. Rountree (ed.), *Contemporary Pagan and Native Faith Movements in Europe: Colonialist and Nationalist Impulses*, New York, NY: Berghahn, pp. 64–85.

Griffin, W. (2000), *Daughters of the Goddess: Studies of Healing, Identity and Empowerment*, Walnut Creek, CA: Altamira.

Grill, J. (2011), 'From street busking in Switzerland to meat factories in the UK: a comparative study of two Roma migration networks from Slovakia', in D. Kaneff and F. Pine (eds), *Global Connections and Emerging Inequalities in Europe: Perspectives on Poverty and Transnational Migration*, London, UK and New York, NY: Anthem Press, pp. 79–102.

Grill, J. (2012a), '"It's building up to something and it won't be nice when it erupts": the making of Roma/Gypsy migrants in post-industrial Scotland', *Focaal – Journal of Global and Historical Anthropology*, 62: 42–54.

Grill, J. (2012b), '"Going up to England": exploring mobilities among Roma from Eastern Slovakia', *Journal of Ethnic and Migration Studies*, 38(8): 1269–87.

Gross, Z. and Ziebertz, H. G. (2010), 'Religion and xenophobia', in H. G. Ziebertz, W. K. Kay and U. Riegel (eds), *Youth in Europe III*, Berlin, Germany: LIT-Verlag, pp. 181–99.

Grötsch, F. (2009), 'The mobilization of religion in the EU (1976-2007). From "blindness to religion" to the anchoring of religious norms in the EU', *Journal of Religion*, 2(3): 231–56.

Grötsch, F. and Schnabel, A. (2012), 'Integration – what integration? The religious framing of the European integration process between 1990 and 2000', *European Societies*, 14(4): 586–610.

Grube, D. (2011), 'How can "Britishness" be re-made?', *Political Quarterly*, 82(4): 628–35.

Guéhenno, J.-M. (2011), 'The Arab Spring is 2011, not 1989', *The New York Times*, 21 April [online], http://www.nytimes.com/2011/04/22/opinion/22iht-edguehenno22.html [accessed 13 March].

Gustafsson, G. (2003), 'Church–state separation Swedish-style', *West European Politics*, 26(1): 51–72.

Habermas, J. (1989), *The Structural Transformation of the Public Sphere: An Inquiry Into a Category of Bourgeois Society*, Cambridge, UK: Polity Press.

Habermas, J. (1992), 'Zur Rolle von Zivilgesellschaft und politischer Öffentlichkeit', in J. Habermas (ed.), *Faktizität und Geltung*, Frankfurt, Germany: Suhrkamp, pp. 399–467.

Habermas, J. (2006), 'Religion in the public sphere', *European Journal of Philosophy*, 14: 1–25.

Habermas, J. (2008), 'Notes on a post-secular society', *Sign and Sight*, http://print.signandsight.com/features/1714 [accessed 16 September 2014].

Habermas, J. (2011), '"The Political": the rational meaning of a questionable inheritance of political theology', in E. Mendieta and J. VanAntwerpen (eds), *The Power of Religion in the Public Sphere*, New York, NY: Colombia University Press.

Hadden, J. (1987), 'Toward desacralizing secularization theory', *Social Forces*, 65(3): 587–611.

Halikiopoulou, D. (2008), 'The changing dynamics of religion and national identity: Greece and the Republic of Ireland in a comparative perspective', *Journal of Religion in Europe*, 1(3): 302–28.

Hall, A. and Midgley, J. (2004), *Social Policy for Development*, London, UK: Sage.

Hall, S. (1992), *New Ethnicities in Race, Culture and Difference*, London, UK: Sage.

Hall, S. (1996), *Questions of Cultural Identity*, London, UK: Sage.

Hallin, D. C. and Mancini, P. (2004), *Comparing Media Systems: Three Models of Media and Politics*, Cambridge, UK: Cambridge University Press.

Harding, S. F. (1991), 'Representing fundamentalism: the problem of the repugnant cultural other', *Social Research*, 58(2): 373–93.

Harik, J. (1994), *The Public and Social Services of the Lebanese Militias*, Papers on Lebanon no. 14, Oxford, UK: Centre for Lebanese Studies.

Harvey, G. (1997), *Listening People, Speaking Earth: Contemporary Paganism*, London, UK: Hurst & Co.

Harvey, G. (2005), *Animism: Respecting the Living World*, London, UK: Hurst & Co.

Harvey, G. (2011), *Contemporary Paganism: Religions of the Earth from Druids and Witches to Heathens and Ecofeminists*, New York, NY: New York University Press.

Hasan, M. (2014), 'What the jihadists who bought "Islam for Dummies" on Amazon tell us about radicalisation', *New Statesman*, 21 August, http://www.newstatesman.com/religion/2014/08/what-jihadists-who-bought-islam-dummies-amazon-tell-us-about-radicalisation [accessed 17 September].

Hasanović, M. (2001), 'Poglavlje X Odnos drustvene zajednice prema problemima ovisnosti', in O. Sinanovic (ed.), *Ovisnost o drogama: Uzroci i posljedice, prevencija i ljecenje: Multidisciplinarni pristup*, Tuzla, Bosnia and Herzegovina: Behram – Begova Medresa u Tuzli, Medicinski Fakultet Univerziteta u Tuzli.

Haynes, J. (2010), 'Religion and politics in Europe, the Middle East and North Africa', in J. Haynes (ed.), *Religion and Politics in Europe, the Middle East and North Africa*, London, UK: Routledge, pp. 1–20.

Heath, A. F., Fisher, S. D., Sanders, D. and Sobolewska, M. (2011), 'Ethnic heterogeneity in the social bases of voting at the 2010 British general election', *Journal of Elections, Public Opinion & Parties*, 21(2): 255–77.

Hedman, H. (2009), 'Suomen romanikieli. Sen asema yhteisössään, käyttö ja romanien kieliasenteet', *Kotimaisten Kielten Tutkimuskeskuksen Verkkojulkaisuja*, Helsinki, Finland: Kotimaisten kielten tutkimuskeskus. http://scripta.kotus.fi/www/verkkojulkaisut/julk8/.

Heelas, P. (2009), 'The spiritual revolution: from "religion" to "spirituality"', in L. Woodhead (ed.), *Religions in the Modern World Traditions and Transformations*, London, UK: Routledge.

Heikkilä, M., Knuutila, J. and Scheinin, M. (2005), 'State and church in Finland', in G. Robbers (ed.), *State and Church in the European Union*, 2nd edn, Baden-Baden, Germany: Nomos, pp. 519–36.

Helms, E. (2008), 'East and West Kiss: gender, Orientalism, and Balkanism in Muslim-majority Bosnia-Herzegovina', *Slavic Review*, 67(1): 88–119.

Henry, C. M. and Springborg, R. (2001), *Globalization and the Politics of Development in the Middle East*, Cambridge, UK: Cambridge University Press.

Herbert, D. (2011), 'Theorizing religion and media in contemporary societies: an account of religious "publicization"', *European Journal of Cultural Studies*, 14(6): 626–48.

Hernesniemi, P. and Hannikainen, L. (2000), *Roma Minorities in the Nordic and Baltic Countries: Are Their Rights Realized?*, Rovaniemi, Finland: Lapland University Press.

Heyneman, S. (2004), 'Introduction', in S. P. Heyneman (ed.), *Islam and Social Policy*, Nashville, TN: Vanderbilt University Press, pp. 1–12.

Hickman, M., Crowley, H. and Mai, N. (2008), *Immigration and Social Cohesion in the UK: The Rhythms and Realities of Everyday Life*, York, UK: Joseph Rowntree Foundation.

Hill, M. (2006), *Social Policy in the Modern World: A Comparative Text*, Chichester, UK: Wiley-Blackwell.

Hill, M. (2010), 'Voices in the wilderness: the established Church of England and the European Union', in L. N. Leustean and J. T. S. Madeley (eds), *Religion, Politics and Law in the European Union*, London, UK: Routledge, pp. 161–74.

Hirschi, T. and Stark, R. (1969), 'Hellfire and delinquency', *Social Problems*, 17(2): 202–13.

Hjarvard, S. (2011), 'The mediatisation of religion: theorising religion, media and social change', *Culture and Religion*, 12: 119–35.

Hjarvard, S. (2012), 'Three forms of mediatized religion. Changing the public face of religion', in S. Hjarvard and M. Lövheim (eds), *Mediatization and Religion: Nordic Perspectives*, Gothenburg, Sweden: Nordicom, pp. 21–44.

Hjarvard, S. and Lövheim, M. (eds) (2012), *Mediatization and Religion: Nordic Perspectives*, Gothenburg, Sweden: Nordicom.

Hjelm, T. (2011), 'Religion and social problems: three perspectives', in T. Hjelm (ed.), *Religion and Social Problems*, New York, NY: Routledge, pp. 1–11.

Hjelm, T. (2012), 'Introduction: Islam and Muslims in European news media', *Journal of Religion in Europe*, 5(2): 137–39.

Hjelm, T. (2013), 'Religion, discourse and power: a contribution towards a critical sociology of religion', *Critical Sociology*, published online 4 March, doi:10.1177/0896920513477664.

Hjelm, T. (2014a), 'National piety: religious equality, freedom of religion and
    national identity in Finnish political discourse', *Religion*, 44(1): 25–48.
Hjelm, T. (2014b), 'Paradoxes of religious legitimacy and authenticity in an age
    of expediency', A paper presented at the annual conference of the British
    Sociological Association, 24 April.
Hjelm, T. (2014c), 'Religion, discourse and power: outline of a critical agenda for
    the sociology of religion', *Critical Sociology*, 40(6): 855–71.
Hjelm, T. (2014d), *Social Constructionisms: Approaches to the Study of the
    Human World*, Basingstoke, UK: Palgrave Macmillan.
Hjerm, M. (1998), 'National Identities, national pride and xenophobia: a
    comparison of four Western countries', *Acta Sociologica*, 41(4): 335–47.
Hjerm, M. (2007), 'Are we the people? National sentiments in a changing
    political landscape', in S. Svallfors (ed.), *The Political Sociology of the
    Welfare State: Institutions, Cleavages, Orientations*, Stanford, CA:
    Stanford University Press.
Hobsbawm, E. (1987), *The Age of Empire, 1875–1914*, London, UK: Abacus.
Hobsbawm, E. (1990), *Nations and Nationalism since 1780*, Cambridge, UK:
    Cambridge University Press.
Hokkanen, S. (2007), 'The Pentecostal movement in Finland', a Finnish
    Institutions Research Paper, University of Tampere, Finland, http://www.uta.fi/
    FAST/FIN/REL/sh-pente.html.
Hollinger, F., Haller, M. and Valle-Hollinger, A. (2007), 'Christian religion, society
    and the state in the modern world', *Innovation: The European Journal of Social
    Science Research*, 20(2): 133–57.
Holyoake, G. J. (1871), *The Principles of Secularism*, London, UK: Book Store.
Hood, D. E. (2011), *Addiction Treatment: Comparing Religion and Science in
    Application*, Somerset, NJ: Transaction.
House of Commons Debates, 2 December 2007.
House of Commons Debates, 12 December 2012.
Houston, K. (2010), 'The logic of structured dialogue between religious
    associations and the institutions of the European Union', in L. N. Leustean
    and J. T. S. Madeley (eds), *Religion, Politics and Law in the European Union*,
    London, UK: Routledge, pp. 201–16.
Hox, J. (2002), *Multilevel Analysis: Techniques and Applications*, Mahwah, NJ:
    Taylor & Francis.
Hox, J. and Kreft, I. G. G. (1994), 'Multilevel analysis methods', *Sociological
    Methods Research*, 22(3): 283–301.
Hunt, S. J. (2007), 'The rhetoric of rights in UK Christian churches regarding non-
    heterosexual citizenship', *Politics and Religion*, 4(2): 183–200.
Hutton, R. (1999), *The Triumph of the Moon: A History of Modern Pagan
    Witchcraft*, Oxford, UK: Oxford University Press.
Ivakhiv, A. (2005), 'The revival of Ukrainian Native Faith', in M. Strmiska (ed.),
    Modern Paganism in World Cultures: Comparative Perspectives, Santa
    Barbara, CA: ABC-CLIO, pp. 209–39.
Ivakhiv, A. (2009), 'Nature and ethnicity in East European Paganism: an
    environmental ethic of the religious right?', in B. Davy (ed.), *Paganism:
    Critical Concepts in Religious Studies*, vol. 2, London, UK and New York, NY:
    Routledge, pp. 213–42.
Jawad, R. (2009), *Social Welfare and Religion in the Middle East*, Bristol, UK: The
    Policy Press.

Jelen, T. D. (2005), 'Political Esperanto: rhetorical resources and limitations of the Christian Right in the United States', *Sociology of Religion*, 66(3): 303–21.

Jelen, T. D. (2010), 'Religious liberty as a democratic institution', in D. H. Davis (ed.), *Church and State in the United States*, Oxford, UK: Oxford University, pp. 311–29.

Jenkins, R. (1996), *Social Identity*, Mahwah, NJ: Taylor & Francis.

Jensen, D. (2011), 'Classifying church-state arrangements. Beyond religious versus secular', in N. Hosen and R. Mohr (eds), *Law and Religion in Public Life: The Contemporary Debate*, London, UK: Routledge, pp. 15–33.

Jepperson, R. J. (2002), 'Political modernities: disentangling two underlying dimensions of institutional differentiation', *Sociological Theory*, 20(1): 61–85.

Jepperson, R. J. and Meyer, J. W. (2000), 'Ordine pubblico e costruzione di organizzazioni formali', in W. W. Powell, J. W. Meyer and P. J. DiMaggio (eds), *Il neoistituzionalismo nell'analisi organizzativa*, Turin, Italy: Edizioni di Comunità, pp. 275–312.

Jones, F. L. and Smith, P. (2001), 'Individual and societal bases of national identity. A comparative multi-level analysis', *European Sociological Review*, 17(2): 103–18.

Jones, S., Hooper, J. and Kington, K. (2010), 'Pope Benedict XVI goes to war with "atheist extremism"', *Guardian*, 16 September.

Juva, M. (1960), *Valtiokirkosta kansankirkoksi*, Helsinki, Finland: Suomen Kirkkohistoriallinen Seura.

Kääriäinen, K., Ketola, K., Niemelä, K., Palmu, H. and Salomäki, H. (2009), *Facing Diversity. The Evangelical Lutheran Church of Finland from 2004 to 2007*, Tampere, Finland: Church Research Institute.

Kagan, R. (2011), 'A foreign policy that needs realism and pragmatism', *The Washington Post*, 28 April [online], http://www.washingtonpost.com/opinions/a-foreign-policy-that-needs-realism-and-pragmatism/2011/04/28/AFu8uy8E_story.html [accessed 13 March].

Kahl, S. (2005), 'The religious roots of modern poverty policy: Catholic, Lutheran and Reformed Protestant traditions compared', *Archives Européennes de Sociologie* (*European Journal of Sociology*), XLVI(1): 91–126.

Karshenas, M. and Moghadam, V. (2006), 'Social policy in the Middle East: introduction and overview', in M. Karshenas and V. Moghadam (eds), *Social Policy in the Middle East*, UNRISD Social Policy in a Development Context Series, New York, NY: Palgrave Macmillan, pp. 1–30.

Katbamna, S., Ahmad, W., Bhakta, P., Baker, R. and Parker, G. (2004), 'Do they look after their own? Informal support for South Asian carers', *Health and Social Care in the Community*, 12(5): 398–406.

Kettell, S. (2012), 'Religion and the Big Society: a match made in heaven?', *Policy and Politics*, 40(2): 281–96.

Kettell, S. (2013), 'Faithless: the politics of New Atheism', *Secularism and Non-Religion*, 2: 61–78.

Khalidi-Beyhum, R. (1999), *Poverty Reduction Policies in Jordan and Lebanon: An Overview*, Eradicating Poverty Series no. 10, Economic and Social Commission for Western Asia, New York, NY: United Nations.

Khanfar, W. (2011), 'Those who support democracy must welcome the rise of political Islam', *The Guardian*, 27 November [online], http://www.guardian.co.uk/commentisfree/2011/nov/27/islamist-arab-spring-west-fears?INTCMP=SRCH [accessed 30 March].

King, R. D. and Wheelock, D. (2007), 'Group threat and social control: race, perceptions of minorities and the desire to punish', *Social Forces*, 85(3): 1255–80.

Klimova-Alexander, I. (2005), *The Romani Voice in World Politics: The United Nations and Non-State Actors*, Aldershot, UK: Ashgate.

Knippenberg, H. (2006), 'The political geography of religion: historical state–church relations in Europe and recent challenges', *GeoJournal*, 67: 253–65.

Knott, K., Poole, E. and Taira, T. (2013), *Media Portrayals of Religion and the Secular Sacred. Representation and Change*, Farnham, UK: Ashgate.

Knutsen, O. (2004), 'Religious denomination and party choice in Western Europe: a comparative longitudinal study from eight countries, 1970 – 97', *International Political Science Review*, 25: 97–128.

Knutson, K. E. (2011), 'Breaking the chains?: constraint and the political rhetoric of religious interest groups', *Politics and Religion*, 4: 312–37.

Köhrsen, J. (2012), 'How religious is the public sphere? A critical stance on the debate about public religion and post-secularity', *Acta Sociologica*, 55: 273–88.

Kolstoe, P. (2000), *Political Construction Sites: Nation-building in Russia and the Post-Soviet States*, Boulder, CO: Westview Press.

Kosmin, B. A. (2009), 'Contemporary secularity and secularism', in B. Kosmin and A. Keysar (eds), *Secularism and Secularity: Contemporary International Perspectives*, San Francisco, CA: Institute for the Study of Secularism in Society and Culture.

Kotler-Berkowitz, L. A. (2001), 'Religion and voting behaviour in Great Britain: a reassessment', *British Journal of Political Science*, 31(3): 523–54.

Kourounis, A. (2007), 'Greece: exploring the revival of ancient religious traditions', *Deutsche Welle*, http://www.dw.de/greece-exploring-the-revival-of-ancient-religious-traditions/a-2786954-1 [accessed 19 February 2014].

Kraft, S.-E. (2015), 'Sami neo-shamanism in Norway: colonial grounds, ethnic revival and Pagan pathways', in K. Rountree (ed.), *Contemporary Pagan and Native Faith Movements in Europe: Colonialist and Nationalist Impulses*, New York, NY: Berghahn, pp. 25–42.

Krohn, I. (2006), 'Tiedote 15.2.2006', http://www.vihreat.fi/yleviarkisto/2_2006/0045.html [accessed 14 July 2012].

Kumlin, S. and Svallfors, S. (2007), 'Social stratification and political articulation: why attitudinal class differences vary across countries', in S. Mau and B. Veghte (eds), *Social Justice, Legitimacy and the Welfare State*, Aldershot, UK: Ashgate, pp. 19–46.

Kuru, A. T. (2007), 'Passive and assertive secularism. Historical conditions, ideological struggles, and state policies toward religion', *World Politics*, 59: 568–94.

LA 157/2005vp (2005), Laki Suomen perustuslain 76 §:n kumoamisesta sekä eräiden siihen liittyvien lakien kumoamisesta ja muuttamisesta, http://www.eduskunta.fi/faktatmp/utatmp/akxtmp/la_157_2005_p.shtml [accessed 14 July 2012].

Ladányi, J. and Szelényi, I. (2006), *Patterns of Exclusion: Constructing Gypsy Ethnicity and the Making of an Underclass in Transitional Societies of Europe*, New York, NY: Columbia University Press.

Lampinen, T. (1984), 'Preaching of state – civil religion in the proclamation of church and state in Finland', in B. Harmati (ed.), *The Church and Civil Religion in the Nordic Countries of Europe*, Geneva, Switzerland: Lutheran World Federation, pp. 41–8.

Larsen, T. (2007), 'Defining and locating evangelicalism', in T. Larsen and D. J. Treier (eds), *The Cambridge Companion to Evangelical Theology*, Cambridge, UK: Cambridge University Press, pp. 1–14.

Lehtinen, Sanna (2011), 'Fighting against unemployment: Finnish parishes as agents in European Social Fund Projects', in Titus Hjelm (ed.), *Religion and Social Problems*, New York: Routledge, pp. 67–81.

Lesiv, M. (2013), *The Return of Ancestral Gods: Modern Ukrainian Paganism as an Alternative Vision for a Nation*, Montreal and Kingston, Canada: McGill–Queen's University Press.

Lewis, J. R. (2012), 'The Pagan explosion revisited: a statistical postmortem on the Teen Witch fad', *The Pomegranate*, 14(1): 128–39.

Lilli, W. and Diehl, M. (1999), 'Measuring national identity. Mannheimer Zentrum für Europäische Sozialforschung', Arbeitspapiere – Mannheimer Zentrum für Europäische Sozialforschung, 10.

Lincoln, B. (2003), *Holy Terrors: Thinking about Religion after September 11*, Chicago, IL: The University of Chicago Press.

Lindberg, J. (2014), 'Politicisation of religion in Nordic parliamentary debates 1988–2009', *Politics, Religion & Ideology*, 15(4): 565–82.

Linderman, A. (2013), 'Resultat och iakttagelser delstudie 1. Working paper'.

Lindquist, G. (2011), 'Ethic identity and religious competition: Buddhism and shamanism in southern Siberia', in G. Lindquist and D. Handelman (eds), *Religion, Politics and Globalization: Anthropological Approaches*, New York, NY: Berghahn, pp. 69–90.

Lipset, S. M. and Rokkan, S. (1967), *Party Systems and Voter Alignments: Cross-national Perspectives*, New York, NY: Free Press.

Llera Blanes, R. (2007), 'Why Africans do what they do. Arguments, discussions and religious transmission in Angolan Pentecostal churches in Lisbon', *Quaderos de l'Institut Catala d'Antropologia*, 23: 123–37.

Loewe, M. (2004), 'New avenues to be opened for social protection in the Arab World: the case of Egypt', *International Journal of Social Welfare*, 13: 3–14.

Lorentzen, L. (2001), 'Who is Indian? Religion, globalization and Chiapas', in D. H. Hopkins, L. A. Lorentzen, E. Mendieta and D. Batstone (eds), *Religions/Globalizations: Theories and Cases*, Durham, NC: Duke University Press, pp. 84–102.

Lövheim, M. (2012), 'Religious socialisation in a media age', *Nordic Journal of Religion and Society*, 5: 151–68.

Lövheim, M. and Axner, M. (2011), 'Halal-tv: negotiating the place of religion in Swedish public discourse', *Nordic Journal of Religion and Society*, 24: 57–74.

Lövheim, M. and Axner, M. (2014), 'Mediatized religion and public spheres: current approaches and new questions', in K. Granholm, M. Moberg and S. Sjö (eds), *Religion, Media, and Social Change*, New York, NY and London, UK: Routledge, pp. 38–53.

Lövheim, M. and Lundby, K. (2013), 'Mediated religion across time and space. A case study of Norwegian newspapers', *Nordic Journal of Religion and Society*, 26: 25–44.

Lövheim, M. and Lynch, G. (2011), 'The mediatisation of religion debate: an introduction', *Culture and Religion*, 12(2): 111–17.

Luciani, G. (1990), 'Introduction', in G. Luciani (ed.), *The Arab State*, London, UK: Routledge, pp. xvii–xxxii.

Luckmann, T. (1967), *The Invisible Religion: The Problem of Religion in Modern Society*, New York, NY: Macmillan.

Luhmann, N. (1977), *Funktion der Religion*, Frankfurt, Germany: Suhrkamp.

Luhmann, N. (1990), *La differenziazione del diritto*, Bologna, Italy: Il Mulino.

Luhmann, N. (1995), *Das recht der gesellschaft*, Frankfurt, Germany: Suhrkamp.

Luhmann, N. (1997), *Die Gesellchaft der Gesellchaft*, vol. II, Frankfurt, Germany: Suhrkamp.

Luhmann, N. (2002), *I diritti fondamentali come istituzione*, Bari, Italy: Dedalo.

Luhmann, N. (2005), *Organizzazione e decisione*, Milan, Italy: Bruno Mondadori.

Luhrmann, T. (1989), *Persuasions of the Witch's Craft: Ritual Magic in Contemporary England*, Cambridge, MA: Harvard University Press.

Lundby, K. (2009), *Mediatization: Concept, Changes, Consequences*, New York, NY: Lang.

Lundby, K. (2010), 'Medier som ressurs for religion', in P. K. Botvar and U. Schmidt (eds), *Religion i dagens Norge. Mellom sekularisering og sakralisering*, Oslo, Norway: Universitetsforlaget, pp. 111–30.

Maček, I. (2007), '"Imitation of life": negotiating normality in Sarajevo under siege', in X. Bougarel, G. Duijzings and E. Helms (eds), *The New Bosnian Mosaic: Identities, Memories and Moral Claims in a Post-War Society*, Aldershot, UK: Ashgate.

Madeley, J. T. S. (2003), 'European liberal democracies and the principle of state religious neutrality', in J. T. S. Madeley (ed.), *Church and State in Contemporary Europe: The Chimera of Neutrality*, London, UK: Frank Cass, pp. 1–22.

Madeley, J. T. S. (2009), 'Unequally yoked: the antinomies of church-state separation in Europe and the USA', *European Political Science*, 8: 273–88.

Malcolm, N. (1994), *Bosnia: A Short History*, London, UK: Macmillan.

Malik, K. (2008), *Strange Fruit: Why Both Sides Are Wrong in the Race Debate*, London, UK: One World Publishing.

Mannheim, K. (1944), *Diagnosis of Our Time*, New York, NY: Oxford University Press.

Manow, P. (2005), 'Plurale Wohlfahrtswelten. Auf der Suche nach dem Sozialmodell und seinen religiösen Wurzeln', *Jahrbuch für Christliche Sozialwissenschaften*, 46: 207–34.

Manow, P. and van Kersbergen, K. (2009), 'Religion and the Western welfare state – the theoretical context', in P. Manow and K. van Kersbergen (eds), *Religion, Class Coalitions and Welfare States*, Cambridge, UK: Cambridge University Press, pp. 1–38.

Markkanen, A. (2003), *Luonnollisesti: Etnografinen Tutkimus Romaninaisten Elämänkulusta*, Joensuu, Finland: Joensuu Yliopisto.

Markus, R. A. (1970), *Saeculum: History and Society in the Theology of St Augustin*, Cambridge, UK: Cambridge University Press.

Markus, R. A. (2006), *Christianity and the Secular*, Notre Dame, IN: University of Notre Dame Press.

Martin, D. (1978), *A General Theory of Secularization*, Oxford, UK: Blackwell.

Mathews, S. H. and Rosner, T. T. (1988), 'Shared filial responsibility: the family as primary caregiver', *Journal of Marriage and the Family*, 50: 185–95.

Mau, S. (2002), 'Wohlfahrtsregime als Reziprozitätsarrangements. Versuch einer Typisierung', *Berliner Journal*, 12(3): 345–64.

May, T. (2010), *Contemporary Political Movements and the Thought of Jacques Rancière: Equality in Action*, Edinburgh, UK: Edinburgh University Press.

Maynard, M., Afshar, H., Franks, M. and Wray, S. (2008), *Women in Later Life: Exploring Race and Ethnicity*, Maidenhead, UK: Open University Press.

McAnulla, S. (2012), 'Radical atheism and religious power: the politics of New Atheism', *Approaching Religion*, 2(1): 87–99.

McConnell, M. W. (2009), 'Reclaiming the secular and the religious: the primacy of religious autonomy', *Social Research*, 4: 1333–44.

McCrea, R. (2010), *Religion and the Public Order of the European Union*, Oxford, UK: Oxford University Press.

McGarry, A. (2010), *Who speaks for Roma? Political Representation of a Transnational Minority Community*, London, UK: Continuum Publishing.

McGee, J. E. (1948), *A History of The British Secular Movement*, Girard, KS: Haldeman-Julius Publications.

McGraw, B. (2003), *Rediscovering America's Sacred Ground: Public Religion and Pursuit of the Good in a Pluralistic America*, Albany, NY: State University of New York Press.

McLennan, G. (2007), 'Towards postsecular sociology?', *Sociology*, 41(5): 857–70.

Meer, N. (2014), *Key Concepts in Race and Ethnicity*, London, UK: Sage.

Merrel, J., Kinsella, F., Murphy, F., Philpin, S. and Amina, A. (2006), 'Accessibility and equity of health and social care services: exploring the view and experiences of Bangladeshi carers in South Wales, UK', *Health and Social Care in the Community*, 14(3): 197–205.

Messkoub, M. (2006), 'Constitutionalism, modernization and Islamization: the political economy of social policy in Iran', in M. Karshenas and V. Moghadam (eds), *Social Policy in the Middle East*, UNRISD Social Policy in a Development Context Series, New York, NY: Palgrave Macmillan, pp. 190–220.

Methodist Central Hall (2014), 'History overview', http://www.methodist-central-hall.org.uk/index.php?option=com_content&view=category&id=32&Itemid=25.

Meur, W. P. van (1999), 'Die Transformation der baltischen Staaten: Baltische Wirtschaft und russische Diaspora', *Bericht des BIOst (6)*, Cologne, Germany: Bundesinstitut für ostwissenschaftliche und international Studien.

Meyer, B. (1995), 'Magic, mermaids and modernity: the attraction of Pentecostalism in Africa', *Etnofoor*, 2: 47–67.

Meyer, B. (1998), '"Make a complete break with the past": memory and postcolonial modernity in Ghanaian Pentecostal discourse', in R. Werbner (ed.), *Memory and the Postcolony: African Anthropology and the Critique of Power*, London, UK: Zed Books.

Michel, P. and Pace, E. (eds) (2011), *Annual Review of the Sociology of Religion, vol. 2: Religion and Politics*, Leiden, Netherlands: Brill.

Micklethwait, J. and Wooldridge, A. (2009), *God is Back: How the Global Rise of Faith is Changing the World*, London, UK: Penguin.

Miller, C. (1998), 'American Roma and the ideology of defilement', in D. Tong (ed.), *Gypsies: An Interdisciplinary Reader*, New York, NY and London, UK: Garland Publishing, pp. 201–17.

Miller, D. (1993), 'In defence of nationality', *Journal of Applied Philosophy*, 10(1): 3–16.

Minkenberg, M. (2003), 'The policy impact of church–state relations: family policy and abortion in Britain, France, and Germany', *West European Politics*, 26(1): 195–217.

Minkenberg, M. (2010), 'Party politics, religion and elections in Western democracies', *Comparative European Politics*, 8(4): 385–414.

Moberg, M., Granholm, K. and Nynäs, P. (2012), 'Trajectories of post-secular complexity: an introduction', in P. Nynäs, M. Lassander and T. Utriainen (eds), *Post-Secular Society*, New Brunswick, NJ: Transaction Publishers, pp. 1–25.

Modood, T. (2009), 'Muslims, religious equality and secularism', in G. B. Levey and T. Modood (eds), *Secularism, Religion and Multicultural Citizenship*, Cambridge, UK: Cambridge University Press, pp. 164–85.

Modood, T. (2010), 'Moderate secularism, religion as identity and respect for religion', *Political Quarterly*, 81(1): 4–14.

Modood, T. (2012a), 'Is there a crisis of secularism in Western Europe?', *Sociology of Religion*, 73(2): 130–49.

Modood, T. (2012b), 'Moderate secularism, religion as identity and respect for religion', in E. Reed and M. Dumper (eds), *Civil Liberties, National Security and Prospects for Consensus*, Cambridge, UK: Cambridge University Press, pp. 62–80.

Monsma, S. V. (2000), 'Substantive neutrality as a basis for free exercise-no establishment common ground', *Journal of Church & State*, 42(1): 13–36.

Monsma, S. V. and Soper, J. C. (2009), *The Challenge of Pluralism: Church and State in Five Democracies*, 2nd edn, Lanham, MD: Rowman and Littlefield.

Moreton, C. (2012), 'The battle for Britain's soul begins here', *Daily Telegraph*, 18 March.

Moriarty, J. and Butt, J. (2004), 'Inequalities in quality of life among older people from different ethnic groups', *Ageing and Society*, 24(5): 729–53.

Morrison, I. A. (2013), 'Rancière, religion and the political', *Citizenship Studies*, 17(6/7): 886–900.

Morrison, I. A. (2014), 'Orientalism and the construction of the apolitical Buddhist Subject', in E. F. Isin and P. Nyers (eds), *The Routledge Handbook of Global Citizenship Studies*, London, UK: Routledge, pp. 325–34.

Muir, R. (2007), 'The new identity politics', London, UK: Institute for Public Policy Research.

Muir, R. and Wetherell, M. (2010), 'Identity, politics and public policy', London, UK: Institute for Public Policy Research.

Murphy-O'Connor, C. (2006), 'Time to stand up for our beliefs', *Times*, 25 November.

Nämnden för statligt stöd till trossamfund, http://www.sst.a.se/statistik/statisktik 2012.4.524fbdf71429b7641b72f86.html [accessed 10 March 2014].

Napolitano, Andrew P. (2012), 'The Arab spring becomes a western winter', FoxNews.com, 27 September, http://www.foxnews.com/opinion/2012/09/27/arab-spring-becomes-western-winter [accessed 13 March].

National Secular Society (2014a), 'MOD spends 22 million a year on Christian chaplains', http://www.secularism.org.uk/mod-spends-gbp22-million-a-year.html.

National Secular Society (2014b), 'Chaplaincy funding and the NHS', http://www.secularism.org.uk/nhs-chaplaincy-funding.html.

Nayak, A. and Kehily, M. J. (2008), *Gender, Youth and Culture: Young Masculinities and Femininities*, New York, NY: Palgrave.

Nelson-Becker, H., Ai, L. A., Hopp, F., McCormick, T. R., Schlueter, J. O. and Camp, J. K. (2013), 'Spirituality in end-of-life and palliative care: what matters?', *Journal of Social Work*, 9(2/3): 112–16.

New Statesman (2013), 'New Year Leader: the moral challenges of our times' [online], http://www.newstatesman.com/2013/12/moral-challenges-our-time [accessed 10 February 2014].

Niemelä, K. and Christensen, H. C. (2013), 'Religion in the newspapers in the Nordic countries 1988–2008', *Nordic Journal of Religion and Society*, 26: 5–24.

Nobles, M. (2002), 'Racial categorisation and censuses', in D. Kertzer and D. Arel (eds), *Census and Identity: The Politics of Race, Ethnicity and Language in National Censuses*, Cambridge, UK: Cambridge University Press, pp. 43–71.

Nolan, M., Davies, S., Brown, J., Keady, J. and Nolan, J. (2004), 'Beyond person centred care: a new vision for gerontological nursing', *Journal of Clinical Nursing*, 13: 45–53.

Nord, L. (2001), *Vår tids ledare. En studie av den svenska dagspressens politiska opinionsbildning*, Stockholm, Sweden: Carlssons.

Nordberg, C. (2005), 'Integrating a traditional minority into a Nordic society: elite discourse on Finnish Roma', *Social Work and Society*, 3(2): 158–73.

Nordicom, http://www.nordicom.gu.se/en/media-trends/media-statistics [accessed 10 March 2014].

Office for National Statistics (2011), 'Religion in England and Wales 2011', December.

Okely, J. (1983), *The Traveller-Gypsies*, Cambridge, UK: Cambridge University Press.

Okely, J. (1996), *Own and Other Culture*, London, UK and New York, NY: Routledge.

O'Nions, H. (2007), *Minority Rights Protection in International Law: The Roma of Europe*, Aldershot, UK: Ashgate.

Orloff, A. S. (2005), 'Social provision and regulation: theories of states, social policies and modernity', in J. Adams, E. S. Clements and A. Shola Orloff (eds), *Remaking Modernity: Politics, History and Sociology*, Durham/London, UK: Duke University Press, pp. 190–224.

Østebø, M. T., Haukanes, H. and Blystad, A. (2013), 'Strong state policies on gender and aid: threats and opportunities for Norwegian Faith-Based Organisations', *Forum for Development Studies*, 40(2): 193–216.

Palonen, K. (2008), 'Speaking *Pro et Contra*: the rhetorical intelligibility of parliamentary politics and the political intelligibility of parliamentary rhetoric', in S. Soininen and T. Turkka (eds), *The Parliamentary Style of Politics*, Helsinki, Finland: The Finnish Political Science Association, pp. 82–105.

Pearson, J. (2009), 'Demarcating the field: Paganism, Wicca and Witchcraft', in B. Davy (ed.), *Paganism: Critical Concepts in Religious Studies*, vol. 1, London, UK and New York, NY: Routledge, pp. 228–40.

Pekonen, K. (2008), 'Two versions of representative talk in Finnish parliament', in S. Soininen and T. Turkka (eds), *The Parliamentary Style of Politics*, Helsinki, Finland: The Finnish Political Science Association, pp. 208–27.

Pelkmans, M. (2009), 'Introduction: Post-Soviet space and the unexpected turns of religious life', in M. Pelkmans (ed.), *Conversion after Socialism: Disruptions, Modernisms and Technologies of Faith in the Former Soviet Union*, New York, NY and Oxford, UK: Berghahn Books.

Perica, V. (2002), *Balkan Idols: Religion and Nationalism in Yugoslav States*, Oxford, UK: Oxford University Press.

Petersson, O. and Carlberg, I. (1990), *Makten över tanken: en bok om det svenska massmediesamhället* [*Power Over Thought: a Book on Swedish Mass Media Society*], Stockholm, Sweden: Carlsson.

Pettersson, T. (2009), 'Religion och samhällspraktik. En jämförande analys av det sekulariserade Sverige', *Socialvetenskaplig tidskrift*, 3–4: 233–64.

PEW Forum on Religion and Public Life (2011), 'Religion in the news: Islam was no. 1 topic in 2010', http://www.pewforum.org/Politics-and-Elections/Religion-in-the-News--Islam-Was-No--1-Topic-in-2010.aspx#1 [accessed 18 February 2013].

Philippopoulos-Mihailopoulos, A. (2011), *Niklas Luhmann: Law, Justice, Society*, London, UK: Routledge.

Phillips, J. (2012), 'The Arab Spring descends into Islamist winter: implications for U.S. policy', *The Heritage Foundation Backgrounder*, 20 December, pp. 1–10.

Pickles, E. (2010), 'Why this government wants faith groups to play a leading part in the Big Society', Conservative Home Blogs, 27 November, http://conservativehome.blogs.com/localgovernment/2010/11/eric-pickles-mp-why-this-government-wants-faith-groups-to-play-a-leading-part-in-big-society.html.

Pierson, P. (2000), 'Increasing returns, path dependence, and the study of politics', *American Political Science Review*, 94(2): 251–67.

Pizza, M. and Lewis, J. R. (eds) (2009), *Handbook of Contemporary Paganism*, Leiden, Netherlands and Boston, MA: Brill.

Pollock, D. (2008), 'Religious change in Europe: theoretical considerations and empirical findings', *Social Compass*, 55(2): 168–86.

Potter, J. (1996), *Representing Reality: Discourse, Rhetoric, and Social Construction*, London, UK: Sage.

Putnam, R. D. (1993), *Making Democracy Work: Civic Traditions in Modern Italy*, Princeton, NJ: Princeton University Press.

Putnam, R. D. (1995a), 'Bowling alone: America's declining social capital', *Journal of Democracy*, 6(1): 65–78.

Putnam, R. D. (1995b), 'Bowling alone: America's declining social capital', in J. Lin and Ch. Mele (eds), *The Urban Sociology Reader*, Oxon, UK and New York, NY: Routledge, pp. 120–8.

Putnam, R. D. (2000), *Bowling Alone: The Collapse and Revival of American Community*, New York, NY: Simon and Schuster.

Rancière, J. (1995), *Dis-agreement*, trans. J. Rose, Minneapolis, MN and London, UK: University of Minnesota Press.

Rancière, J. (2001), 'Ten theses on politics', *Theory and Event*, 5(3). http://muse.jhu.edu/journals/theory_and_event/.

Rancière, J. (2004), 'Who is the subject of the rights of man?', *The South Atlantic Quarterly*, 103(2/3): 297–310.

Rancière, J. (2005), *Hatred of Democracy*, London, UK and New York, NY: Verso.

Rawls, J. (1997), 'The idea of public reason revisited', *University of Chicago Law Review*, 64: 765–807.

Raymond, C. (2011), 'The continued salience of religious voting in the United States, Germany, and Great Britain', *Electoral Studies*, 30: 125–35.

Richards, D. and Smith, M. (2002), *Governance and Public Policy in the United Kingdom*, Oxford, UK: Oxford University Press.

Richardson, J. E. (2007), *Analysing Newspapers: An Approach from Critical Discourse Analysis*, Basingstoke, UK: Palgrave Macmillan.

Richardson, J. T. (2006), 'The sociology of religious freedom: a structural and socio-legal analysis', *Sociology of Religion*, 3: 271–94.

Richardson, J. T. (2014), 'The social construction of legal pluralism', in A. Possamai, J. T. Richardson and B. S. Turner (eds), *Legal Pluralism and Shari'a Law*, London, UK: Routledge, pp. 80–95.

Ries, J. (2011) 'Romany/Gypsy church or people of God? The dynamics of Pentecostal Mission and Romani/Gypsy ethnicity management', in M. Stewart and M. Rövid (eds), *Multi-disciplinary Approaches to Romani Studies*, Budapest, Hungary: CEU Press, pp. 271–9.

Riis, O. (1989), 'The role of religion in legitimating the modern structuration of society', *Acta Sociologica*, 32(2): 137–53.

Ringwald, C. D. (2002), *The Soul of Recovery: Uncovering the Spiritual Dimension in the Treatment of Addictions*, Oxford, UK and New York, NY: Oxford University Press.

Rivers, J. (2012), 'The secularisation of the British constitution', *Ecclesiastical Law Journal*, 14(3): 371–99.

Robbers, G. (2005). 'State and church in the European Union', in G. Robbers (ed.), *State and Church in the European Union*, 2nd edn, Baden-Baden, Germany: Nomos, pp. 577–89.

Robertson, R. (1990), 'After nostalgia? Wilful nostalgia and the phase of globalisation', in B. S. Turner (ed.), *Theories of Modernity and Postmodernity*, London: Sage, pp. 25–44.

Robertson, W. S. (1950), 'Ecological correlations and the behavior of individuals', *American Sociological Review*, 15(3): 351–7.

Rogers, D. (2005), 'Introductory essay: the anthropology of religion after Socialism', *Religion, State and Society*, 33: 5–18.

Ross, T., Moreton, C. and Kirkup, J. (2014), 'Former Archbishop of Canterbury: we are a post-Christian nation', *Sunday Telegraph*, 26 April.

Rountree, K. (2004), *Embracing the Witch and the Goddess: Feminist Ritual-makers in New Zealand*, London, UK: Routledge.

Rountree, K. (2010), *Crafting Contemporary Pagan Identities in a Catholic Society*, London, UK: Ashgate.

Rountree, K. (2011), 'Localising neo-Paganism: integrating global and indigenous traditions in a Mediterranean Catholic society', *Journal of the Royal Anthropological Institute*, 17(4): 846–72.

Rountree, K. (2012), 'Neo-Paganism, animism, and kinship with nature', *Journal of Contemporary Religion*, 27(2): 305–20.

Rountree, K. (2014), 'Neo-Paganism, Native Faith and indigenous religion: a case study of Malta within the European context', *Social Anthropology/ Anthropologie Sociale*, 22(1): 81–100.

Rousseau, J.-J. (1974), *Il contratto sociale*, Milan, Italy: Mursia.

Rubin, J. (2011), 'Egypt's Arab Spring turns frosty', *The Washington Post*, 29 March [online], http://www.washingtonpost.com/blogs/right-turn/post/egypts-arab-spring-turns-frosty/2011/03/29/gIQAcFh1cL_blog.html [accessed 30 March].

Ruohomäki, J. (2014), *Suomen Helluntalailiikkeen Synty, Leviäminen ja Yhteisönmuodotus 1907–1922*, Keuruu, Finland: Aikamedia.

Sabry, S. (2005), 'The social aid and assistance programme of the government of Egypt – a critical review', *Environment and Urbanization*, 17(2): 27–41.

Saeidi, A. (2004), 'The accountability of para-governmental organizations (bonyads): the case of Iranian foundations', *The International Society for Iranian Studies*, 37(3): 479–98.

Salamey, I. and Pearson, F. (2007), 'Hezbollah: a proletarian party with an Islamic manifesto – a sociopolitical analysis of Islamist populism in Lebanon and the Middle East', *Small Wars and Insurgencies*, 18(3): 416–38.

Sandberg, R. and Doe, N. (2007), 'Religious exemptions in discrimination law', *Cambridge Law Journal*, 66(2): 302–12.

Sanders, D., Heath, A., Fisher, S. and Sobolewska, M. (2013), 'The calculus of ethnic minority voting in Britain', *Political Studies*, 62: 231–51.

Sanderson, T. (2012), 'Prime minister's dissembling, hypocritical and disingenuous speech to religious leaders', National Secular Society, 3 April, http://www.secularism.org.uk/blog/2012/04/prime-ministers-dissembling-hypocritical-and-disingenuous-speech-to-religious-leaders.

Santoro, E. (2003), '"Rule of law" e "libertà degli inglesi" L'interpretazione di Albert Venn Dicey', in P. Costa and D. Zolo (eds), *Lo Stato di diritto. Storia, teoria e critica*, Milan, Italy: Milano, pp. 173–223.

Savelli, M. (2012), 'Diseased, depraved or just drunk? The psychiatric panic over alcoholism in Communist Yugoslavia', *Social History of Medicine*, 25(2): 462–80.

Schmitt, C. (1996), *Roman Catholicism and Political Form*, trans. G. L. Ulmen, Westport, CT: Greenwood Press.

Schmitt, C. (2005), *Political Theology*, Chicago, IL: University of Chicago Press.

Scolnicov, A. (2010), 'Does constitutionalisation lead to secularisation? The case law of the European Court of Human Rights and its effect on European secularisation', in I. Katznelson and G. Stedman Jones (eds), *Religion and the Political Imagination*, Cambridge, UK: Cambridge University Press, pp. 295–313.

Scotsman (2006), 'Mark your vote with a cross', http://www.scotsman.com/news/mark-your-vote-with-a-cross-1-1415981.

Scott, S. L. (1994), '"They don't have to live by the old traditions": saintly men, sinner women and an Appalachian Pentecostal revival', *American Ethnologist*, 21(2): 227–44.

Scottish Government (2014), 'Scotland's future', http://www.scotreferendum.com.

Seppo, J. (1998), 'The freedom of religion and conscience in Finland', *Journal of Church and State*, 40(4): 847–72.

Seppo, J. (2003). 'Die Religionsfreiheit im Spiegel des Staat-Kirche-Verhältnisses in Finnland', *Studia Theologica – Nordic Journal of Theology*, 57(1): 20–35.

Shakman Hurd, E. (2008), *The Politics of Secularism in International Relations*, Princeton, NJ: Princeton University Press.

Shnirelman, V. (2000), 'Perun, Svarog and others: Russian neo-Paganism in search of itself', *Cambridge Anthropology*, 21(3): 18–36.

Shnirelman, V. (2002), '"Christians! Go home": a revival of neo-Paganism between the Baltic Sea and Transcaucasia', *Journal of Contemporary Religion*, 17(2): 197–211.

Shnirelman, V. (2007), 'Ancestral wisdom and ethnic nationalism: a view from Eastern Europe', *The Pomegranate: The International Journal of Pagan Studies*, 9(1): 41–61.

Shohet, M. (2007), 'Narrating anorexia: "full" and "struggling" genres of recovery', *Ethos*, 35(3): 344–82.

Siddiqui, H. (2012a), 'Clichés cloud view of Egypt and Turkey', *Toronto Star*, 19 December [online], http://www.thestar.com/opinion/2012/12/19/siddiqui_clichs_cloud_view_of_egypt_and_turkey.html [accessed 13 March].

Siddiqui, H. (2012b), 'In Egypt, it's the elite vs. the unwashed', *Toronto Star*, 15 December [online], http://www.thestar.com/opinion/editorialopinion/2012/12/15/siddiqui_in_egypt_its_the_elite_vs_the_unwashed.html [accessed 13 March].

Sigona, N. and Trehan, N. (2010), *Romani Politics in Contemporary Europe: Poverty, Ethnic Mobilization, and the Neoliberal Order*, Basingstoke, UK: Palgrave Macmillan.

Sihvo, J. (1991), 'The Evangelical-Lutheran church and state in Finland', *Social Compass*, 38(1): 17–24.

Simpson, S. (2000), *Native Faith: Polish Neo-Paganism at the Brink of the Twenty-First Century*, Krakow, Poland: Nomos.

Sin, C. (2006), 'Expectations of support among White British and Asian-Indian older people in Britain: the interdependence of the formal and informal spheres', *Health and Social Care in the Community*, 14(3): 215–24.

Slavkova, M. (2007), 'Evangelical Gypsies in Bulgaria: way of life and performance of identity', *Romani Studies*, 17(2): 205–46.

Smidt, C. (2003), *Religion as Social Capital: Producing a Common Good*, Waco, TX: Baylor University Press.

Smith, A. D. (1991), *National Identity*, Reno, NV: University of Nevada Press.

Snijders, T. A. and Bosker, R. J. (1999), 'Standard errors and sample sizes for two-level research', *Journal of Educational and Behavioral Statistics*, 18(3): 237–59.

Sobolewska, M. (2005), 'Ethnic agenda: relevance of political attitudes to party choice', *Journal of Elections, Public Opinion & Parties*, 15(2): 197–214.

Sorabji, C. (1994), 'Mixed motives, Islam, nationalism and *Mevluds* in an unstable Bosnia', in C. Fawzi El-Solh and J. Mabro (eds), *Muslim Women's Choices: Religious Belief and Social Reality*, Providence, RI: Berg.

Spickard, J. V. (2006), 'What is happening to religion? Six sociological narratives', *Nordic Journal of Religion and Society*, 19(1): 13–29.

Spohn, W. (2009), 'Europeanization, religion and collective identities in an enlarging Europe: a multiple modernities perspective', *European Journal of Social Theory*, 12(3): 358–74.

Stark, R. (1996), 'Religion as context: hellfire and delinquency, one more time', *Sociology of Religion*, 57(2): 163–73.

Stark, R. and Bainbridge, W. (1987), *A Theory of Religion*, Bern, Switzerland: Peter Lang.

Steenbergen, M. R. and Jones, B. S. (2002), 'Modeling multilevel data structures', *American Journal of Political Science*, 46(1): 218–37.

Stefansson, A. (2007), 'Urban exile: locals, newcomers and the cultural transformations of Sarajevo', in X. Bougarel, G. Duijzings and E. Helms (eds), *The New Bosnian Mosaic: Identities, Memories and Moral Claims in a Post-War Society*, Aldershot, UK: Ashgate.

Stepan, A. (2000), 'Religion, democracy, and the "Twin Tolerations"', in
    L. Diamons, M. F. Plottner and P. J. Costopulos (eds), *World Religions and
    Democracy*, Baltimore, MD: Johns Hopkins University Press, pp. 37–57.
Stepan, A. (2001), *Arguing Comparative Politics*, Oxford, UK: Oxford University
    Press.
Stepan, A. (2011), 'The multiple secularisms of modern democratic and non-
    democratic regimes', in C. Calhoun, M. Juergensmeyer and J. VanAntwerper
    (eds), *Rethinking Secularism*, Oxford, UK: Oxford University Press,
    pp. 114–44.
Stephens, B. (2011), 'Egypt's silhouette of fire', *The Wall Street Journal*, 11
    October [online], http://online.wsj.com/news/articles/SB10001424052970203
    4997045766228001074901 80?mg=reno64-wsj&url=http%3A%2F%2Fonline.
    wsj.com%2Farticle%2FSB100014240529702034997045766228001074901 80.
    html [accessed 30 March].
Stewart, M. (1997), *The Time of the Gypsies*, Boulder, CO: Westview.
Stewart, M. (1998), 'Brothers and orphans: two egalitarian models of community
    among Hungarian Rom', in S. Day, M. Stewart and E. Papataxiarchis (eds),
    Lilies of the Field: Marginal Peoples who Live for the Moment, Boulder, CO:
    Westview, pp. 27–44.
Stone, L. and Muir, R. (2007), 'Who are we? Identities in Britain, 2007', London,
    UK: Institute for Public Policy Research.
Strhan, A. (2012), 'Discipleship and desire: conservative evangelicals, coherence,
    and the moral lives of the metropolis', PhD dissertation, Canterbury, UK:
    University of Kent.
Strhan, A. (2013a), 'The metropolis and evangelical life: coherence and
    fragmentation in the "lost city of London"', *Religion*, 43(3): 331–52.
Strhan, A. (2013b), 'Christianity and the city: Simmel, space, and urban
    subjectivities', *Religion and Society: Advances in Research*, 4: 125–49.
Strhan, A. (2014), 'English, evangelicals, equality and the city', in H. Shipley (ed.),
    Globalized Religion and Sexual Identity: Contexts, Contestations, Voices,
    Leiden, Netherlands: Brill, pp. 236–54.
Strmiska, M. (ed.) (2005), *Modern Paganism in World Cultures: Comparative
    Perspectives*, Santa Barbara, CA: ABC-CLIO.
Stychin, C. F. (2004), 'Same-sex sexualities and the globalization of human rights
    discourse', *McGill Law Journal*, 49(4): 951–68.
Sumiala, J. (2013), *Media and Ritual. Death, Community and Everyday Life*,
    London, UK and New York, NY: Routledge.
Sundback, S. (1984), 'Folk church religion – a new kind of civil religion?', in
    B. Harmati (ed.), *The Church and Civil Religion in the Nordic Countries of
    Europe*, Geneva, Switzerland: Lutheran World Federation, pp. 35–40.
Survation (2014), Scottish Independence Issues Poll, 19 February 2014, http://
    survation.com/archive/archive-2014/ [accessed 26 July]
Sutherland, A. (1975), *Gypsies: The Hidden Americans*, New York, NY: Taylor &
    Francis Group, Routledge.
Sutton, P. W. and Vertigans, S. (2005), *Resurgent Islam: A Sociological Approach*,
    Cambridge, UK: Polity Press.
Svallfors, S. (2012), *Contested Welfare States: Welfare Attitudes in Europe and
    Beyond*, Stanford, CA: Stanford University Press.
Svenskakyrkan.se, http://www.svenskakyrkan.se/statistik [accessed 10 March
    2014].

Szilágyi, T. (2011), 'Quasi-religious character of the Hungarian right-wing radical ideology: an international comparison', in A. Máté-Tóth and C. Rughinis (eds), *Spaces and Borders: Current Research on Religion in Central and Eastern Europe*, Berlin, Germany: De Gruyter Verlag, pp. 251–65.

Szilágyi, T. (2012), 'The Neopagan intellectual orientation and its effects on contemporary Hungarian mentality and politics: some remarks', in B. Gábor and O. László (eds), *Hereditas*, Szeged, Hungary: Gerhardus kiadó, pp. 111–21.

Szilágyi, T. (2015), 'Emerging identity markets of contemporary Pagan ideologies in Hungary', in K. Rountree (ed.), *Contemporary Pagan and Native Faith Movements in Europe: Colonialist and Nationalist Impulses*, New York, NY: Berghahn, pp. 154–74.

Szilárdi, R. (2009), 'Ancient gods – new ages: lessons from Hungarian Paganism', *The Pomegranate: The International Journal of Pagan Studies*, 11(1): 44–57.

Takeyh, R. (2011), 'U.S. must take sides to keep the Arab Spring from Islamist takeover', *The Washington Post*, 24 March [online], http://www.washingtonpost.com/opinions/us-must-take-sides-to-keep-the-arab-spring-from-islamist-takeover/2011/03/23/ABNhI2KB_story.html [accessed 30 March].

Tanke, J. J. (2011), *Jacques Rancière: An Introduction*, New York, NY: Continuum.

Taylor, A. (1965), *English History 1914–1945*, Oxford, UK: Clarendon.

Taylor, C. (2007), *A Secular Age*, Cambridge, MA and London, UK: Belknap Press.

Taylor, C. (2009), 'What is secularism?', in G. B. Levey and T. Modood (eds), *Secularism, Religion and Multicultural Citizenship*, Cambridge, UK: Cambridge University Press, pp. xxi–xxii.

Taylor, C. (2011), 'Why we need a radical redefinition of secularism', in E. Mendieta and J. VanAntwerpen (eds), *The Power of Religion in the Public Sphere*, New York, NY: Columbia University Press.

Taylor, G. H. (1957), 'A chronology of British secularism', London UK: National Secular Society, http://www.secularism.org.uk/uploads/a-chronology-of-british-secularism.pdf.

Teahan, M. (2012), 'Archbishop: secularists are holding back the faithful', *Catholic Herald*, 15 February.

Tervonen, M. (2010), *'Gypsies', 'Travelers' and 'Peasants'. A Study on Ethnic Boundary Drawing in Finland and Sweden, c. 1860–1925*, Florence, Italy: European University Institute.

The Christian Institute (2009), *Marginalising Christians: Instances of Christians Being Sidelined in Modern Britain*, Newcastle, UK: Christian Institute.

The Independent (2011), 'Egypt: a moment of hope, but also of peril', 2 February [online], http://www.independent.co.uk/voices/editorials/leading-article-egypt-a-moment-of-hope-but-also-of-peril-2201248.html?origin=internalSearch [accessed 13 March].

Thompson, J. B. (1990), *Ideology and Modern Culture*, Stanford, CA: Stanford University Press.

Thompson, J. B. (1995), *Media and Modernity: A Social Theory of the Media*, Cambridge, UK: Polity Press.

Thurfjell, D. (2013), *Faith and Revivalism in a Nordic Romani Community. Pentecostalism amongst the Kaale Roma of Sweden and Finland*, London, UK and New York, NY: I.B. Tauris.

Tilly, J. (2014), '"We don't do God?" Religion and party choice in Britain', *British Journal of Political Science* (published online, April): 1–21.

Todorova, M. (1997), *Imagining the Balkans*, New York, NY and Oxford, UK: Oxford University Press.

Tomalin, E. (2008), 'Faith and development', in V. Desai and R. B. Potter (eds), *The Companion to Development Studies*, London, UK: Hodder Education, pp. 485–9.

Triandafyllidou, A. (1998), 'National identity and the "other"', *Ethnic and Racial Studies*, 21(4): 593–612.

Trigg, R. (2012), *Equality, Freedom and Religion*, Oxford, UK: Oxford University Press.

Tripp, C. (2006), *Islam and the Moral Economy: The Challenge of Capitalism*, Cambridge, UK: Cambridge University Press.

Turner, B. S. (1991), *Religion and Social Theory*, 2nd edn, London, UK: Sage.

UK Ministry of Defence (2014), 'Faith and diversity', http://www.army.mod.uk/join/20225.aspx.

UK Monarchy (2014), 'The Act of Settlement', http://www.royal.gov.uk/HistoryoftheMonarchy/KingsandQueensoftheUnitedKingdom/TheStuarts/MaryIIWilliamIIIandTheActofSettlement/TheActofSettlement.aspx.

UK Parliament (2011), 'Prayers', http://www.parliament.uk/about/how/business/prayers.

United Nations (2003), *Arab Human Development Report*, Oxford, UK: Oxford University Press.

Valiente, D. (1978), *Witchcraft for Tomorrow*, Blaine, WA: Phoenix Publishing.

Van Baar, H. (2011), 'Europe's Romaphobia', *Environment and Planning: Society and Space*, 29(2): 203–12.

Van der Brug, W. (2010), 'Structural and ideological voting in age cohorts', *West European Politics*, 33(3): 586–607.

Van der Brug, W., Hobolt, S. B. and De Vrees, C. H. (2009), 'Religion and party choice in Europe', *West European Politics*, 32(6): 1266–83.

Van Dijk, T. A. (1997), 'Political discourse and racism: describing others in Western parliaments', in S. H. Riggins (ed.), *The Language and Politics of Exclusion: Others in Discourse*, Thousand Oaks, CA: Sage, pp. 31–64.

Van Horn Melton, J. (2001), *The Rise of the Public in Enlightenment Europe*, Cambridge, UK: Cambridge University Press.

Van Kersbergen, K. (1995), *Social Capitalism: A Study of Christian Democracy and the Welfare State*, London, UK and New York, NY: Routledge.

Västrik, E.-H. (2015), 'In search of genuine religion: the contemporary Estonian Maausulised movement and nationalist discourse', in K. Rountree (ed.), *Contemporary Pagan and Native Faith Movements in Europe: Colonialist and Nationalist Impulses*, New York, NY: Berghahn, pp. 130–53.

Velkoborská, K. (2015), 'The Brotherhood of Wolves, Czech Republic: from Ásatrú to primitivism', in K. Rountree (ed.), *Contemporary Pagan and Native Faith Movements in Europe: Colonialist and Nationalist Impulses*, New York, NY: Berghahn, pp. 86–109.

Vermeersch, P. (2006), *The Romani Movement: Minority Politics and Ethnic Mobilization in Contemporary Central Europe*, Oxford, UK and New York, NY: Berghahn Books.

Victor, C. and Zubair, M. (2015), 'Expectations of care and support in old age by Bangladeshi and Pakistani elders', in U. Karl and S. Torres (eds), *Ageing in the Context of Migration*, London, UK: Routledge.

Victor, C., Martin, W. and Zubair, M. (2012), 'Families and caring amongst older people in South Asian communities in the UK: a pilot study', *European Journal of Social Work*, 15(91): 81–96.

Victor, C., Burholt, V., Ahmet, A. and Dobbs, C. (2014), 'Who cares and why?'. Paper presented at the British Society of Gerontology Annual Conference, University of Southampton, September.

Virkkunen, S. (1981), *Suomalainen fraasisanakirja*, Helsinki, Finland: Otava.

Voas, D., Crockett, A. and Olson, D. V. (2002), 'Religious pluralism and participation: why previous research is wrong', *American Sociological Review*, 67(2): 212–30.

Von Stuckrad, K. (2013), 'Secular religion: a discourse–historical approach to religion in contemporary Western Europe', *Journal of Contemporary Religion*, 28(1): 1–14.

Vrcan, S. (1986), *Od krize religije k religiji krize: prilog raspravi o religiji u uvjetima suvremene krize*, Zagreb, Croatia: Školska knj.

Vrcan, S. (2006), *Nacija, nacionalizam, moderna država: izme u etnonacionalizma, liberalnog i kulturnog nacionalizma ili građanske nacije i postnacionalnih konstelacija*, Zagreb, Croatia: Golden marketing-Technička knjiga.

Vučetić, R. (2012), *Koka-Kola Socijalizam: Amerikanizacija jugoslavenske popularne culture sezdesetih godina XX veka*, Belgrade, Serbia: Službeni glasnik.

Wacquant, L. (2004), 'Following Pierre Bourdieu into the field', *Ethnography*, 5(4): 387–414.

Wahl-Jorgensen, K. (2004), 'Playground of the pundits or voice of the people? Comparing British and Danish opinion pages', *Journalism Studies*, 5(1): 59–70.

Walker, A. J., Pratt, C. C. and Eddy, L. (1995), 'Informal caregiving to aging family members: a critical review', *Family Relations*, 44: 402–11.

Walters, S. and Carlin, B. (2012), 'Defiant speaker vows there will be no prayer ban in the Commons', *Daily Mail*, 12 February.

Walton, A. with Hatcher, A. and Spencer, N. (2013), *Is There a 'Religious Right' Emerging in Britain?*, London, UK: Theos.

Wanless, D. (2006), 'Wanless social care review: securing good care for older people, taking a long-term view', Kings Fund.

Ward, G. and Hoelzl, M. (2008), 'Introduction', in G. Ward and M. Hoelzl (eds), *The New Visibility of Religion: Studies in Religion and Cultural Hermeneutics*, London: Continuum, pp. 1–14.

Warner, R. (2007), *Reinventing English Evangelicalism, 1966–2001*, Milton Keynes, UK: Paternoster Press.

Warsi, S. (2012), speech to the Vatican, 14 February, http://www.cabinetoffice. gov.uk/news/baroness-warsi-speech-holy-see.

Weber, M. (1978), *Economy and Society: An Outline of Interpretative Sociology*, Oakland, CA: University of California Press.

Weber, M. (2006[1922]), *Wirtschaft und Gesellschaft: Grundriss der verstehenden Soziologie*, Tübingen, Germany: Mohr Siebeck.

Wehler, H.-U. (2004), *Nationalisms*, Munich, Germany: C. H. Beck.

Weiner, M. (1997), *Japan's Minorities: The Illusion of Homogeneity*, New York, NY: Routledge.

Weintraub, J. A. (1997), 'The theory and politics of the public/private distinction', in J. A. Weintraub and K. Kumar (eds), *Public and Private in Thought and Practice: Perspectives on a Grand Dichotomy*, Chicago, IL: University of Chicago Press, pp. 1–42.

Welch, M. R., Sikkink, D., and Loveland, M. T. (2007), 'The radius of trust: Religion, social embeddedness and trust in strangers.' *Social Forces* 86(1): 23–46.

Welch, M., Sikkinik, D., Sartain, E. and Bond, C. (2004), 'Trust in God and trust in man', *Journal of the Scientific Study of Religion*, 43(3): 317–43.

Welsh, M. R., Tittle, C. R. and Petee, T. (1991), 'Religion and deviance among adult Catholics: a test of the "moral communities" hypothesis', *Journal for the Scientific Study of Religion*, 30(2): 159–72.

Wiktorowicz, Q. (ed.) (2003), *Islamic Activism: A Social Movement Theory Approach* (Indiana Series in Middle East Studies), Paperback – 25 November 2003.

Wilber, C. K. and Jameson, K. P. (1980), 'Religious values and social limits to development', *World Development*, 8(7/8): 467–80.

Wilford, J. G. (2012), *Sacred Subdivisions: The Postsuburban Transformation of American Evangelicalism*, New York, NY: New York University Press.

Williams, P. (1987), 'Le développement du Pentecôtisme chez les Tsiganes en France: mouvement messianique, stéréotypes et affirmation d'identité', *Vers des Sociétés Pluriculturelles: études Comparatives et Situation en France*, Actes du Colloque International de l'AFA – Association Française des Anthropologues (9-11 janvier 1986, Ministère de la Recherche et de la Technologie, Paris), Paris, France: ORSTOM, pp. 325–31.

Williams, P. (2003), *Gypsy World: The Silence of the Living and the Voices of the Dead*, Chicago, IL: Chicago University Press.

Williams, R. (2012), *Faith in the Public Square*, London, UK: Bloomsbury.

Williamson, P. (2007), 'The monarchy and public values', in A. Olechnowicz (ed.), *The Monarchy and the British Nation*, Cambridge, UK: Cambridge University Press, pp. 223–57.

Winter, S. (2008), *Kharis: Hellenic Polytheism Explored*, US: Createspace.

Witte Jr, J. (2000), *Religion and the American Constitutional Experiment. Essential Rights and Liberties*, Boulder, CO: Westview Press.

Witte Jr, J. and Nichols, J. A. (2011), *Religion and the American Constitutional Experiment*, Boulder, CO: Westview Press.

Wodak, R. (2008), 'Introduction: discourse studies – important concepts and terms', in R. Wodak and M. Krzyzanowski (eds), *Qualitative Discourse Analysis in the Social Sciences*, Basingstoke, UK: Palgrave, pp. 1–29.

Wolfe, A. and Klausen, J. (1997), 'Identity politics and the welfare state', *Social Philosophy and Policy*, 14(2): 231–55.

Wolffe, J. (2000), *Great Deaths*, Oxford, UK: British Academy/Oxford University Press.

Woodhead, L. (2012), 'Introduction', in L. Woodhead and R. Catto (eds), *Religion and Change in Modern Britain*, London: Routledge, pp. 1–33.

Woodhead, L. (2013), 'Liberal religion and illiberal secularism', in G. D'Costa, M. Evans, T. Modood and J. Rivers (eds), *Religion in a Liberal State*, Cambridge: Cambridge University Press, pp. 93–116.

Woodhead, L. (2014), 'Telling the truth about Christian Britain', AHRC/ESRC Faith Debates.

Woodhead, L. and Heelas, P. (2000), *Religion in Modern Times: An Interpretive Anthology*, Oxford, UK: Blackwell Publishers.

Wray, S. (2007), 'Making sense of mid-life ethnic and cultural diversity', *Journal of Ageing Studies*, 21(1): 31–42.

Wright, O. (2011), 'Cameron shows off his faith with a swipe at Archbishop', *Independent*, 17 December.

Yosso, T. J. (2005), 'Whose culture has capital? A critical race theory discussion of community cultural wealth', *Race, Ethnicity and Education*, 8(1): 69–91.

YouGov (2012), poll research, February, http://cdn.yougov.com/cumulus_uploads/document/pe06bnkf18/YG-Archives-YouGov-ChristianCountryPrayers-160212.pdf.

YouGov–Cambridge (2012), poll research, August, http://d25d2506sfb94s.cloudfront.net/cumulus_uploads/document/md6rf2qvws/Reputation%20UK%20Report_21-Aug-2012_F.pdf.

Yuval-Davis, N. (2010), *Intersectional Politics of Belongings*, London, UK: Sage.

Zack, N. (2002), *Philosophy of Science and Race*, London, UK: Routledge.

Zolo, D. (2003), 'Teoria e critica dello Stato di diritto', in P. Costa and D. Zolo (eds), *Lo Stato di diritto. Storia, teoria e critica*, Milan, Italy: Feltrinelli, pp. 17–88.

Index